Modern Critical Views

Chinua Achebe
Henry Adams
Aeschylus
S. Y. Agnon
Edward Albee
Raphael Alberti
Louisa May Alcott
A. R. Ammons
Sherwood Anderson
Aristophanes
Matthew Arnold
Antonin Artaud
John Ashbery
Margaret Atwood
W. H. Auden
Jane Austen
Isaac Babel
Sir Francis Bacon
James Baldwin
Honoré de Balzac
John Barth
Donald Barthelme
Charles Baudelaire
Simone de Beauvoir
Samuel Beckett
Saul Bellow
Thomas Berger
John Berryman
The Bible
Elizabeth Bishop
William Blake
Giovanni Boccaccio
Heinrich Böll
Jorge Luis Borges
Elizabeth Bowen
Bertolt Brecht
The Brontës
Charles Brockden Brown
Sterling Brown
Robert Browning
Martin Buber
John Bunyan
Anthony Burgess
Kenneth Burke
Robert Burns
William Burroughs
George Gordon, Lord
  Byron
Pedro Calderón de la Barca
Italo Calvino
Albert Camus
Canadian Poetry: Modern
  and Contemporary
Canadian Poetry through
  E. J. Pratt
Thomas Carlyle
Alejo Carpentier
Lewis Carroll
Willa Cather
Louis-Ferdinand Céline
Miguel de Cervantes

Geoffrey Chaucer
John Cheever
Anton Chekhov
Kate Chopin
Chrétien de Troyes
Agatha Christie
Samuel Taylor Coleridge
Colette
William Congreve & the
  Restoration Dramatists
Joseph Conrad
Contemporary Poets
James Fenimore Cooper
Pierre Corneille
Julio Cortázar
Hart Crane
Stephen Crane
e. e. cummings
Dante
Robertson Davies
Daniel Defoe
Philip K. Dick
Charles Dickens
James Dickey
Emily Dickinson
Denis Diderot
Isak Dinesen
E. L. Doctorow
John Donne & the
  Seventeenth-Century
  Metaphysical Poets
John Dos Passos
Fyodor Dostoevsky
Frederick Douglass
Theodore Dreiser
John Dryden
W. E. B. Du Bois
Lawrence Durrell
George Eliot
T. S. Eliot
Elizabethan Dramatists
Ralph Ellison
Ralph Waldo Emerson
Euripides
William Faulkner
Henry Fielding
F. Scott Fitzgerald
Gustave Flaubert
E. M. Forster
John Fowles
Sigmund Freud
Robert Frost
Northrop Frye
Carlos Fuentes
William Gaddis
Federico García Lorca
Gabriel García Márquez
André Gide
W. S. Gilbert
Allen Ginsberg
J. W. von Goethe

Nikolai Gogol
William Golding
Oliver Goldsmith
Mary Gordon
Günther Grass
Robert Graves
Graham Greene
Thomas Hardy
Nathaniel Hawthorne
William Hazlitt
H. D.
Seamus Heaney
Lillian Hellman
Ernest Hemingway
Hermann Hesse
Geoffrey Hill
Friedrich Hölderlin
Homer
A. D. Hope
Gerard Manley Hopkins
Horace
A. E. Housman
William Dean Howells
Langston Hughes
Ted Hughes
Victor Hugo
Zora Neale Hurston
Aldous Huxley
Henrik Ibsen
Eugène Ionesco
Washington Irving
Henry James
Dr. Samuel Johnson and
  James Boswell
Ben Jonson
James Joyce
Carl Gustav Jung
Franz Kafka
Yasonari Kawabata
John Keats
Søren Kierkegaard
Rudyard Kipling
Melanie Klein
Heinrich von Kleist
Philip Larkin
D. H. Lawrence
John le Carré
Ursula K. Le Guin
Giacomo Leopardi
Doris Lessing
Sinclair Lewis
Jack London
Robert Lowell
Malcolm Lowry
Carson McCullers
Norman Mailer
Bernard Malamud
Stéphane Mallarmé
Sir Thomas Malory
André Malraux
Thomas Mann

Modern Critical Views

Modern Critical Views

WILLIAM
SHAKESPEARE
THE TRAGEDIES

Modern Critical Views

WILLIAM
SHAKESPEARE
THE TRAGEDIES

Edited with an introduction by

Harold Bloom

Sterling Professor of the Humanities
Yale University

CHELSEA HOUSE PUBLISHERS
New York

THE COVER:
The ghost of Hamlet's father, armed for war, represents the crisis of Shakespeare's major tragedy, in which the spirit of revenge dominates the divided consciousness of his son.
—H.B.

PROJECT EDITORS: Emily Bestler, James Uebbing
EDITORIAL COORDINATOR: Karyn Gullen Browne
EDITORIAL STAFF: Julia Myer, Laura Ludwig, Linda Grossman, Marena Fisher, Peter Childers
DESIGN: Susan Lusk

Cover illustration by Kye Carbone

Printed and bound in the United States of America

10

Library of Congress Cataloging in Publication Data

William Shakespeare.
    (Modern critical views)
    Bibliography: p.
    Includes index.
    1. Shakespeare, William, 1564–1616—Criticism and interpretation—Addresses, essays, lectures.   I. Bloom, Harold.   II. Series.
PR2976.W535   1985   822.3'3   85–3815
ISBN 0–87754–617–7 (v. 1)

Contents

Editor's Note

This volume gathers together a representative selection of the best critical essays devoted to Shakespeare's tragedies during the last half-century. It begins with the editor's introductory essay on the originality of Shakespeare's mimetic art, which centers upon *Hamlet*. G. Wilson Knight's eloquent analysis of *King Lear* commences the chronological sequence, which continues with two very different but now equally classical essays; Harold Goddard's passionate reading of *Romeo and Juliet* and Harry Levin's skeptical exegesis of *Hamlet*.

Two highly individual scholars of the Elizabethan period, the late A. P. Rossiter and Alvin Kernan, follow with greatly contrasting essays on *Troilus and Cressida* and *Othello*, respectively, in which Rossiter's baroque elaborations are offset by Kernan's powerfully naturalistic mode of commentary. Kenneth Burke's highly characteristic exuberance as he analyzes *Coriolanus* finds its foil in Northrop Frye's systematic and judicious ana-gogical treatment of *Julius Caesar* and of *Macbeth*. The essay by David Daiches on *Antony and Cleopatra* is marked by a lively eclecticism in the relation of imagery to poetic meaning.

The two final essays, by Howard Felperin and A. D. Nuttall, are recent efforts to illuminate the crucial problems of Shakespearean representation, in the context of contemporary Post-Structuralist criticism, which has repudiated mimesis and insisted that any text, in order to come into existence as a text, must suspend its referential aspects almost entirely. Felperin, following the late Paul de Man, reads *Macbeth* as an implicit poetics of modernity, while Nuttall examines *Othello* as a supreme instance of a true representation of given reality. This volume thus comes full circle to the issue obsessively engaged by the "Introduction," which is the perpetually unmatched originality of Shakespeare's powers of representation in his greatest tragedies, and in *Hamlet* above all.

Introduction

I

The last we see of Hamlet at the court in Act IV is his exit for England:

HAMLET: For England?
CLAUDIUS: Ay, Hamlet.
HAMLET: Good.
CLAUDIUS: So is it, if thou knew'st our purposes.
HAMLET: I see a cherub that sees them. But come, for England. Farewell, dear mother.
CLAUDIUS: Thy loving father, Hamlet.
HAMLET: My mother. Father and mother is man and wife, man and wife is one flesh; so my mother. Come, for England.

Exit.

It is a critical commonplace to assert that the Hamlet of Act V is a changed man: mature rather than youthful, certainly quieter, if not quietistic, and somehow more attuned to divinity. Perhaps the truth is that he is at last himself, no longer afflicted by mourning and melancholia, by murderous jealousy and incessant rage. Certainly he is no longer haunted by his father's ghost. It may be that the desire for revenge is fading in him. In all of Act V he does not speak once of his dead father directly. There is a single reference to "my father's signet" which serves to seal up the doom of those poor schoolfellows, Rosencrantz and Guildenstern, and there is the curious phrasing of "my king" rather than "my father" in the half-hearted rhetorical question the prince addresses to Horatio:

Does it not, think thee, stand me now upon—
He that hath kill'd my king and whor'd my mother,
Popp'd in between th'election and my hopes,
Thrown out his angle for my proper life
And with such coz'nage—is't not perfect conscience
To quit him with this arm?

When Horatio responds that Claudius will hear shortly from England, presumably that Rosencrantz and Guildenstern have been executed, Hamlet rather ambiguously makes what might be read as a final vow of revenge:

It will be short. The interim is mine.
And a man's life's no more than to say 'one.'

However this is to be interpreted, Hamlet forms no plot, and is content with a wise passivity, knowing that Claudius must act. Except for the scheme of Claudius and Laertes, we and the prince might be confronted by a kind of endless standoff. What seems clear is that the urgency of the earlier Hamlet has gone. Instead, a mysterious and beautiful disinterestedness dominates this truer Hamlet, who compels a universal love precisely because he is beyond it, except for its exemplification by Horatio. What we overhear is an ethos so original that we still cannot assimilate it:

Sir, in my heart there was a kind of fighting
That would not let me sleep. Methought I lay
Worse than the mutines in the bilboes. Rashly—
And prais'd be rashness for it: let us know
Our indiscretion sometimes serves us well
When our deep plots do pall; and that should learn us
There's a divinity that shapes our ends,
Rough-hew them how we will—

Weakly read, that divinity is Jehovah, but more strongly "ends" here are not our intentions but rather our fates, and the contrast is between a force that can *shape* stone, and our wills that only hew roughly against implacable substance. Nor would a strong reading find Calvin in the echoes of the Gospel of Matthew as Hamlet sets aside his own: "Thou wouldst not think how ill all's here about my heart." In his heart, there is again a kind of fighting, but the readiness, rather than the ripeness, is now all:

Not a whit. We defy augury. There is special providence in the fall of a sparrow. If it be now, 'tis not to come; if it be not to come, it will be now; if it be not now, yet it will come. The readiness is all. Since no man, of aught he leaves, knows aught, what is't to leave betimes? Let be.

The apparent nihilism more than negates the text cited from Matthew, yet the epistemological despair does not present itself as despair, but as an achieved serenity. Above all else, these are not the accents of an avenger, or even of someone who still mourns, or who continues to suffer the selfish virtues of the natural heart. Not nihilism but authentic disinterestedness, and yet what is that? No Elizabethan lore, no reading in Aristotle, or even in Montaigne, can help to answer that question. We know the ethos of disinterestedness only because we know Hamlet. Nor can we hope to know Hamlet any better by knowing Freud. The dead father indeed was, during four acts, more powerful than even the living one could be, but by Act V the dead father is not even a numinous shadow. He is merely a precursor, Hamlet the Dane before this one, and this one matters much more. The tragic hero in Shakespeare, at his most universally moving, is a representation so original that conceptually *he contains us*, and fashions our psychology of motives permanently. Our map or general theory of the mind may be Freud's, but Freud, like all the rest of us, inherits the representation of mind, at its most subtle and excellent, from Shakespeare. Freud could say that the aim of all life was death, but not that readiness is all.

II

Originality in regard to Shakespeare is a bewildering notion, because we have no rival to set him against. "The originals are not original," Emerson liked to remark, but he withdrew that observation in respect to Shakespeare. If Shakespeare had a direct precursor it had to be Marlowe, who was scarcely six months older. Yet, in comparison to Shakespeare, Marlowe represents persons only by caricature. The Chaucer who could give us the Pardoner or the Wife of Bath appears to be Shakespeare's only authentic English precursor, if we forget the English renderings of the Bible. Yet we do not take our psychology from Chaucer or even from the Bible. Like Freud himself, we owe our psychology to Shakespeare. Before Shakespeare, representations in literature may change *as* they speak, but they do not change *because* of what they say. Shakespearean representation turns upon his persons listening to themselves simultaneously with our listening, and learning and changing even as we learn and change. Falstaff delights himself as much as he delights us, and Hamlet modifies himself by studying his own modifications. Ever since, Falstaff has been the inescapable model for nearly all wit, and Hamlet the paradigm for all introspection. When Yorick's skull replaces the helmeted ghost, then the mature Hamlet has replaced the self-chastising revenger, and a different sense of death's power over life has been created, and in more than a play or a dramatic poem:

> HAMLET: To what base uses we may return, Horatio! Why may not imagination trace the noble dust of Alexander till a find it stopping a bunghole?
> HORATIO: 'Twere to consider too curiously to consider so.
> HAMLET: No, faith, not a jot, but to follow him thither with modesty enough, and likelihood to lead it.

Probability leads possibility, likelihood beckons imagination on, and Alexander is essentially a surrogate for the dead father, the Danish

Alexander. Passionately reductive, Hamlet would consign his own dust to the same likelihood, but there we part from him, with Horatio as our own surrogate. Hamlet's unique praise of Horatio sets forever the paradigm of the Shakespearean reader or playgoer in relation to the Shakespearean tragic hero:

> Dost thou hear?
> Since my dear soul was mistress of her choice,
> And could of men distinguish her election,
> Sh'ath seal'd thee for herself; for thou hast been
> As one, in suff'ring all, that suffers nothing . . .

Which means, not that Horatio and the reader do not suffer with Hamlet, but rather that truly they suffer nothing precisely because they learn from Hamlet the disinterestedness they themselves cannot exemplify, though in possibility somehow share. And they survive, to tell Hamlet's story "of accidental judgments" not so accidental and perhaps not judgments, since disinterestedness does not judge, and there are no accidents.

Only Hamlet, at the last, is disinterested, since the hero we see in Act V, despite his protestations, is now beyond love, which is not to say that he never loved Gertrude, or Ophelia, or the dead father, or poor Yorick for that matter. Hamlet is an actor? Yes, earlier, but not in Act V, where he has ceased also to be a play director, and finally even abandons the profession of poet. Language, so dominant as such in the earlier Hamlet, gives almost the illusion of transparency in his last speech, if only because he verges upon saying what cannot be said:

> You that look pale and tremble at this chance,
> That are but mutes or audience to this act,
> Had I but time—as this fell sergeant, Death,
> Is strict in his arrest—O, I could tell you—
> But let it be.

Evidently he does know something of what he leaves, and we ache to know what he could tell us, since it is Shakespeare's power to persuade us that Hamlet has gained a crucial knowledge. One clue is the abiding theatrical trope of "but mutes or audience," which suggests that the knowledge is itself "of" illusion. But the trope is framed by two announcements to Horatio and so to us. "I am dead," and no other figure in Shakespeare seems to stand so authoritatively on the threshold between the worlds of life and death. When the hero's last speech moves between "O, I die, Horatio" and "the rest is silence," there is a clear sense again that much more might be said, concerning our world and not the "undiscovered country" of death. The hint is that Hamlet could tell us something he has learned about the nature of representation, because he has learned what it is that he himself represents.

Shakespeare gives Fortinbras the last word on this, but that word is irony, since Fortinbras represents only the formula of repetition: like father, like son. "The soldier's music and the rite of war" speak loudly for the dead father, but not for this dead son, who had watched the army of Fortinbras march past to gain its little patch of ground and had mused that: "Rightly to be great/Is not to stir without great argument." The reader's last word has to be Horatio's, who more truly than Fortinbras has Hamlet's dying voice: "and from his mouth whose voice will draw on more," which only in a minor key means draw more supporters to the election of Fortinbras. Horatio represents the audience, while Fortinbras represents all the dead fathers.

III

We love Hamlet, then, for whatever reasons Horatio loves him. Of Horatio we know best that what distinguishes him from Rosencrantz and Guildenstern, and indeed from Polonius, Ophelia, Laertes, and Gertrude, is that Claudius *cannot use him.* Critics have remarked upon Horatio's ambiguously shifting status at the court of Denmark, and the late William Empson confessed a certain irritation at Hamlet's discovery of virtues in Horatio that the prince could not find in himself. Yet Shakespeare gives us a Hamlet we must love while knowing our inferiority, since he has the qualities we lack, and so he also gives us Horatio, our representative, who loves so stoically for the rest of us. Horatio is loyal, and limited; skeptical as befits a fellow-student of the profoundly skeptical Hamlet, yet never skeptical about Hamlet. Take Horatio out of the play, and you take us out of the play. The plot could be rearranged to spare the wretched Rosencrantz and Guildenstern, even to spare Laertes, let alone Fortinbras, but remove Horatio, and Hamlet becomes so estranged from us that we scarcely can hope to account for that universality of appeal which is his, and the play's, most original characteristic.

Horatio, then, represents by way of our positive association with him; it is a commonplace, but not less true for that, to say that Hamlet represents by negation. I think this negation is Biblical in origin, which is why it seems so Freudian to us, because Freudian negation is Biblical and not Hegelian, as it were. Hamlet is Biblical rather than Homeric or Sophoclean. Like the Hebrew hero confronting Yahweh, Hamlet needs to be everything in himself yet knows the sense in which he is nothing in himself. What Hamlet takes back from repression is returned only cognitively, never affectively, so that in him thought is liberated from its sexual past, but at the high expense of a continued and augmenting sense of sexual disgust. And what Hamlet at first loves is what Biblical and Freudian man loves: the image of authority, the dead father, and the object of the dead father's love, who is also the object of Claudius' love. When Hamlet matures, or returns fully to himself, he transcends the love of authority, and ceases to love at all, and perhaps he can be said to be dying throughout all of Act V, and not just in the scene of the duel.

In Freud, we love authority, but authority does not love us in return. Nowhere in the play are we told, by Hamlet or by anyone else, of the love of the dead king for his son, but only for Gertrude. That Hamlet hovers always beyond our comprehension must be granted, yet he is not so far beyond as to cause us to see him with the vision of Fortinbras, rather than the vision of Horatio. We think of him not necessarily as royal, but more as noble, in the archaic sense of "noble" which is to be a seeing soul. It is surely no accident that Horatio is made to emphasize the word "noble" in his elegy for Hamlet, which contrasts angelic song to "the soldier's music" of Fortinbras. As a noble or seeing heart, Hamlet indeed sees feelingly. Short of T. S. Eliot's judgment that the play is an aesthetic failure, the oddest opinion in the *Hamlet* criticism of our time was that of W. H. Auden in his Ibsen essay, "Genius and Apostle," which contrasts Hamlet as a mere actor to Don Quixote as the antithesis of an actor:

> Hamlet lacks faith in God and in himself. Consequently he must define his existence in terms of others, e.g., I am the man whose mother married his uncle who murdered his father. He would like to become what the Greek tragic hero is, a creature of situation. Hence his inability to act, for he can only 'act,' i.e., play at possibilities.

Harold Goddard, whose *The Meaning of Shakespeare* (1951) seems to me still the most illuminating single book on Shakespeare, remarked that, "Hamlet is his own Falstaff." In Goddard's spirit, I might venture the formula that Brutus plus Falstaff equals Hamlet, though "equals" is hardly an accurate word here. A better formula was proposed by A. C. Bradley, when he suggested that Hamlet was the only Shakespearean character whom we could think had written Shakespeare's plays. Goddard built on this by saying of Shakespeare: "He is an unfallen Hamlet." From a scholarly or any Formalist perspective, Goddard's aphorism is not criticism, but neither historical research nor Formalist modes of criticism have helped us much in learning to describe the unassimilated originality that

Shakespearean representation still constitutes. Because we are formed by Shakespeare, paradoxically most fully where we cannot assimilate him, we are a little blinded by what might be called the originality of this originality. Only a few critics (A. D. Nuttall among them) have seen that the central element in this originality is its cognitive power. Without Shakespeare (and the Bible as his precursor text) we would not know of a literary representation that worked so as to compel "reality" (be it Platonic or Humean, Hegelian or Freudian) to reveal aspects of itself we previously could not discern. Such a representation cannot be considered anti-mimetic or an effect of language alone.

IV

One way, by no means unproductive, of accounting for the force of Shakespearean representation is to see it as the supreme instance of what the late Paul de Man called a poetics of modernity, of a revisionism of older literary conventions that at once subsumed and cancelled the illusions always present in all figurative language. Howard Felperin, working in de Man's mode, adroitly reads Macbeth's "modernity" as the dilemma of a figure totally unable to take his own nature for granted: "He cannot quite rest content in an action in which his role and his nature are determined in advance, but must continuously re-invent himself in the process of acting them out." In such a view, Macbeth is a strong misreading of a figure like Herod in the old morality plays. I would go further and suggest that the drama, *Macbeth*, is an allusive triumph over more formidable precursors, just as *King Lear* is. The Shakespearean Sublime, too strong to find agonists in Seneca or in the native tradition (even in Marlowe), and too remote from Athenian drama to feel its force, confronts instead the Sublime of the Bible. What breaks loose in the apocalyptic cosmos of *Macbeth* or of *Lear* is an energy of the abyss or the original chaos that is ignored in the priestly first chapter of Genesis, but which wars fiercely against Jehovah in crucial passages of Job, the Psalms and Isaiah. To subsume and supersede the Bible could not have been the conscious ambition of Shakespeare, but if we are to measure the preternatural energies of *Macbeth* or of *Lear*, then we will require Job or Isaiah or certain Psalms as the standard of measurement.

What is the advance, cognitive and figurative, that Shakespearean representation achieves over Biblical depiction? The question is absurdly difficult, yet anything but meaningless. If Shakespeare has a true Western rival, then he is either the Yahwist, the Hebrew Bible's great original, or the Homer of the *Iliad.* Can there *be* an advance over Jacob or Achilles as representations of reality, whatever that is taken to be? What the question reduces to is the unanswerable: can there be advances in reality? The arts, as Hazlitt insisted, are not progressive, and if reality is, then its progression suspiciously resembles a speeding up of what Freud called the death drive. Reality testing, like the reality principle, is Freud's only transcendentalism, his last vestige of Platonism. Freud's own originality, as he deeply sensed, tends to evaporate when brought too near either to the originality of the Yahwist or to the originality of Shakespeare. This may be the true cause of the disaster that is *Moses and Monotheism,* and of Freud's own passion for the lunatic thesis that Shakespeare's plays were written by the Earl of Oxford.

By Nietzsche's genealogical test for the memorable, which is cognitive pain, Job is no more nor less forgettable than *Macbeth* or *Lear.* The rhetorical economy of Job's wife, in her one appearance, unmatchable even out of context, is overwhelming within context, and may have set for Shakespeare one of the limits of representation:

> So went Satan forth from the presence of the Lord, and smote Job with sore boils from the sole of his foot unto his crown.
> And he took him a potsherd to scrape himself withal; and he sat down among the ashes.
> Then said his wife unto him, Dost thou still retain thine integrity? Curse God, and die.

Lear's Queen, the mother of Goneril, Regan and Cordelia, had she survived to accompany her husband onto the heath, hardly could have said more in less. In Shakespeare's tragedies there are moments of compressed urgency that represent uncanny yet persuasive change with Biblical economy. The dying Edmund sees the bodies of Goneril and Regan brought in, and belatedly turns his lifetime about in four words: "Yet Edmund was belov'd." The phrase is a vain attempt to countermand his own order for the murder of Cordelia. "Yet Edmund was belov'd"—though loved by two fiends, the shock of knowing he *was* loved, unto death, undoes "mine own nature." One thinks of Hamlet's "Let be" that concludes his "We defy augury" speech, as he goes into the trap of Claudius' last plot. "Let be" epitomizes what I have called "disinterestedness," though Horatio's word "noble" may be more apt. That laconic "Let be," repeated as "Let it be" in Hamlet's death speech, is itself a kind of catastrophe creation, even as it marks another phase in Hamlet's release from what Freud called the family romance, and even as it compels another transference for our veneration to Hamlet. Catastrophe creation, family romance, transference: these are the stigmata and consequently the paradigms for imaginative originality in the Bible and, greatly shadowed, in Freud, and I suggest now that they can be useful paradigms for the apprehension of originality in Shakespeare's tragic representations. The fantasy of rescuing the mother from degradation is palpable in Hamlet; less palpable and far more revelatory is the sense in which the prince has molded himself into a pragmatic changeling. The ghost is armed for war, and Hamlet, grappling with Laertes in the graveyard, accurately warns Laertes (being to that extent his father's son) that as the prince he has something dangerous in him. But is Hamlet psychically ever armed for war? Claudius, popping in between the election and Hamlet's hopes, could have shrewdly pled more than his nephew's youth and inexperience while properly arguing that his own nature was better qualified for the throne. Hamlet, in the graveyard, shocked back from beyond affect, accurately indicates whose true son he first became as changeling:

> Alas, poor Yorick. I knew him, Horatio, a fellow of infinite jest, of most excellent fancy. He hath bore me on his back a thousand times, and now—how abhorred in my imagination it is. My gorge rises at it. Here hung those lips that I have kissed I know not how oft . . .

Harry Levin, for whom strong misreading is not serendipity but misfortune, advises us that "Hamlet without *Hamlet* has been thought about all too much." One might reply, in all mildness, that little memorable has been written about *Hamlet* that does not fall into the mode of "Hamlet without *Hamlet*." Far more even than *Lear* or *Macbeth*, the play is the figure; the question of *Hamlet* only can be Hamlet. He does not move in a Sublime cosmos, and truly has no world except himself, which would appear to be what he has learned in the interim between Acts IV and V. Changelings who move from fantasy to fact are possible only in romance, and alas Shakespeare wrote the tragedy of Hamlet, and not the romance of Hamlet instead. But the originality of Shakespearean representation in tragedy, and particularly in *Hamlet*, hardly can be overstressed. Shakespeare's version of the Family Romance always compounds it with two other paradigms for his exuberant originality: with a catastrophe that creates and with a carrying across from earlier ambivalences within the audience to an ambivalence that is a kind of taboo settling in about the tragic hero like an aura. At the close of *Hamlet*, only Horatio and Fortinbras are survivors. Fortinbras presumably will be another warrior-king of Denmark. Horatio does not go home with us, but vanishes into the aura of Hamlet's after-light, perhaps to serve as witness of Hamlet's story over and over again. The hero leaves us with a sense that finally he has fathered himself, that he was beyond our touch though not beyond our affections, and that the catastrophes he helped provoke have brought about, not a new creation, but a fresh revelation of what was latent in reality but not evident without his own disaster.

V

As a coda, I return to my earlier implication that Shakespearean originality is the consequence of diction or a will over language changing his characters, and not of language itself. More than any other writer, Shakespeare is able to exemplify how meaning gets started rather than just renewed. Auden remarked that Falstaff is free of the superego; there is no over-I or above-I for that triumph of wit. Nietzsche, attempting to represent a man without a superego, gave us Zarathustra, a mixed achievement in himself, but a very poor representation when read side by side with Falstaff. Falstaff or Zarathustra? No conceivable reader would choose the Nietzschean rather than the Shakespearean over-man. Falstaff indeed *is* how meaning gets started: by excess, overflow, emanation, contamination, the will to life. Zarathustra is a juggler of perspectives, a receptive will to interpretation. Poor Falstaff ends in tragedy; his catastrophe is his dreadfully authentic love for Hal. Zarathustra loves only a trope, the solar trajectory, and essentially is himself a trope; he is Nietzsche's metalepsis or transumption of the philosophical tradition. A Formalist critic would say that Falstaff is a trope also, a gorgeous and glowing hyperbole. Say rather that Falstaff is a representation, in himself, of how meaning gets started, of how invention is accomplished and manifested. But we remember Falstaff as we want to remember him, triumphant in the tavern, and not rejected in the street. We remember Hamlet as he wanted us to remember him, as Horatio remembers him, without having to neglect his end. Perhaps Hamlet is a representation, in himself, not just of how meaning gets started, but also of how meaning itself is invention, of how meaning refuses to be deferred or to be ended. Perhaps again that is why we can imagine Hamlet as the author of *Hamlet*, as the original we call Shakespeare.

G. WILSON KNIGHT

"King Lear" and the Comedy of the Grotesque

It may appear strange to search for any sort of comedy as a primary theme in a play whose abiding gloom is so heavy, whose reading of human destiny and human actions so starkly tragic. Yet it is an error of aesthetic judgement to regard humour as essentially trivial. Though its impact usually appears vastly different from that of tragedy, yet there is a humour that treads the brink of tears, and tragedy which needs but an infinitesimal shift of perspective to disclose the varied riches of comedy. Humour is an evanescent thing, even more difficult of analysis and intellectual location than tragedy. To the coarse mind lacking sympathy an incident may seem comic which to the richer understanding is pitiful and tragic. So, too, one series of facts can be treated by the artist as either comic or tragic, lending itself equivalently to both. Sometimes a great artist may achieve significant effects by a criss-cross of tears and laughter. Chekov does this, especially in his plays. A shifting flash of comedy across the pain of the purely tragic both increases the tension and suggests, vaguely, a resolution and a purification. The comic and the tragic rest both on the idea of incompatibilities, and are also, themselves, mutually exclusive: therefore to mingle them is to add to the meaning of each; for the result is then but a new sublime incongruity.

King Lear is roughly analogous to Chekov where *Macbeth* is analogous to Dostoievsky. The wonder of Shakespearian tragedy is ever a mystery—a vague, yet powerful, tangible, presence; an interlocking of the mind with a profound meaning, a disclosure to the inward eye of vistas undreamed,

From *The Wheel of Fire.* Copyright © 1930 by Oxford University Press.

and but fitfully understood. *King Lear* is great in the abundance and richness of human delineation, in the level focus of creation that builds a massive oneness, in fact, a universe, of single quality from a multiplicity of differentiated units; and in a positive and purposeful working out of a purgatorial philosophy. But it is still greater in the perfect fusion of psychological realism with the daring flights of a fantastic imagination. The heart of a Shakespearian tragedy is centred in the imaginative, in the unknown; and in *King Lear*, where we touch the unknown, we touch the fantastic. The peculiar dualism at the root of this play which wrenches and splits the mind by a sight of incongruities displays in turn realities absurd, hideous, pitiful. This incongruity is Lear's madness; it is also the demonic laughter that echoes in the *Lear* universe. In pure tragedy the dualism of experience is continually being dissolved in the masterful beauty of passion, merged in the sunset of emotion. But in comedy it is not so softly resolved—incompatibilities stand out till the sudden relief of laughter or its equivalent of humour: therefore incongruity is the especial mark of comedy. Now in *King Lear* there is a dualism continually crying in vain to be resolved either by tragedy or comedy. Thence arises its peculiar tension of pain: and the course of the action often comes as near to the resolution of comedy as to that of tragedy. So I shall notice here the imaginative core of the play, and, excluding much of the logic of the plot from immediate attention, analyse the fantastic comedy of *King Lear*.

From the start, the situation has a comic aspect. It has been observed that Lear has, so to speak, staged an interlude, with himself as chief actor, in which he grasps expressions of love to his heart, and resigns his sceptre to a chorus of acclamations. It is childish, foolish—but very human. So, too, is the result. Sincerity forbids play-acting, and Cordelia cannot subdue her instinct to any judgement advising tact rather than truth. The incident is profoundly comic and profoundly pathetic. It is, indeed, curious that so storm-furious a play as *King Lear* should have so trivial a domestic basis: it is the first of our many incongruities to be noticed. The absurdity of the old King's anger is clearly indicated by Kent:

> Kill thy physician, and the fee bestow
> Upon the foul disease.
>
> (I. i. 166)

The result is absurd. Lear's loving daughter Cordelia is struck from his heart's register, and he is shortly, old and grey-haired and a king, cutting a cruelly ridiculous figure before the cold sanity of his unloving elder daughters. Lear is selfish, self-centred. The images he creates of his three daughters' love are quite false, sentimentalized: he understands the nature of none of his children, and demanding an unreal and impossible love from all three, is disillusioned by each in turn. But, though sentimental, this love is not weak. It is powerful and firm-planted in his mind as a mountain rock embedded in earth. The tearing out of it is hideous, cataclysmic. A tremendous soul is, as it were, incongruously geared to a puerile intellect. Lear's senses prove his idealized love-figments false, his intellect snaps, and, as the loosened drive flings limp, the disconnected engine of madness spins free, and the ungeared revolutions of it are terrible, fantastic. This, then, is the basis of the play: greatness linked to puerility. Lear's instincts are themselves grand, heroic—noble even. His judgement is nothing. He understands neither himself nor his daughters:

> REGAN: 'Tis the infirmity of his age: yet he hath ever but slenderly known himself.
> GONERIL: The best and soundest of his time hath been but rash . . .
> (I. i. 296)

Lear starts his own tragedy by a foolish misjudgement. Lear's fault is a fault of the mind, a mind unwarrantably, because selfishly, foolish. And he knows it:

> O Lear, Lear, Lear!
> Beat at this gate that let thy folly in,
> And thy dear judgement out!
> (I. iv. 294)

His purgatory is to be a purgatory of the mind, of madness. Lear has trained himself to think he cannot be wrong: he finds he is wrong. He has fed his heart on sentimental knowledge of his children's love: he finds their love is not sentimental. There is now a gaping dualism in his mind, drawn asunder by incongruities, and he endures madness. So the meaning of the play is embodied continually into a fantastic incongruity, which is implicit in the beginning—in the very act of Lear's renunciation, retaining the 'title and addition' of King, yet giving over a king's authority to his children. As he becomes torturingly aware of the truth, incongruity masters his mind, and fantastic madness ensues; and this peculiar fact of the Lear-theme is reflected in the *Lear* universe:

> GLOUCESTER: These late eclipses in the sun and moon portend no good to us: though the wisdom of nature can reason it thus and thus, yet nature finds itself scourged by the sequent effects: love cools, friendship falls off, brothers divide: in cities, mutinies; in countries, discord; in palaces, treason; and the bond cracked 'twixt son and father. This villain of mine comes under the prediction; there's son against father: the King falls from bias of nature; there's father

against child. We have seen the best of our time: machinations, hollowness, treachery, and all ruinous disorders, follow us disquietly to our graves.

(I. ii. 115)

Gloucester's words hint a universal incongruity here: the fantastic incongruity of parent and child opposed. And it will be most helpful later to notice the Gloucester-theme in relation to that of Lear.

From the first signs of Goneril's cruelty, the Fool is used as a chorus, pointing us to the absurdity of the situation. He is indeed an admirable chorus, increasing our pain by his emphasis on a humour which yet will not serve to merge the incompatible in a unity of laughter. He is not all wrong when he treats the situation as matter for a joke. Much here that is always regarded as essentially pathetic is not far from comedy. For instance, consider Lear's words:

> I will have such revenges on you both
> That all the world shall—I will do such things—
> What they are, yet I know not; but they shall be
> The terrors of the earth.

(II. iv. 282)

What could be more painfully incongruous, spoken, as it is, by an old man, a king, to his daughter? It is not far from the ridiculous. The very thought seems a sacrilegious cruelty, I know: but ridicule is generally cruel. The speeches of Lear often come near comedy. Again, notice the abrupt contrast in his words:

> But yet thou art my flesh, my blood, my daughters;
> Or rather a disease that's in my flesh,
> Which I must needs call mine: thou art a boil,
> A plague-sore, an embossed carbuncle,
> In my corrupted blood. But I'll not chide thee . . .

(II. iv. 224)

This is not comedy, nor humour. But it is exactly the stuff of which humour is made. Lear is mentally a child; in passion a titan. The absurdity of his every act at the beginning of his tragedy is contrasted with the dynamic fury which intermittently bursts out, flickers—then flames and finally gives us those grand apostrophes lifted from man's stage of earth to heaven's rain and fire and thunder:

> Blow, winds, and crack your cheeks! rage! blow!
> You cataracts and hurricanoes, spout
> Till you have drench'd our steeples, drown'd the cocks!

(III. ii. 1)

Two speeches of this passionate and unrestrained volume of Promethean curses are followed by:

> No, I will be the pattern of all patience;
> I will say nothing.
>
> (III. ii. 37)

Again we are in touch with potential comedy: a slight shift of perspective, and the incident is rich with humour. A sense of self-directed humour would have saved Lear. It is a quality he absolutely lacks.

Herein lies the profound insight of the Fool: he sees the potentialities of comedy in Lear's behaviour. This old man, recently a king, and, if his speeches are fair samples, more than a little of a tyrant, now goes from daughter to daughter, furious because Goneril dares criticize his pet knights, kneeling down before Regan, performing, as she says, 'unsightly tricks' (II. iv. 159)—the situation is excruciatingly painful, and its painfulness is exactly of that quality which embarrasses in some forms of comedy. In the theatre, one is terrified lest some one laugh: yet, if Lear could laugh—if the Lears of the world could laugh at themselves—there would be no such tragedy. In the early scenes old age and dignity suffer, and seem to deserve, the punishments of childhood:

> Now, by my life,
> Old fools are babes again; and must be used
> With checks as flatteries.
>
> (I. iii. 19)

The situation is summed up by the Fool:

LEAR: When were you wont to be so full of songs, sirrah?
FOOL: I have used it, nuncle, ever since thou madest thy daughters thy
      mother: for when thou gavest them the rod, and put'st down thine
      own breeches . . .

> (I. iv. 186)

The height of indecency in suggestion, the height of incongruity. Lear is spiritually put to the ludicrous shame endured bodily by Kent in the stocks: and the absurd rant of Kent, and the unreasonable childish temper of Lear, both merit in some measure what they receive. Painful as it may sound, that is, provisionally, a truth we should realize. The Fool realizes it. He is, too, necessary. Here, where the plot turns on the diverging tugs of two assurances in the mind, it is natural that the action be accompanied by some symbol of humour, that mode which is built of unresolved incompatibilities. Lear's torment is a torment of this dualistic kind, since he scarcely believes his senses when his daughters resist him. He repeats the histoy of Troilus, who cannot understand the faithlessness of Cressid. In *Othello* and *Timon of Athens* the transition is swift from extreme love to revenge or hate. The movement of Lear's mind is less direct: like Troilus, he is suspended between two separate assurances. Therefore Pandarus, in the latter acts of *Troilus and Cressida*, plays a part similar to the Fool in *King Lear*: both attempt to heal the gaping wound of the mind's incongruous knowledge by the unifying, healing release of laughter. They make no attempt to divert, but rather to direct the hero's mind to the present incongruity. The Fool sees, or tries to see, the humorous potentialities in the most heart-wrenching of incidents:

> LEAR: O me, my heart, my rising heart! but, down!
> FOOL: Cry to it, nuncle, as the cockney did to the eels when she put 'em
> i' the paste alive; she knapped 'em o' the coxcombs with a stick, and
> cried 'Down, wantons, down!' 'Twas her brother that, in pure
> kindness to his horse, buttered his hay.
>
> (II. iv. 122)

Except for the last delightful touch—the antithesis of the other—that is a cruel, ugly sense of humour. It is the sinister humour at the heart of this play: we are continually aware of the humour of cruelty and the cruelty of humour. But the Fool's use of it is not aimless. If Lear could laugh he might yet save his reason.

But there is no relief. Outside, in the wild country, the storm grows more terrible:

> KENT: . . . Since I was man
> Such sheets of fire, such bursts of horrid thunder,
> Such groans of roaring wind and rain, I never
> Remember to have heard . . .
>
> (III. ii. 45)

Lear's mind keeps returning to the unreality, the impossibility of what has happened:

> Your old kind father, whose frank heart gave all—
> O, that way madness lies; let me shun that;
> No more of that.
>
> (III. iv. 20)

He is still self-centred; cannot understand that he has been anything but a perfect father; cannot understand his daughters' behaviour. It is

> as this mouth should tear this hand
> For lifting food to't . . .
>
> (III. iv. 15)

It is incongruous, impossible. There is no longer any 'rule in unity itself'. Just as Lear's mind begins to fail, the Fool finds Edgar disguised as 'poor Tom'. Edgar now succeeds the Fool as the counterpart to the breaking sanity of Lear; and where the humour of the Fool made no contact with Lear's mind, the fantastic appearance and incoherent words of Edgar are immediately assimilated, as glasses correctly focused to the sight of oncoming madness. Edgar turns the balance of Lear's wavering mentality. His fantastic appearance and lunatic irrelevancies, with the storm outside, and the Fool still for occasional chorus, create a scene of wraith-like unreason, a vision of a world gone mad:

> . . . Bless thy five wits! Tom's a-cold—O, do de, do de, do de. Bless thee from whirlwinds, star-blasting, and taking! Do poor Tom some charity, whom the foul fiend vexes: there could I have him now—and there—and there again, and there.
>
> (III. iv. 57)

To Lear his words are easily explained. His daughters 'have brought him to this pass'. He cries:

> LEAR: Is it the fashion that discarded fathers
> Should have thus little mercy on their flesh?
> Judicious punishment! 'twas this flesh begot
> Those pelican daughters.
> EDGAR: Pillicock sat on Pillicock-hill:
> Hallo, halloo, loo, loo!
> FOOL: This cold night will turn us all to fools and madmen.
>
> (III. iv. 71)

What shall we say of this exquisite movement? Is it comedy? Lear's profound unreason is capped by the blatant irrelevance of Edgar's couplet suggested by the word 'pelican'; then the two are swiftly all but unified, for us if not for Lear, in the healing balm of the Fool's conclusion. It is the process of humour, where two incompatibles are resolved in laughter. The Fool does this again. Lear again speaks a profound truth as the wild night and Edgar's fantastic impersonation grip his mind and dethrone his conventional sanity:

> LEAR: Is man no more than this? Consider him well. Thou owest the worm no silk, the beast no hide, the sheep no wool, the cat no perfume. Ha! Here's three on 's are sophisticated! Thou art the thing itself: unaccommodated man is no more but such a poor, bare, forked animal as thou art. Off, off, you lendings! come unbutton here. (*Tearing off his clothes.*)
> FOOL: Prithee, nuncle, be contented; 'tis a naughty night to swim in.
>
> (III. iv. 105)

This is the furthest flight, not of tragedy, but of philosophic comedy. The autocratic and fiery-fierce old king, symbol of dignity, is confronted with the meanest of men: a naked lunatic beggar. In a flash of vision he attempts to become his opposite, to be naked, 'unsophisticated'. And then the opposing forces which struck the lightning-flash of vision tail off, resolved into a perfect unity by the Fool's laughter, reverberating, trickling, potent to heal in sanity the hideous unreason of this tempest-shaken night: ' 'tis a naughty night to swim in'. Again this is the process of humour: its flash of vision first bridges the positive and negative poles of the mind, unifying them, and then expresses itself in laughter.

This scene grows still more grotesque, fantastical, sinister. Gloucester enters, his torch flickering in the beating wind:

> FOOL: . . . Look, here comes a walking fire.
> (*Enter* GLOUCESTER, *with a torch.*)
> EDGAR: This is the foul fiend Flibbertigibbet: he begins at curfew and
>   walks till the first cock . . .
>
> (III. iv. 116)

Lear welcomes Edgar as his 'philosopher', since he embodies that philosophy of incongruity and the fantastically-absurd which is Lear's vision in madness. 'Noble philosopher', he says (III. iv. 176), and 'I will still keep with my philosopher' (III. iv. 180). The unresolved dualism that tormented Troilus and was given metaphysical expression by him (*Troilus and Cressida*, V. ii. 134–57) is here more perfectly bodied into the poetic symbol of poor Tom: and since Lear cannot hear the resolving laugh of foolery, his mind is focused only to the 'philosopher' mumbling of the foul fiend. Edgar thus serves to lure Lear on: we forget that he is dissimulating. Lear is the centre of our attention, and as the world shakes with tempest and unreason, we endure something of the shaking and the tempest of his mind. The absurd and fantastic reign supreme. Lear does not compass for more than a few speeches the 'noble anger' (II. iv. 279) for which he prayed, the anger of Timon. From the start he wavered between affection and disillusionment, love and hate. The heavens in truth 'fool' (II. iv. 278) him. He is the 'natural fool of fortune' (IV. vi. 196). Now his anger begins to be a lunatic thing, and when it rises to any sort of magnificent fury or power it is toppled over by the ridiculous capping of Edgar's irrelevancies:

> LEAR: To have a thousand with red burning spits
>   Come hissing in upon 'em—
> EDGAR: The foul fiend bites my back.
>
> (III. vi. 17)

The mock trial is instituted. Lear's curses were for a short space terrible, majestic, less controlled and purposeful than Timon's but passionate and grand in their tempestuous fury. Now, in madness, he flashes on us the ridiculous basis of his tragedy in words which emphasize the indignity and incongruity of it, and make his madness something nearer the ridiculous than the terrible, something which moves our pity, but does not strike awe:

> Arraign her first; 'tis Goneril. I here take my oath before this honourable assembly, she kicked the poor king her father.
>
> (III. vi. 49)

This stroke of the absurd—so vastly different from the awe we experience in face of Timon's hate—is yet fundamental here. The core of the play is an absurdity, an indignity, an incongruity. In no tragedy of Shakespeare does incident and dialogue so recklessly and miraculously walk the tight-rope of our pity over the depths of bathos and absurdity.

This particular region of the terrible bordering on the fantastic and absurd is exactly the playground of madness. Now the setting of Lear's madness includes a sub-plot where these same elements are presented in stark nakedness, with no veiling subtleties. The Gloucester-theme is a certain indication of our vision and helps us to understand, and feel, the enduring agony of Lear. As usual, the first scene of this play strikes the dominant note. Gloucester jests at the bastardy of his son Edmund, remarking that, though he is ashamed to acknowledge him, 'there was good sport at his making' (I. i. 23). That is, we start with humour in bad taste. The whole tragedy witnesses a sense of humour in 'the gods' which is in similar bad taste. Now all the Lear effects are exaggerated in the Gloucester theme. Edmund's plot is a more Iago-like, devilish, intentional thing than Goneril's and Regan's icy callousness. Edgar's supposed letter is crude and absurd:

> . . . I begin to find an idle and fond bondage in the oppression of aged tyranny . . .
>
> (I. ii. 53)

But then Edmund, wittiest and most attractive of villains, composed it. One can almost picture his grin as he penned those lines, commending them mentally to the limited intellect of his father. Yes—the Gloucester theme has a beginning even more fantastic than that of Lear's tragedy. And not only are the Lear effects here exaggerated in the directions of villainy and humour: they are even more clearly exaggerated in that of horror. The gouging out of Gloucester's eyes is a thing unnecessary, crude, disgusting: it is meant to be. It helps to provide an accompanying exaggeration of one element—that of cruelty—in the horror that makes Lear's madness. And not only horror: there is even again something satanically comic bedded deep in it. The sight of physical torment, to the uneducated, brings laughter. Shakespeare's England delighted in watching both physical torment and the comic ravings of actual lunacy. The dance of madmen in Webster's *Duchess of Malfi* is of the same ghoulish humour as Regan's plucking Gloucester by the beard: the groundlings will laugh at both. Moreover, the sacrilege of the human body in torture must be, to a human mind, incongruous, absurd. This hideous mockery is consummated in Regan's final witticism after Gloucester's eyes are out:

> Go, thrust him out at gates, and let him smell
> His way to Dover.
>
> (III. vii. 93)

The macabre humoresque of this is nauseating: but it is there, and integral to the play. These ghoulish horrors, so popular in Elizabethan drama, and the very stuff of the *Lear* of Shakespeare's youth, *Titus Andronicus*, find an exquisitely appropriate place in the tragedy of Shakespeare's maturity which takes as its especial province this territory of the grotesque and the fantastic which is Lear's madness. We are clearly pointed to this grim fun, this hideous sense of humour, at the back of tragedy:

> As flies to wanton boys are we to the gods;
> They kill us for their sport.
>
> (IV. i. 36)

This illustrates the exact quality I wish to emphasize: the humour a boy—even a kind boy—may see in the wriggles of an impaled insect. So, too, Gloucester is bound, and tortured, physically; and so the mind of Lear is impaled, crucified on the cross-beams of love and disillusion.

There follows the grim pilgrimage of Edgar and Gloucester towards Dover Cliff: an incident typical enough of *King Lear*—

> 'Tis the times' plague when madmen lead the blind.
> (IV. i. 46)

They stumble on, madman and blind man, Edgar mumbling:

> . . . five fiends have been in poor Tom at once; of lust, as Obidicut; Hobbididance, prince of dumbness; Mahu, of stealing; Modo, of murder; Flibbertigibbet, of mopping and mowing, who since possesses chambermaids and waiting-women . . .
>
> (IV. i. 59)

They are near Dover. Edgar persuades his father that they are climbing steep ground, though they are on a level field, that the sea can be heard beneath:

GLOUCESTER: Methinks the ground is even.
EDGAR: Horrible steep.
    Hark, do you hear the sea?
GLOUCESTER: No, truly.
EDGAR: Why, then your other senses grow imperfect
    By your eyes' anguish.

(IV. vi. 3)

Gloucester notices the changed sanity of Edgar's speech, and remarks thereon. Edgar hurries his father to the supposed brink, and vividly describes the dizzy precipice over which Gloucester thinks they stand:

> How fearful
> And dizzy 'tis to cast one's eyes so low!
> The crows and choughs that wing the midway air
> Show scarce so gross as beetles: half way down
> Hangs one that gathers samphire, dreadful trade! . . .

(IV. vi. 12)

Gloucester thanks him, and rewards him; bids him move off; then kneels, and speaks a prayer of noble resignation, breathing that stoicism which permeates the suffering philosophy of this play:

> O you mighty gods!
> This world I do renounce, and, in your sights,
> Shake patiently my great affliction off:
> If I could bear it longer, and not fall
> To quarrel with your great opposeless wills,
> My snuff and loathed part of nature should
> Burn itself out.

(IV. vi. 35)

Gloucester has planned a spectacular end for himself. We are given these noble descriptive and philosophical speeches to tune our minds to a noble, tragic sacrifice. And what happens? The old man falls from his kneeling posture a few inches, flat, face foremost. Instead of the dizzy circling to crash and spill his life on the rocks below—just this. The grotesque merged into the ridiculous reaches a consummation in this bathos of tragedy: it is the furthest, most exaggerated, reach of the poet's towering fantasticality. We have a sublimely daring stroke of technique, unjustifiable, like Edgar's emphasized and vigorous madness throughout, on the plane of plot-logic, and even to a superficial view somewhat out of place imaginatively in so dire and stark a limning of human destiny as is *King Lear*; yet this scene is in reality a consummate stroke of art. The Gloucester-theme throughout reflects and emphasizes and exaggerates all the percurrent qualities of the Lear-theme. Here the incongruous and fantastic element of the Lear-theme is boldly reflected into the tragically-absurd. The stroke is audacious, unashamed, and magical of effect. Edgar keeps up the deceit; persuades his father that he has really fallen; points to the empty sky, as to a cliff:

> . . . the shrill-gorged lark
> Cannot be heard so far . . .
> (IV. vi. 59)

and finally paints a fantastic picture of a ridiculously grotesque devil that stood with Gloucester on the edge:

> As I stood here below, methought his eyes
> Were two full moons; he had a thousand noses,
> Horns whelk'd and waved like the enridged sea;
> It was some fiend . . .
> (IV. vi. 70)

Some fiend, indeed.

There is masterful artistry in all this. The Gloucester-theme has throughout run separate from that of Lear, yet parallel, and continually giving us direct villainy where the other shows cold callousness; horrors of physical torment where the other has a subtle mental torment; culminating in this towering stroke of the grotesque and absurd to balance the fantastic incidents and speeches that immediately follow. At this point we suddenly have our first sight of Lear in the full ecstasy of his later madness. Now, when our imaginations are most powerfully quickened to the grotesque and incongruous, the whole surge of the Gloucester-theme, which has just reached its climax, floods as a tributary the main stream of our sympathy with Lear. Our vision has thus been uniquely focused to understand that vision of the grotesque, the incongruous, the fantastically-horrible, which is the agony of Lear's mind:

> Enter Lear, fantastically dressed with wild flowers.
> (IV. vi. 81)

So runs Capell's direction. Lear, late 'every inch a king', the supreme pathetic figure of literature, now utters the wild and whirling language of furthest madness. Sometimes his words hold profound meaning. Often they are tuned to the orthodox Shakespearian hate and loathing, especially sex-loathing, of the hate-theme. Or again, they are purely ludicrous, or would be, were it not a Lear who speaks them:

> . . . Look, look, a mouse! Peace, peace; this piece of toasted cheese will do't . . .
> (IV. vi. 90)

It is certainly as well that we have been by now prepared for the grotesque. Laughter is forbidden us. Consummate art has so forged plot and incident that we may watch with tears rather than laughter the cruelly comic actions of Lear:

> LEAR: I will die bravely, like a bridegroom. What!
>   I will be jovial: come, come; I am a king,
>   My masters, know you that?
> GENTLEMAN: You are a royal one, and we obey you.
> LEAR: Then there's life in't. Nay, if you get it, you shall get it with
>   running. Sa, sa, sa, sa.
>
> (IV. vi. 203)

Lear is a child again in his madness. We are in touch with the exquisitely pathetic, safeguarded only by Shakespeare's masterful technique from the bathos of comedy.

This recurring and vivid stress on the incongruous and the fantastic is not a subsidiary element in *King Lear*: it is the very heart of the play. We watch humanity grotesquely tormented, cruelly and with mockery impaled: nearly all the persons suffer some form of crude indignity in the course of the play. I have noticed the major themes of Lear and Gloucester: there are others. Kent is banished, undergoes the disguise of a servant, is put to shame in the stocks; Cornwall is killed by his own servant resisting the dastardly mutilation of Gloucester; Oswald, the prim courtier, is done to death by Edgar in the role of an illiterate country yokel—

> . . . keep out, che vor ye, or ise try whether your costard or my
> ballow be the harder . . .
>
> (IV. vi. 247)

Edgar himself endures the utmost degradation of his disguise as 'poor Tom', begrimed and naked, and condemned to speak nothing but idiocy. Edmund alone steers something of an unswerving tragic course, brought to a fitting, deserved, but spectacular end, slain by his wronged brother, nobly repentant at the last:

> EDMUND: What you have charged me with, that have I done;
>   And more, much more; the time will bring it out:
>   'Tis past, and so am I. But what art thou
>   That hast this fortune on me? If thou'rt noble,
>   I do forgive thee.
> EDGAR: Let's exchange charity.
>   I am no less in blood than thou art, Edmund;
>   If more, the more thou hast wrong'd me.
>   My name is Edgar . . .
>
> (V. iii. 164)

The note of forgiving chivalry reminds us of the deaths of Hamlet and Laertes. Edmund's fate is nobly tragic: 'the wheel has come full circle; I am here' (V. iii. 176). And Edmund is the most villainous of all. Again, we have incongruity; and again, the Gloucester-theme reflects the Lear-theme. Edmund is given a noble, an essentially tragic, end, and Goneril and Regan, too, meet their ends with something of tragic fineness in pursuit of their evil desires. Regan dies by her sister's poison; Goneril with a knife. They die, at least, in the cause of love—love of Edmund. Compared with these deaths, the end of Cordelia is horrible, cruel, unnecessarily cruel—the final grotesque horror in the play. Her villainous sisters are already dead. Edmund is nearly dead, repentant. It is a matter of seconds—and rescue comes too late. She is hanged by a common soldier. The death which Dostoievsky's Stavrogin singled out as of all the least heroic and picturesque, or rather, shall we say, the most hideous and degrading: this is the fate that grips the white innocence and resplendent love-strength of Cordelia. To be hanged, after the death of her enemies, in the midst of friends. It is the last hideous joke of destiny: this—and the fact that Lear is still alive, has recovered his sanity for this. The death of Cordelia is the last and most horrible of all the horrible incongruities I have noticed:

> Why should a dog, a horse, a rat have life,
> And thou no breath at all?
>
> (V. iii. 308)

We remember: 'Upon such sacrifices, my Cordelia, the gods themselves throw incense' (V. iii. 20). Or do they laugh, and is the *Lear* universe one ghastly piece of fun?

We do not feel that. The tragedy is most poignant in that it is purposeless, unreasonable. It is the most fearless artistic facing of the ultimate cruelty of things in our literature. That cruelty would be less were there not this element of comedy which I have emphasized, the insistent incongruities, which create and accompany the madness of Lear, which leap to vivid shape in the mockery of Gloucester's suicide, which are intrinsic in the texture of the whole play. Mankind is, as it were, deliberately and comically tormented by 'the gods'. He is not even allowed to die tragically. Lear is 'bound upon a wheel of fire' and only death will end the victim's agony:

> Vex not his ghost: O, let him pass! he hates him
> That would upon the rack of this tough world
> Stretch him out longer.
>
> (V. iii. 315)

King Lear is supreme in that, in this main theme, it faces the very absence of tragic purpose: wherein it is profoundly different from *Timon of Athens*. Yet, as we close the sheets of this play, there is no horror, nor resentment. The tragic purification of the essentially untragic is yet complete.

Now in this essay it will, perhaps, appear that I have unduly emphasized one single element of the play, magnifying it, and leaving the whole distorted. It has been my purpose to emphasize. I have not not exaggerated. The pathos has not been minimized: it is redoubled. Nor does the use of the words 'comic' and 'humour' here imply disrespect to the poet's purpose: rather I have used these words, crudely no doubt, to cut out for analysis the very heart of the play—the thing that man dares scarcely face: the demonic grin of the incongruous and absurd in the most pitiful of human struggles with an iron fate. It is this that wrenches, splits, gashes the mind till it utters the whirling vapourings of lunacy. And, though love and music—twin sisters of salvation—temporarily may heal the racked consciousness of Lear, yet, so deeply planted in the facts of our life is this unknowing ridicule of destiny, that the uttermost tragedy of the incongruous ensues, and there is no hope save in the broken heart and limp body of death. This is of all the most agonizing of tragedies to endure: and if we are to feel more than a fraction of this agony, we must have sense of this quality of grimmest humour. We must beware of sentimentalizing the cosmic mockery of the play.

And is there, perhaps, even a deeper, and less heart-searing, significance in its humour? Smiles and tears are indeed most curiously interwoven here. Gloucester was saved from his violent and tragic suicide that he might recover his wronged son's love, and that his heart might

> 'Twixt two extremes of passion, joy and grief,
> Burst smilingly.
>
> (V. iii. 200)

Lear dies with the words

> Do you see this? Look on her, look, her lips,
> Look there, look there!
>
> (V. iii. 312)

What smiling destiny is this he sees at the last instant of racked mortality? Why have we that strangely beautiful account of Cordelia's first hearing of her father's pain:

> . . . patience and sorrow strove
> Who should express her goodliest. You have seen
> Sunshine and rain at once: her smiles and tears

Were like a better way: those happy smilets,
That play'd on her ripe lip, seem'd not to know
What guests were in her eyes; which parted thence,
As pearls from diamonds dropp'd. In brief,
Sorrow would be a rarity most belov'd,
If all could so become it.

(IV. iii. 18)

What do we touch in these passages? Sometimes we know that all human pain holds beauty, that no tear falls but it dews some flower we cannot see. Perhaps humour, too, is inwoven in the universal pain, and the enigmatic silence holds not only an unutterable sympathy, but also the ripples of an impossible laughter whose flight is not for the wing of human understanding; and perhaps it is this that casts its darting shadow of the grotesque across the furrowed pages of *King Lear*.

HAROLD GODDARD

"*Romeo and Juliet*"

One word has dominated the criticism of *Romeo and Juliet:* "star-cross'd."

> From forth the fatal loins of these two foes,

says the Prologue-Chorus,

> A pair of star-cross'd lovers take their life.

"Star-cross'd" backed by "fatal" has pretty much surrendered this drama to the astrologers. "In this play," says one such interpreter, "simply the Fates have taken this young pair and played a cruel game against them with loaded dice, unaided by any evil in men." That is merely an extreme expression of the widely held view that makes *Romeo and Juliet*, in contrast with all Shakespeare's later tragedies, a tragedy of accident rather than of character and on that account a less profound and less universal work. That this play betrays signs of immaturity and lacks some of the marks of mastery that are common to the other tragedies may readily be granted. But that its inferiority is due to the predominance of accident over character ought not to be conceded without convincing demonstration. The burden of proof is certainly on those who assert it, for nowhere else does Shakespeare show any tendency to believe in fate in this sense. The integrity of his mind makes it highly unlikely that in just one instance he would have let the plot of the story he was dramatizing warp his convictions about freedom.

The theme of *Romeo and Juliet* is love and violence and their interactions. In it these two mightiest of mighty opposites meet each other

---

squarely—and one wins. And yet the other wins. This theme in itself makes *Romeo and Juliet* an astrological play in the sense that it is concerned throughout with Venus and Mars, with love and "war," and with little else. Nothing ever written perhaps presents more simply what results from the conjunction of these two "planets." But that does not make it a fatalistic drama. It all depends on what you mean by "stars." If by stars you mean the material heavenly bodies exercising from birth a predestined and inescapable occult influence on man, Romeo and Juliet were no more star-crossed than any lovers, even though their story was more unusual and dramatic. But if by stars you mean—as the deepest wisdom of the ages, ancient and modern, does—a psychological projection on the planets and constellations of the unconsciousness of man, which in turn is the accumulated experience of the race, then Romeo and Juliet and all the other characters of the play are star-crossed as every human being is who is passionately alive.

> In tragic life, God wot,
> No villain need be! Passions spin the plot,
> We are betrayed by what is false within.

The "villain" need not be a conspicuous incarnation of evil like Richard III or Iago; the "hero" himself may be the "villain" by being a conspicuous incarnation of weakness as was another Richard or a Troilus. Or the "villain" may consist in a certain chemical interplay of the passions of two or more characters. To seek a special "tragic flaw" in either Romeo or Juliet is foolish and futile. From pride down, we all have flaws enough to make of every life and of life itself a perpetual and universal tragedy. Altering his source to make the point unmistakable, Shakespeare is at pains to show that, however much the feud between Capulets and Montagues had to do with it incidentally, the tragedy of this play flowed immediately from another cause entirely. But of that in its place. Enough now if we have raised a suspicion that the "star-cross'd" of the Prologue should be taken in something other than a literal sense, or, better, attributed to the Chorus, not to the poet. The two are far from being the same.

In retrospect, Shakespeare's plays, which in one sense culminate in *King Lear* and in another in *The Tempest*, are seen to deal over and over with the same underlying subject that dominates the Greek drama: the relation of the generations. *Romeo and Juliet*, as the first play of its author in which this subject is central, assumes a profound seminal as well as intrinsic interest on that account. It points immediately in this respect to *Henry IV* and *Hamlet*, and ultimately to *King Lear* and *The Tempest*.

This theme of "the fathers" is merely another way of expressing the theme of "the stars." For the fathers are the stars and the stars are the fathers in the sense that the fathers stand for the accumulated experience of the past, for tradition, for authority, and hence for the two most potent forces that mold and so impart "destiny" to the child's life. Those forces, of course, are heredity and training, which between them create that impalpable mental environment, inner and outer, that is even more potent than either of them alone. The hatred of the hostile houses in *Romeo and Juliet* is an inheritance that every member of these families is born into as truly as he is born with the name Capulet or Montague. Their younger generations have no more choice in the matter than they have choice of the language they will grow up to speak. They suck in the venom with their milk. "So is the will of a living daughter curbed by the will of a dead father," as Portia puts it in *The Merchant of Venice*. The daughter may be a son and the father may be living, but the principle is the same. Thus the fathers cast the horoscopes of the children in advance— and are in that sense their stars. If astrology is itself, as it is, a kind of primitive and unconscious psychology, then the identity of the stars and the fathers becomes even more pronounced.

Now there is just one agency powerful enough in youth to defy and cut across this domination of the generations, and that is love. Love also is a "star" but in another and more celestial sense. Romeo, of the Montagues, after a sentimental and unrequited languishing after one Rosaline, falls in love at first sight with Juliet, of the Capulets, and instantly the instilled enmity of generations is dissipated like mist by morning sunshine, and the love that embraces Juliet embraces everything that Juliet touches or that touches her.

> My bounty is as boundless as the sea,
> My love as deep; the more I give to thee,
> The more I have, for both are infinite.

The words—music, imagery, and thought uniting to make them as won-derful as any ever uttered about love—are Juliet's, but Romeo's love is as deep—almost. It is love's merit, not his, that his enemies suddenly become glorified with the radiance of the medium through which he now sees everything. Hostility simply has nothing to breathe in such a transcen-dental atmosphere. It is through this effect of their love on both lovers, and the poetry in which they spontaneously embody it, that Shakespeare convinces us it is no mere infatuation, but love indeed in its divine sense. Passion it is, of course, but that contaminated term has in our day become helpless to express it. Purity would be the perfect word for it if the world had not forgotten that purity is simply Greek for fire.

II

Shakespeare sees to it that we shall not mistake this white flame of Romeo's love, or Juliet's, for anything lower by opposing to the lovers two of the impurest characters he ever created, Mercutio and the Nurse. And yet, in spite of them, it has often been so mistaken. Mercutio and the Nurse are masterpieces of characterization so irresistible that many are tempted to let them arrogate to themselves as virtue what is really the creative merit of their maker. They are a highly vital pair, brimming with life and fire—but fire in a less heavenly sense than the one just mentioned. Juliet, at the most critical moment of her life, sums up the Nurse to all eternity in one word. When, in her darkest hour, this woman who has acted as mother to her from birth goes back on her completely, in a flash of revelation the girl sees what she is, and, reversing in one second the feeling of a lifetime, calls her a fiend ("most wicked fiend"). She could not have chosen a more accurate term, for the Nurse is playing at the moment precisely the part of the devil in a morality play. And Juliet's "ancient damnation" is an equally succinct description of her sin. What more ancient damnation is there than sensuality—and all the other sins it brings in its train? Those who dismiss the Nurse as just a coarse old woman whose loquacity makes us laugh fail hopelessly to plumb the depth of her depravity. It was the Nurse's desertion of her that drove Juliet to Friar Laurence and the desperate expedient of the sleeping potion. Her cowardice was a link in the chain that led to Juliet's death.

The Nurse has sometimes been compared with Falstaff—perhaps the poet's first comic character who clearly surpassed her. Any resemblance between them is superficial, for they are far apart as the poles. Falstaff was at home in low places but the sun of his imagination always accompanied him as a sort of disinfectant. The Nurse had no imagination in any proper sense. No sensualist—certainly no old sensualist—ever has. Falstaff loved Hal. What the Nurse's "love" for Juliet amounted to is revealed when she advises her to make the best of a bad situation and take Paris (bigamy and all). The man she formerly likened to a toad suddenly becomes superior to an eagle.

> Go, counsellor,

cries Juliet, repudiating her Satan without an instant's hesitation,

> Thou and my bosom henceforth shall be twain.

It is the rejection of the Nurse. But unlike Falstaff, when he is rejected, she carries not one spark of our sympathy or pity with her, and a pathetic account of her death, as of his, would be unthinkable. We scorn her as utterly as Juliet does.

III

The contrast between Friar Laurence and the Nurse even the most casual reader or spectator could scarcely miss. The difference between the spiritual adviser of Romeo and the worldly confidant of Juliet speaks for itself. The resemblance of Mercutio to the Nurse is more easily overlooked, together with the analogy between the part he plays in Romeo's life and the part she plays in Juliet's. Yet it is scarcely too much to say that the entire play is built around that resemblance and that analogy.

The indications abound that Shakespeare created these two to go together. To begin with, they hate each other on instinct, as two rival talkers generally do, showing how akin they are under the skin. "A gentleman, nurse," says Romeo of Mercutio, "that loves to hear himself talk, and will speak more in a minute than he will stand to in a month." The cap which Romeo thus quite innocently hands the Nurse fits her so perfectly that she immediately puts it on in two speeches about Mercutio which are typical examples of *her* love of hearing herself talk and of saying things *she* is powerless to stand by:

> An a' speak any thing against me, I'll take him down, an 'a were lustier than he is, and twenty such Jacks; and if I cannot, I'll find those that shall. Scurvy knave! I am none of his flirt-gills; I am none of his skains-mates. (*Turning to* PETER, *her man*) And thou must stand by too, and suffer every knave to use me at his pleasure! . . . Now, afore God, I am so vexed, that every part about me quivers. Scurvy knave!

That last, and the tone of the whole, show that there was a genuinely vicious element in the Nurse under her superficial good nature, as there invariably is in an old sensualist; and I do not believe it is exceeding the warrant of the text to say that the rest of the speech in which she warns Romeo against gross behavior toward her young gentlewoman—quite in the manner of Polonius and Laertes warning Ophelia against Hamlet—proves that in her heart she would have been delighted to have him corrupt her provided she could have shared the secret and been the go-between. "A bawd, a bawd, a bawd!" is Mercutio's succinct description of her.

But, as usual, when a man curses someone else, he characterizes himself. In what sense Mercutio is a bawd appears only too soon. In the meantime what a pity it is that he is killed off so early in the action as to allow no full and final encounter between these two fountains of loquacity! "Nay, an there were two such, we should have none shortly." Mercutio himself says it in another connection, but it applies perfectly to this incomparable pair. Their roles are crowded with parallelisms even down to what seem like the most trivial details. "We'll to dinner thither," says Mercutio, for example, parting from Romeo in Act II, scene 4. "Go, I'll to dinner," says the Nurse on leaving Juliet at the end of scene 5. A tiny touch. But they are just the two who would be certain never to miss a meal. In Shakespeare even such trifles have significance.

The fact is that Mercutio and the Nurse are simply youth and old age of the same type. He is aimed at the same goal she has nearly attained. He would have become the same sort of old man that she is old woman, just as she was undoubtedly the same sort of young girl that he is young man. They both think of nothing but sex—except when they are so busy eating or quarreling that they can think of nothing. (I haven't forgotten Queen Mab; I'll come to her presently.) Mercutio cannot so much as look at the clock without a bawdy thought. So permeated is his language with indecency that most of it passes unnoticed not only by the innocent reader but by all not schooled in Elizabethan smut. Even on our own unsqueamish stage an unabridged form of his role in its twentieth-century equivalent would not be tolerated. Why does Shakespeare place the extreme example of this man's soiled fantasies precisely before the balcony scene? Why but to stress the complete freedom from sensuality of Romeo's passion? Place Mercutio's dirtiest words, as Shakespeare does, right beside Romeo's apostrophe to his "bright angel" and all the rest of that scene where the lyricism of young love reaches one of its loftiest pinnacles in all poetry—and what remains to be said for Mercutio? Nothing—except that he is Mercutio. His youth, the hot weather, the southern temperament, the fashion among Italian gentlemen of the day, are unavailing pleas; not only Romeo, but Benvolio, had those things to contend with also. And they escaped. Mercury is close to the sun. But it was the material sun, Sol, not the god, Helios, that Mercutio was close to. Beyond dispute, this man had vitality, wit, and personal magnetism. But personal magnetism combined with sexuality and pugnacity is one of the most dangerous mixtures that can exist. The unqualified laudation that Mercutio has frequently received, and the suggestion that Shakespeare had to kill him off lest he quite set the play's titular hero in the shade, are the best proof of the truth of that statement. Those who are themselves seduced by Mercutio are not likely to be good judges of him. It may be retorted that Mercutio is nearly always a success on the stage, while Romeo is likely to be insipid. The answer to that is that while Mercutios are relatively common, Romeos are excessively rare. If Romeo proves insipid, he has been wrongly cast or badly acted.

"But how about Queen Mab?" it will be asked. The famous description of her has been widely held to be quite out of character and has been set down as an outburst of poetry from the author put arbitrarily in Mercutio's mouth. But the judgment "out of character" should always be a last resort. Undoubtedly the lines, if properly his, do reveal an unsuspected side of Mercutio. The prankish delicacy of some of them stands out in pleasing contrast with his grosser aspects. The psychology of this is sound. The finer side of a sensualist is suppressed and is bound to come out, if at all, incidentally, in just such a digression as this seems to be. Shakespeare can be trusted not to leave such things out. Few passages in his plays, however, have been more praised for the wrong reasons. The account of Queen Mab is supposed to prove Mercutio's imagination: under his pugnacity there was a poet. It would be nearer the truth, I think, to guess that Shakespeare put it in as an example of what poetry is popularly held to be and is not. The lines on Queen Mab are indeed delightful. But imagination in any proper sense they are not. They are sheer fancy. Moreover, Mercutio's anatomy and philosophy of dreams prove that he knows nothing of their genuine import. He dubs them

> the children of an idle brain,
> Begot of nothing but vain fantasy.

Perhaps his are—the Queen Mab lines would seem to indicate as much. Romeo, on the other hand, holds that dreamers "dream things true," and gives a definition of them that for combined brevity and beauty would be hard to better. They are "love's shadows." And not only from what we can infer about his untold dream on this occasion, but from all the dreams and premonitions of both Romeo and Juliet throughout the play, they come from a fountain of wisdom somewhere beyond time. Primitives distinguish between "big" and "little" dreams. (Aeschylus makes the same distinction in *Prometheus Bound.*) Mercutio, with his aldermen and gnats and coachmakers and sweetmeats and parsons and drums and ambuscadoes, may tell us a little about the littlest of little dreams. He thinks that dreamers are still in their day world at night. Both Romeo and Juliet know that there are dreams that come from as far below the surface of that world as was that prophetic tomb at the bottom of which she saw him "as one dead" at their last parting. Finally, how characteristic of Mercutio that he should make Queen Mab a midwife and blemish his description of her by turning her into a "hag" whose function is to bring an end to maidenhood. Is this another link between Mercutio and the Nurse? Is Shakespeare here preparing the way for his intimation that she would be quite capable of assisting in Juliet's corruption? It might well be. When Shakespeare writes a speech that seems to be out of character, it generally, as in this case, deserves the closest scrutiny.

And there is another justification of the Queen Mab passage. Romeo and Juliet not only utter poetry; they are poetry. The loveliest comment on Juliet I ever heard expressed this to perfection. It was made by a girl only a little older than Juliet herself. When Friar Laurence recommends philosophy to Romeo as comfort in banishment, Romeo replies:

> Hang up philosophy!
> Unless philosophy can make a Juliet . . .
> It helps not, it prevails not. Talk no more.

"Philosophy can't," the girl observed, "but poetry can—and it did!" Over against the poetry of Juliet, Shakespeare was bound, by the demands of contrast on which all art rests, to offer in the course of his play examples of poetry in various verbal, counterfeit, or adulterate estates.

> This precious book of love, this unbound lover,
> To beautify him, only lacks a cover.

That is Lady Capulet on the prospective bridegroom, Paris. It would have taken the play's booby prize for "poetry" if Capulet himself had not outdone it in his address to the weeping Juliet:

> How now! a conduit, girl? What, still in tears?
> Evermore showering? In one little body
> Thou counterfeit'st a bark, a sea, a wind;
> For still thy eyes, which I may call the sea,
> Do ebb and flow with tears; the bark thy body is,
> Sailing in this salt flood; the winds, thy sighs;
> Who, raging with thy tears, and they with them,
> Without a sudden calm, will overset
> Thy tempest-tossed body.

It is almost as if Shakespeare were saying in so many words: That is how poetry is not written. Yet, a little later, when the sight of his daughter, dead as all suppose, shakes even this egotist into a second of sincerity, he can say:

> Death lies on her like an untimely frost
> Upon the sweetest flower of all the field.

There is poetry, deep down, even in Capulet. But the instant passes and he is again talking about death as his son-in-law—and all the rest. The

Nurse's vain repetitions in this scene are further proof that she is a heathen. Her O-lamentable-day's only stress the lack of one syllable of genuine grief or love such as Juliet's father shows. These examples all go to show what Shakespeare is up to in the Queen Mab speech. It shines, and even seems profound, beside the utterances of the Capulets and the Nurse. But it fades, and grows superficial, beside Juliet's and Romeo's. It is one more shade of what passes for poetry but is not.

IV

The crisis of *Romeo and Juliet,* so far as Romeo is concerned, is the scene (just after the secret marriage of the two lovers) in which Mercutio and Tybalt are slain and Romeo banished. It is only two hundred lines long. Of these two hundred lines, some forty are introduction and sixty epilogue to the main action. As for the other hundred that come between, it may be doubted whether Shakespeare to the end of his career ever wrote another hundred that surpasssed them in the rapidity, inevitability, and psychologic truth of the succession of events that they comprise. There are few things in dramatic literature to match them. And yet I think they are generally misunderstood. The scene is usually taken as the extreme precipitation in the play of the Capulet-Montague feud; whereas Shakespeare goes out of his way to prove that at most the feud is merely the occasion of the quarrel. Its cause he places squarely in the temperament and character of Mercutio, and Mercutio, it is only too easy to forget, is neither a Capulet nor a Montague, but a kinsman of the Prince who rules Verona, and, as such, is under special obligation to preserve a neutral attitude between the two houses.

This will sound to some like mitigating the guilt of Tybalt. But Tybalt has enough to answer for without making him responsible for Mercutio's sins.

The nephew of Lady Capulet is as dour a son of pugnacity as Mercutio is a dashing one:

> What, drawn, and talk of peace! I hate the word,
> As I hate hell.

These words—almost the first he speaks in the play—give Tybalt's measure. "More than prince of cats," Mercutio calls him, which is elevated to "king of cats" in the scene in which he mounts the throne of violence. (It is a comment on the Nurse's insight into human nature that she speaks of this fashionable desperado as "O courteous Tybalt! honest gentleman!") Mercutio's contempt for Tybalt is increased by the latter's affectation of the latest form in fencing: "He fights as you sing prick-song, keeps time, distance, and proportion. . . . The pox of such antic, lisping, affecting fantasticoes; these new tuners of accents!" Yet but a moment later, in an exchange of quips with Romeo, we find Mercutio doing with his wit just what he has scorned Tybalt for doing with his sword. For all their differences, as far as fighting goes Mercutio and Tybalt are two of a kind and by the former's rule are predestined to extinction: "an there were two such, we should have none shortly, for one would kill the other." When one kills the other, there is not one left, but none. That is the arithmetic of it. The encounter is not long postponed.

Tybalt is outraged when he discovers that a Montague has invaded the Capulet mansion on the occasion of the ball when Romeo first sees Juliet. But for his uncle he would assail the intruder on the spot:

> Patience perforce with wilful choler meeting
> Makes my flesh tremble in their different greeting.
> I will withdraw; but this intrusion shall
> Now seeming sweet convert to bitter gall.

He is speaking of the clash between patience and provocation in himself. But he might be prophesying his meeting with Romeo. As the third act opens, he is hunting his man.

Tybalt is not the only one who is seeking trouble. The first forty lines of the crisis scene are specifically devised to show that Mercutio was out to have a fight under any and all circumstances and at any price. As well ask a small boy and a firecracker to keep apart as Mercutio and a quarrel. Sensuality and pugnacity are the poles of his nature. In the latter respect he is a sort of Mediterranean Hotspur, his frank southern animality taking the place of the idealistic "honour" of his northern counterpart. He is as fiery in a literal as Romeo is in a poetic sense.

The scene is a public place. Enter Mercutio and Benvolio. Benvolio knows his friend:

> I pray thee, good Mercutio, let's retire.
> The day is hot, the Capulets abroad,
> And, if we meet, we shall not 'scape a brawl,
> For now, these hot days, is the mad blood stirring.

Mercutio retorts with a description of the cool-tempered Benvolio that makes him out an inveterate hothead:

Thou! why, thou wilt quarrel with a man that hath a hair more, or a hair less, in his beard, than thou hast. Thou wilt quarrel with a man for cracking nuts, having no other reason but because thou hast hazel eyes. What eye but such an eye would spy out such a quarrel? Thy head is as full of quarrels as an egg is full of meat, and yet thy head hath been beaten as addle as an egg for quarrelling. Thou hast quarrelled with a man for coughing in the street, because he hath wakened thy dog that hath lain asleep in the sun. Didst thou not fall out with a tailor for wearing his new doublet before Easter? with another, for tying his new shoes with old riband?

This, the cautious and temperate Benvolio! As Mercutio knows, it is nothing of the sort. It is an ironic description of himself. It is he, not his friend, who will make a quarrel out of anything—out of nothing, rather, and give it a local habitation and a name, as a poet does with the creatures of his imagination. Mercutio is pugnacity in its pure creative state. At the risk of the Prince's anger, he makes his friend Romeo's cause his own and roams the streets in the hope of encountering some Capulet with whom to pick a quarrel. The feud is only a pretext. If it hadn't been that, it would have been something else. The Chorus may talk about "stars," but in this case Mars does not revolve in the skies on the other side of the Earth from Venus, but resides on earth right under the jerkin of this particular impulsive youth, Mercutio. Or if this "fate" be a god rather than a planet, then Mercutio has opened his heart and his home to him with unrestrained hospitality. So Romeo is indeed "star-cross'd" in having Mercutio for a friend.

Mercutio has no sooner finished his topsy-turvy portrait of Benvolio than Tybalt and his gang come in to reveal which of the two the description fits. Tybalt is searching for Romeo, to whom he has just sent a challenge, and recognizing Romeo's friends begs "a word with one of you." He wishes, presumably, to ask where Romeo is. But Mercutio, bent on provocation, retorts, "make it a word and a blow." Benvolio tries in vain to intervene. Just as things are getting critical, Romeo enters, and Tybalt turns from Mercutio to the man he is really seeking:

> Romeo, the love I bear thee can afford
> No better term than this,—thou art a villain.

Here is the most direct and galling of insults. Here are Mercutio, Benvolio, and the rest waiting to see how Romeo will take it. The temperature is blistering in all senses. And what does Romeo say?

> Tybalt, the reason that I have to love thee
> Doth much excuse the appertaining rage
> To such a greeting; villain am I none;
> Therefore farewell; I see thou know'st me not.

We who are in the secret know that "the reason" is Juliet and that his love for her is capable of wrapping all Capulets in its miraculous mantle, even "the king of cats."

But Tybalt is intent on a fight and will not be put off by kindness however sincere or deep. "Boy," he comes back insolently,

> this shall not excuse the injuries
> That thou hast done me; therefore turn and draw.

Romeo, however, is in the power of something that makes him impervious to insults:

> I do protest I never injur'd thee,
> But love thee better than thou canst devise
> Till thou shalt know the reason of my love;
> And so, good Capulet,—which name I tender
> As dearly as my own,—be satisfied.

The world has long since decided what to think of a man who lets himself be called a villain without retaliating. Romeo, to put it in one word, proves himself, according to the world's code, a mollycoddle. And indeed a mollycoddle might act exactly as Romeo appears to. But if Romeo is a mollycoddle, then Jesus was a fool to talk about loving one's enemies, for Romeo, if anyone ever did, is doing just that at this moment. And Juliet was demented to talk about love being boundless and infinite, for here Romeo is about to prove that faith precisely true. Those who think that Jesus, and Juliet, and Romeo were fools will have plenty of backing. The "fathers" will be on their side. They will have the authority of the ages and the crowd. Only a philosopher or two, a few lovers, saints, and poets will be against them. The others will echo the

> O calm, dishonourable, vile submission!

with which Mercutio draws his rapier and begins hurling insults at Tybalt that make Tybalt's own seem tame:

> MER: Tybalt, you rat-catcher, will you walk?
> TYB: What wouldst thou have with me?
> MER: Good king of cats, nothing but one of your nine lives.

And Mercutio threatens to stick him before he can draw if he does not do so instantly. What can Tybalt do but draw? "I am for you," he cries, as he does so.

Such, however, is the power of Romeo's love that even now he attempts to prevent the duel:

> Gentle Mercutio, put thy rapier up.

But Mercutio pays no attention and the two go to it. If ever a quarrel scene defined the central offender and laid the responsibility at one man's door, this is the scene and Mercutio is the man. It takes two to make a quarrel. Romeo, the Montague, will not fight. Tybalt, the Capulet, cannot fight if Romeo will not. With Mercutio Tybalt has no quarrel. The poet takes pains to make that explicit in a startling way. "Peace be with you, sir," are the words Tybalt addresses to Mercutio when Romeo first enters. *That* from the man who once cried,

> peace! I hate the word,
> As I hate hell.

Now we see why Shakespeare had him say it. It was in preparation for this scene. Thus he lets one word exonerate Tybalt of the responsibility for what ensues between himself and Mercutio.

And now, condensed into the fractional part of a second, comes the crisis in Romeo's life. Not later, when he decides to kill Tybalt, but now. Now is the moment when two totally different universes wait as it were on the turning of a hand. There is nothing of its kind to surpass it in all Shakespeare, not even in *Hamlet* or *King Lear*, not, one is tempted to think, in all the drama of the world. Here, if anywhere, Shakespeare shows that the fate we attribute to the stars lies in our own souls.

> Our remedies oft in ourselves do lie,
> Which we ascribe to heaven: the fated sky
> Gives us free scope.

Romeo had free scope. For, if we are free to choose between two compulsions, we are in so far free. Romeo was free to act under the compulsion of force or under the compulsion of love—under the compulsion of the stars, that is, in either of two opposite senses. Granted that the temptation to surrender to the former was at the moment immeasurably great, the power of the latter, if Juliet spoke true, was greater yet:

> My bounty is as boundless as the sea,
> My love as deep; the more I give to thee,
> The more I have, for both are *infinite.*

Everything that has just preceded shows that the real Romeo wanted to have utter faith in Juliet's faith. "Genius trusts its faintest intimation," says Emerson, "against the testimony of all history." But Romeo, whose intimations were not faint but strong, falls back on the testimony of all history that only force can overcome force. He descends from the level of love to the level of violence and attempts to part the fighters with his sword.

> Draw, Benvolio; beat down their weapons.
> Gentlemen, for shame, forbear this outrage!

> Tybalt, Mercutio, the prince expressly hath
> Forbidden bandying in Verona streets.
> Hold, Tybalt! good Mercutio!

Here, if anywhere, the distinction between drama and poetry becomes clear. Drama is a portrayal of human passions eventuating in acts. Poetry is a picture of life in its essence. On the level of drama, we are with Romeo absolutely. His purpose is noble, his act endearingly impulsive. We echo that purpose and identify ourselves with that act. In the theater we do, I mean, and under the aspect of time. But how different under the aspect of eternity! There the scene is a symbolic picture of life itself, of faith surrendering to force, of love trying to gain its end by violence—only to discover, as it soon does, and as we do too, that what it has attained instead is death. A noble motive never yet saved a man from the conse-quences of an unwise act, and Romeo's own words to Mercutio as he draws his sword are an unconscious confession in advance of his mistake. Having put aside his faith in Juliet's faith, his appeal is in the name of law rather than of love: "The prince expressly hath forbidden." That, and his "good Mercutio," reveal a divided soul. And it is that divided soul, in a last instant of hesitation, that causes an awkward or uncoordinated motion as he interferes and gives the cowardly Tybalt his chance to make a deadly thrust at Mercutio under Romeo's arm. If Romeo had only let those two firebrands fight it out, both might have lost blood with a cooling effect on their heated tempers, or, if it had gone to a finish, both might have been killed, as they ultimately were anyway, or, more likely, Mercutio would have killed Tybalt. ("An there were two such, we should have none shortly, for one would kill the other.") In any of these events, the feud between the two houses would not have been involved. As it is, the moment of freedom passes, and the rest is fate.

The fallen Mercutio reveals his most appealing side in his good humor at death. But why his reiterated "A plague o' both your houses"? He is one more character in Shakespeare who "doth protest too much." Four times he repeats it, or three and a half to be exact. How ironical of Mercutio to attribute his death to the Capulet-Montague feud, when the Capulet who killed him had plainly been reluctant to fight with him, and the chief Montague present had begged and begged him to desist. That "plague o' both your houses" is Mercutio's unwitting confession that his own intolerable pugnacity, not the feud at all, is responsible. And if that be true, how much that has been written about this tragedy must be retracted.

What follows puts a final confirmation on Romeo's error in trying to part the duelists by force. With Mercutio dead as a direct result of his interference, what can Romeo say? We heard him fall from love to an appeal to law and order while the fight was on. Now it is over, he descends even lower as he bemoans his "reputation stain'd with Tybalt's slander." Reputation! Iago's word.

> O sweet Juliet,
> Thy beauty hath made me effeminate
> And in my temper soften'd valour's steel!

Were ever words more tragically inverted? That fire should soften metal must have seemed a miracle to the man who first witnessed it. How much greater the miracle whereby beauty melts violence into love! That is the miracle that was on the verge of occurring in *Romeo and Juliet.*

Instead, Benvolio enters to announce Mercutio's death. Whereat Romeo, throwing the responsibility of his own mistake on destiny, exclaims:

> This day's black fate on more days doth depend;
> This but begins the woe others must end.

Could words convey more clearly the fact that the crisis has passed? Freedom has had its instant. The consequences are now in control.

Tybalt re-enters. Does Romeo now remember that his love for Juliet makes every Capulet sacred? Does he recall his last words to her as he left the orchard at dawn?—

> Sleep dwell upon thine eyes, peace in thy breast!
> Would I were sleep and peace, so sweet to rest!

Does he now use his sword merely to prevent bloodshed?

> Away to heaven, respective lenity,

he cries, implying without realizing it the infernal character of his decision,

> And fire-ey'd fury be my conduct now!

Fury! Shakespeare's invariable word for animal passion in man gone mad. And in that fury Romeo's willingness to forgive is devoured like a flower in a furnace:

> Now, Tybalt, take the villain back again
> That late thou gav'st me; for Mercutio's soul
> Is but a little way above our heads,
> Staying for thine to keep him company.
> Either thou, or I, or both, must go with him.

The spirit of Mercutio does indeed enter Romeo's body, and though it is Tybalt who is to go with the slain man literally, it is Romeo who goes with him in the sense that he accepts his code and obeys his ghost. Drawing his rapier, he sends Tybalt to instant death—to the immense gratification of practically everyone in the audience, so prone are we in the theater to surrender to the ancestral emotions. How many a mother, suspecting the evil influence of some companion on her small son, has put her arms about him in a desperate gesture of protection. Yet that same mother will attend a performance of *Romeo and Juliet*, and, seduced by the crowd, will applaud Romeo's capitulation to the spirit of Mercutio to the echo. So frail is the tenderness of the mothers in the face of the force of the fathers.

In this respect the scene is like the court scene in *The Merchant of Venice* when we gloat over Shylock's discomfiture. Here, as there, not only our cooler judgment when we are alone but all the higher implications of the tragedy call for a reversal of our reaction when with the crowd. In this calmer retrospect, we perceive that between his hero's entrance and exit in this scene Shakespeare has given us three Romeos, or, if you will, one Romeo in three universes. First we see him possessed by love and a spirit of universal forgiveness. From this he falls, first to reason and an appeal to law, then to violence—but violence in a negative or "preventive" sense. Finally, following Mercutio's death, he passes under the control of passion and fury, abetted by "honour," and thence to vengeance and offensive violence. In astrological terms, he moves from Venus, through the Earth, to Mars. It is as if Dante's *Divine Comedy* were compressed into eighty lines and presented in reverse—Romeo in an inverted "pilgrimage" passing from Paradise, through Purgatory, to the Inferno.

This way of taking the scene acquits Romeo of doing "wrong," unless we may be said to do wrong whenever we fail to live up to our highest selves. Love is a realm beyond good and evil. Under the aspect of time, of common sense, possibly even of reason and morality, certainly of "honour," Romeo's conduct in the swift succession of events that ended in Tybalt's death was unexceptionable. What else could he have done? But under the aspect of eternity, which is poetry's aspect, it was less than that. We cannot blame a man because he does not perform a miracle. But when he offers proof of his power, and the very next moment has the opportunity to perform one, and does not, the failure is tragic. Such was the "failure" of Romeo. And he himself admits it in so many words. Death, like love, lifts us for a moment above time. Just before he drinks the poison, catching sight of the body of Tybalt in the Capulet vault, Romeo cries, "Forgive me, cousin." Why should he ask forgiveness for what he did in honor, if honor be the guide to what is right?

Romeo as an honorable man avenges his friend. But in proving himself a man in this sense, he proves himself less than the perfect lover. "Give all to love," says Emerson:

> Give all to love . . .
> 'Tis a brave master;
> Let it have scope:
> Follow it utterly,
> Hope beyond hope . . .
> Heartily know,
> When half-gods go,
> The gods arrive.

Juliet's love had bestowed on Romeo power to bring down a god, to pass even beyond the biblical seventy times seven to what Emily Brontë calls the "first of the seventy-first." But he did not. The play is usually explained as a tragedy of the excess of love. On the contrary it is the tragedy of a deficiency of it. Romeo did not "follow it utterly," did not give quite "all" to love.

V

Romeo's mental condition following the death of Tybalt is proof of the treason he has committed against his own soul. Up to this point in the scene, as we saw, Shakespeare has given us three Romeos. Now he gives us a fourth: the man rooted to the spot at the sight of what he has done. The citizens have heard the tumult and are coming. "Stand not amaz'd," cries Benvolio—and it is a case where one poet's words seem to have been written to illuminate another's. Wordsworth's lines are like a mental stage direction for the dazed Romeo:

> Action is transitory—a step, a blow,
> The motion of a muscle—this way or that—
> 'Tis done; and in the after-vacancy
> We wonder at ourselves like men betrayed:
> Suffering is permanent, obscure and dark,
> And has the nature of infinity.

"O! I am Fortune's fool," cries Romeo. "Love's not Time's fool," says Shakespeare, as if commenting on this very scene, in that confession of his own faith, the 116th sonnet:

> O, no! it is an ever-fixed mark,
> That looks on tempests and is never shaken;
> It is the star to every wandering bark,
> Whose worth's unknown, although his height be taken.

There is an astrology at the opposite pole from that of the Chorus to this play. Romeo's love looked on a tempest—and it was shaken. He apparently has just strength enough left to escape and seek refuge in Friar Laurence's cell, where, at the word of his banishment, we find him on the floor,

> Taking the measure of an unmade grave,

in a fit of that suicidal despair that so often treads on the heels of "fury." It is not remorse for having killed Tybalt that accounts for his condition, nor even vexation with himself for having spoiled his own marriage, but shame for having betrayed Juliet's faith in the boundlessness of love.

Meanwhile, at the scene of the duels, citizens have gathered, followed by the Prince with Capulets and Montagues. Lady Capulet, probably the weakest character in the play, is the first to demand more blood as a solution of the problem:

> Prince, as thou art true,
> For blood of ours, shed blood of Montague.

But the Prince asks first for a report of what happened.

> Benvolio, who began this bloody fray?

Benvolio mars what is otherwise a remarkably accurate account of the affair by failing utterly to mention Mercutio's part in instigating the first duel, placing the entire blame on Tybalt.

> He is a kinsman to the Montague,

cries Lady Capulet,

> Affection makes him false; he speaks not true.
> Some twenty of them fought in this black strife,
> And all those twenty could but kill one life.

Her sense of reality and character are on a level with her courage.

In Capulet's orchard, the Nurse brings to Juliet the rope ladder by which her husband is to reach her chamber—and with it the news of Tybalt's death and Romeo's banishment.

> O serpent heart, hid with a flowering face!
> Did ever dragon keep so fair a cave?

cries Juliet,

> O nature, what hadst thou to do in hell,
> When thou didst bower the spirit of a fiend
> In mortal paradise of such sweet flesh?

Even in the exaggeration of her anguish, Juliet diagnoses what has happened precisely as Shakespeare does: a fiend—the spirit of Mercutio—has taken possession of her lover-husband's body. Contrast her insight at such a moment with the Nurse's drivellings:

> There's no trust,
> No faith, no honesty in men; all perjur'd,
> All forsworn, all naught, all dissemblers.
> Ah, where's my man?

A fair sample of how well her inane generalizations survive the test of a concrete need.

Back in Friar Laurence's cell, the stunned Romeo is like a drunken man vaguely coming to himself after a debauch. When he draws his sword to make away with himself, the Friar restrains him not by his hand, as Romeo had once sought to restrain Mercutio at a similarly critical moment, but by the force of his words:

> Hold thy desperate hand!
> Art thou a man?

And he seeks to sting him back to manhood by comparing his tears to those of a woman and his fury to that of a beast.

> Thou hast amaz'd me. . . .
> Why rail'st thou on thy birth, the heaven, and earth?
> Since birth, and heaven, and earth, all three do meet
> In thee at once, which thou at once wouldst lose.

No nonsense about "star-cross'd lovers" for Friar Laurence. Shakespeare, like Dante before him and Milton after him, knew where the stars are, knew that heaven and hell, and even earth, are located within the human soul. Romeo is the "skilless soldier" who sets afire the powder in his own flask.

VI

Juliet too in her despair can think of death. But with what relative calmness and in what a different key! The contrast between the two lovers at this stage is a measure of the respectively innocent and guilty states of their souls.

Their meeting at night is left to our imagination, but their parting at dawn is Shakespeare's imagination functioning at its highest lyrical intensity, with interwoven symbols of nightingale and lark, darkness and light, death and love. Then follow in swift succession the mother's announcement of her daughter's impending marriage with Paris, Juliet's ringing repudiation of the idea, the rejection of her, in order, by her father, her mother, and the Nurse—the first brutal, the second supine, the third Satanic. And then, with an instantaneousness that can only be called divine, Juliet's rejection of the Nurse. In a matter of seconds the child has become a woman. This is the second crisis of the drama, Juliet's, which, with Romeo's, gives the play its shape as certainly as its two foci determine the shape of an ellipse. If ever two crises were symmetrical, and opposite, these are.

Romeo, in a public place, lured insensibly through the influence of Mercutio to the use of force, falls, and as a direct result of his fall, kills Tybalt. Juliet, in her chamber, deserted by father and mother and enticed to faithlessness by the Nurse, child as she is, never wavers for an instant, puts her tempter behind her, and consents as the price of her fidelity to be "buried" alive. Can anyone imagine that Shakespeare did not intend this contrast, did not build up his detailed parallelism between Mercutio and the Nurse to effect it? Romeo, as we said, does not give quite "all" for love. But Juliet does. She performs her miracle and receives supernatural strength as her reward. He fails to perform his and is afflicted with weakness. But eventually her spirit triumphs in him. Had it done so at first, the tragedy would have been averted. Here again the heroine transcends the hero. And yet Romeo had Friar Laurence as adviser while Juliet was brought up by the Nurse! The profounder the truth, the more quietly Shakespeare has a habit of uttering it. It is as if he were saying here that innocence comes from below the sources of pollution and can run the fountain clear.

To describe as "supernatural" the strength that enables Juliet "without fear or doubt" to undergo the ordeal of the sleeping potion and the burial vault does not seem excessive:

> Give me, give me! O! tell me not of fear!

Long before—in the text, not in time—when she had wondered how Romeo had scaled the orchard wall below her balcony, he had said:

> With love's light wings did I o'erperch these walls;
> For stony limits cannot hold love out,
> And what love can do that dares love attempt.

Juliet is now about to prove the truth of his words, in a sense Romeo never dreamed of, "in that dim monument where Tybalt lies." The hour comes, and after facing the terrors her imagination conjures up, Juliet goes through her "dismal scene" alone, is found "dead," and following a scene that anticipates but reverses *Hamlet* in that a wedding is turned into a funeral, is placed in the Capulet vault in accordance with Friar Laurence's desperate plan. But after force has had its instant way, fate in the guise of fear usually has its protracted way, and to oppose it is like trying to stay an avalanche with your hand.

VII

The pestilence prevents the Friar's messenger from reaching Romeo. Instead, word is brought to him that Juliet is dead, and, armed with a drug of an apothecary who defies the law against selling poison, he ends his banishment to Mantua and starts back to Verona to seek beside Juliet the eternal banishment of death. The fury with which he threatens his companion Balthasar, on dismissing him when they reach the churchyard, if he should return to pry, reveals Romeo's mood:

> By heaven, I will tear thee joint by joint
> And strew this hungry churchyard with thy limbs.
> The time and my intents are savage-wild,
> More fierce and more inexorable far
> Than empty tigers or the roaring sea.

And when he encounters and slays Paris, the contrast between his death and that of Mercutio, or even Tybalt, shows that we are dealing here not so much with the act of a free agent choosing his course in the present as with the now fatal consequences of an act in the past, of an agent then free but now no longer so. Paris is little more than the branch of a tree that Romeo pushes aside—and his death affects us almost as little. It is all like a dream, or madness. Finding the sleeping—as he supposes the dead—Juliet, Romeo pours out his soul in words which, though incomparable as poetry, err in placing on the innocent heavens the responsibility for his own venial but fatal choice:

> O, here
> Will I set up my everlasting rest,
> And shake the yoke of inauspicious stars
> From this world-wearied flesh.

And then, by one of those strokes that, it sometimes seems, only Shakespeare could achieve, the poet makes Romeo revert to and round out, in parting from Juliet forever, the same metaphor he had used when she first gazed down on him from her balcony and he had tried to give expression

to the scope and range of his love. How magically, placed side by side, the
two passages fit together, how tragically they sum up the story:

> I am no pilot; yet, wert thou as far
> As that vast shore wash'd with the farthest sea,
> I would adventure for such merchandise.

> Come, bitter conduct, come, unsavoury guide!
> Thou desperate pilot, now at once run on
> The dashing rocks thy sea-sick weary bark!
> Here's to my love! (*Drinks.*) O true apothecary!
> Thy drugs are quick. Thus with a kiss I die. (*Dies.*)

Enter Friar Laurence—a moment too late. That fear is with him Shakespeare shows by another echo. "Wisely and slow; they stumble that run
fast," the Friar had warned Romeo on dismissing him after his first
confession of his love for Juliet, and now he says:

> How oft to-night
> Have my old feet stumbled at graves! . . .
> . . . Fear comes upon me.

He discovers the dead Romeo. Just then Juliet awakes. But at the same
moment he hears a noise. The watch is coming! He cannot be found here.

> Come, go, good Juliet, I dare no longer stay,

and when she refuses to follow, he deserts her. With a glance into the
empty cup in Romeo's hand and a kiss on the lips that she hopes keep
poison for her own—anticipating touches at the deaths of both Hamlet
and Cleopatra—she snatches Romeo's dagger and kills herself.

Why did Shakespeare, after building up so noble a character as
Friar Laurence, permit him to abandon Juliet at so fatal a moment? Why
add *his* name to the so different ones of Capulet, Lady Capulet, and the
Nurse, no matter how much better the excuse for his desertion of her? For
two reasons, I think: first, to show how far the infection of fear extends
that Romeo's use of force had created. "Here is a friar, that trembles,
sighs, and weeps," says the Third Watchman, and Laurence himself confesses,
when he tells his story,

> But then a noise did scare me from the tomb.

And then, to show that Juliet, abandoned *even by religion*, must fall back
for courage finally on love alone.

The pestilence plays a crucial part toward the end of the action. It
is a symbol. Whatever literal epidemic there may have been in the region,
it is plain that fear is the real pestilence that pervades the play. It is fear of

the code of honor, not fate, that drives Romeo to seek vengeance on Tybalt. It is fear of the plague, not accident, that leads to the miscarriage of Friar Laurence's message to Romeo. It is fear of poverty, not the chance of his being at hand at the moment, that lets the apothecary sell the poison. It is fear of the part he is playing, not age, that makes Friar Laurence's old feet stumble and brings him to the tomb just a few seconds too late to prevent Romeo's death. It is fear of being found at such a spot at such a time, not coincidence, that lets him desert Juliet at last just when he does. Fear, fear, fear, fear, fear. Fear is the evil "star" that crosses the lovers. And fear resides not in the skies but in the human heart.

VIII

The tragedy ends in the reconciliation of the two houses, compensation, it is generally held, for the deaths of the two lovers. Doubtless the feud was not renewed in its former form. But much superfluous sentiment has been spent on this ending. Is it not folly to suppose that Capulet or Lady Capulet was spiritually transformed by Juliet's death? And as for Montague, the statue of her in pure gold that he promised to erect in Verona is proof in itself how incapable he was of understanding her spirit and how that spirit alone, and not monuments or gold, can bring an end to feuds. (Lady Montague, who died of a broken heart, was far and away the finest of the four parents.) Shakespeare's happy endings are, almost without exception, suspect. Or rather they are to be found, if at all, elsewhere than in the last scene and final speeches, and are "happy" in a quite untheatrical sense.

Cynics are fond of saying that if Romeo and Juliet had lived their love would not have "lasted." Of course it wouldn't—in the cynic's sense. You can no more ask such love to last than you can ask April to last, or an apple blossom. Yet April and apple blossoms do last and have results that bear no resemblance to what they come from—results such as apples and October—and so does such love. Romeo, in his last words, referred to the phenomenon known as "a lightning before death." Here is that lightning, and here, if it have one, is the happy ending of *Romeo and Juliet*:

> ROM: If I may trust the flattering truth of sleep,
> My dreams presage some joyful news at hand.
> My bosom's lord sits lightly in his throne,
> And all this day an unaccustom'd spirit
> Lifts me above the ground with cheerful thoughts.
> I dreamt my lady came and found me dead—

Strange dream, that gives a dead man leave to think!—
And breath'd such life with kisses in my lips,
That I reviv'd and was an emperor.
Ah me! how sweet is love itself possess'd,
When but love's shadows are so rich in joy!
Enter BALTHASAR—*with news of Juliet's death.*

Dreams go by contraries, they say, and this seems to be an example. But is it?

HARRY LEVIN

Interrogation, Doubt, Irony: Thesis, Antithesis, Synthesis

In reconsidering *Hamlet*, we cannot
pretend that we are unaware of what happens next or how it all comes
out. Knowing what will finally be decided, critics have grown impatient
over its agonies of decision, and have blamed Hamlet for undue procrastination. But what may be a foregone conclusion to them must be an open
question to him, as we have reminded ourselves by watching the process
unfold, and observing how the tone is set through the interaction of
questions, answers, and unanswered speculations. Having rehearsed the
play once with an emphasis on the interrogative mood, let us push the
interrogation further by returning to certain indicative passages, tracing
now an inner train of thought, and later placing it in a broader perspective. *Interrogatio* is classified—by the rhetorician, Henry Peacham—as a
form of *pathopoeia*, which in turn is neither more nor less than a device for
arousing emotions: "Examples hereof are common in Tragedies." *Dubitatio*,
our next figure of speech and thought, is less emotional and more deliber-
ative. As it is defined by Abraham Fraunce, in *The Arcadian Rhetorike*,
"Addubitation or doubting is a kinde of deliberation with our selves." The
orator deliberates between rival options: either to revenge or not to
revenge, whether a visitant comes from heaven or hell. For doubt is a
state of mind where the questioner faces no single answer nor the lack of
one, but rather a choice between a pair of alternatives. Etymologically,
the word stems from *dubitare*, which means precisely to hesitate in the face
of two possibilities. The structure of *Hamlet* seems, at every level, to have

been determined by this duality. "A double blessing is a double grace" (I.iii.53).

Similarly, the texture is characterized by a tendency to double and redouble words and phrases. From the very first scene, the speeches abound in hendiadys: "gross and scope," "law and heraldry." Sometimes the paired nouns are redundant synonyms: "food and diet," "pith and moment"—Saxon balancing Latin as in the doublets of Sir Thomas Browne. Adjectives or verbs are coupled at other times: "impotent and bedrid," "countenance and excuse." This reduplication seems to be a habit of courtly diction into which Hamlet himself falls now and then: "the purpose of playing . . . is . . . to show . . . the very age and body of the time his form and pressure" (III.ii.21–25). By the count of R. A. Foakes, no less than 247 such pairings are scattered through the play. They are doubtless more ornamental than functional; yet they charge the air with overtones of wavering and indecision. The Clown goes farther with his equivocations, putting his finger on serious ambiguities. And Hamlet goes too far with his *double entendres*, besmirching the maidenly innocence of Ophelia. Claudius, in his opening address to the Council, establishes himself as a practiced exponent of stately double-talk. With unctuous skill, he manages a transition from the old King's death to himself and his inherited queen. Antithesis is condensed into oxymoron: "delight and dole," "defeated joy." Some of these mannerisms will have their echo in the stilted language of the Play-King: "Grief joys, joy grieves, on slender accident" (III.ii.209). The formal style is a mask, which accords with the dress and etiquette of the court; Claudius is virtually winking, when he speaks of "an auspicious and a dropping eye" (I.ii.11). Hamlet, speaking informally and ironically to Horatio, sums up the paradoxical situation:

> The funeral bak'd meats
> Did coldly furnish forth the marriage tables.
> (180–81)

The incrimination of Claudius by the Ghost, duly recorded in the book of Hamlet's brain, is an object lesson in duplicity. Claudius himself is unremittingly conscious of the distinction between the "exterior" and "the inward man" (II.ii.6). Both in communing with himself and in dealing with others, he seldom fails to distinguish between words and deeds, or face and heart. He introduces Gertrude by publicly casting her in a dual role, "our sometime sister, now our queen," as he does his nephew shortly afterward, "my cousin Hamlet, and my son" (I.ii.8, 64). Hamlet resentfully picks up the implications, and caustically refers to his "uncle-father and aunt-mother" (II.ii.392). On the premise that "man and wife is one flesh," he perversely carries the logic of incest to its conclusion by bidding farewell to Claudius as his "dear mother" (IV.iii.51). He prefaces his interview with Gertrude by resolving to act a part: "My tongue and soul in this be hypocrites" (III.ii.415). He will "speak daggers" to her, and she will admit that his words are "like daggers" (III.iv.95). Addressing her as "your husband's brother's wife," he implores her to keep aloof from Claudius, though she may feel otherwise inclined: "Assume a virtue, if you have it not" (15, 160). It is the recommendation of worldly wisdom that La Rochefoucauld would moralize: "Hypocrisy is the tribute that vice pays to virtue." Molière's *Misanthrope* would reject such sophistications; Alceste stands squarely for virtue disdaining vice; like the ingenuous Hamlet, he knows not "seems." But Hamlet, unlike Alceste, learns to live at court, in an arena where men and women must be actors and actresses. He must learn an etymology which may not have struck him during his humanistic studies at Wittenberg—that the word "hypocrite," in the original Greek, designated an actor.

Claudius, invoking the "twofold force" of prayer, acknowledges his own hypocrisy, caught as he is between guilt and repentance:

> . . . like a man to double business bound,
> I stand in pause where I should first begin.
> (III.iii.1–2)

A moment later, Hamlet will stand in pause before the double business of whether Claudius should be saved or damned, and will give him the benefit of an unforeseen doubt. The smiling villain is a double-dealer; but so is Hamlet, in another sense. ¡At the beginning he is single-minded, all of a piece, all melancholia; then he puts on his mask and plays the antic, carrying his buffoonery to the verge of hysteria; his disposition is manic in the presence of others and depressive when he is by himself. Where the vicious Claudius assumes an air of respectability, the virtuous Hamlet must assimilate the atmosphere of licentiousness.¡ He must set aside the high-minded idealism of Castiglione's *Courtier*, "The courtier's, scholar's, soldier's eye, tongue, sword," and take up the time-serving realism of Machiavelli's *Prince* (III.i.159). It is the role of Polonius, as chamberlain, to profess the one and practice the other. While he privately expounds a philosophy of keeping up appearances, he prides himself on his capacity for seeing through them. Master of ceremonies, he bustles about, arranging formalities according to protocol; but he is also a master of palace intrigue, who sneaks behind curtains to spy; and, with him, the play oscillates between ceremonious public hearings and furtive whisperings behind the scenes, so to speak. With the twin figures of Rosencrantz and Guildenstern, the double-dealing is symmetrically personified. Since they invariably hunt in couples, their roles are interchangeable. Each of them has an introductory speech of exactly the same length and rhythm, and in each case the key word is "both" (II.ii.26–32).

> Thanks, Rosencrantz and gentle Guildenstern.

the King responds, and the Queen preserves the symmetry by adding:

> Thanks, Guildenstern and gentle Rosencrantz.

The Gravedigger, who—like so many of Shakespeare's clowns—is an accomplished dialectician, explains to us that "an act hath three branches—it is to act, to do, and to perform" (V.i.12–13). This is redundant logic, yet it serves a purpose; it rings the changes on a momentous word, and it comments obliquely on Hamlet's inaction. Moreover, lest we dally too long before his dilemmas, it reminds us that the argument must proceed to a third and decisive stage. Our thesis has been singular, in the person of a solitary being wholly surrounded by questions. Doubts, as to his relations with other beings, as to the basis of his continued existence, present themselves under the twofold aspect of an antithesis. These components must be resolved through a synthesis, pieced together out of the playwright's assumptions about the nature of human experience. The conventional five-act structure of tragedy is ignored by the Quartos of *Hamlet*, indicated for only the first two acts of the Folio text, and completed by later editors. Granville-Barker's recommendation, which best accords with modern theatrical usage, is that we conceive the play as a work composed in three movements. "Treble woe" is the fatality that overtakes Polonius and his two children. Threefold also are the consequences of the original sin against the old King, his loss "Of life, of crown, of queen" (I.v.75). The drama might almost be described as a triangle play with a vengeance. The interrelationship of Hamlet the Elder, Claudius, and Gertrude predominates in the mind of Hamlet the Younger. Perhaps it has some bearing upon his tendency to triple his phrases: "O, horrible! O, horrible! most horrible!" (I.v.80). "Words, words, words" (II.ii.194). "Mother, mother, mother!" (II.iv.6).

Our third trope, *ironia*, is more than a figure of speech or even of thought; it may be a point of view, a view of life, and—as such—a resolvent for contrarieties. Its most clear-cut form, designated in Puttenham's *Arte of English Poesie* as "the drye mock," is a statement which means the contrary of what it purports to say. Caesar was ambitious; Brutus was honorable; yet Antony contrives, by his mocking inflection, to carry the opposite impression in both regards. Dubious statements could be reversed by simply adding the Elizabethan interjection *quotha*. Hamlet makes the controversion explicit, when his mother asks him, "What shall I do?" (III.iv.180). He has just told her, directly, "go not to my uncle's bed." Now he elaborates, "Not this, by no means, that I bid you do." In other words, what follows is to be taken ironically: "Let the bloat King tempt you again to bed . . ." And Hamlet dwells, with ambivalent detail, on the endearments he would have her avoid. Given the hypocrisy of the court, where one may not say what one means, honesty must either hold its tongue or express itself through indirection. When Polonius begs to take his leave, Hamlet's tone of politeness thinly disguises his eagerness to confer the favor begged: "You cannot, sir, take from me anything that I will more willingly part withal—" Whereupon his dry mock deepens into a thrice-uttered heartcry: "except my life, except my life, except my life" (II.ii.217–21). To the initial queries of Claudius and Gertrude, his hedging answers are verbal ironies. Gertrude's naïve reaction to the Play-Queen—"The lady doth protest too much, methinks"—unconsciously lays bare her own standards of conduct. Hamlet's double-edged comment, "O, but she'll keep her word," is ostensibly another bit of polite conversation (III.ii.240–41). Actually, he is distorting the play-within-the-play in order to drive home an invidious contrast. The Play-Queen will have no chance to keep her word; the Queen of Denmark had a chance and failed.

As for the King, his usual mode is merely hypocritical; but, under the goading of Hamlet, he too waxes ironic. When he announces the excursion to England, and Hamlet assents with "Good," Claudius says, "So is it, if thou knew'st our purposes" (IV.iii.48–49). He is having his grim little joke, and assuming Hamlet is unaware that what might be good for Claudius would not be good for himself. But the joke is on Claudius; for he does not know that Hamlet knows his purposes, that he himself is rather a step behind than a step ahead of his opponent. Hamlet's retort is enigmatic, if not ironic, with its cryptic allusion to the Ghost: "I see a cherub that sees them." The irony now lies not in the statement but in the situation, which will turn out to be the contrary of what Claudius designs. Hamlet has already ventured a prediction, in his farewell to his mother. There, in hinting at the treachery of Rosencrantz and Guildenstern, whom he will trust as he would "adders fang'd," he has defined the process of dramatic irony:

> For 'tis the sport to have the engineer
> Hoist with his own petar.
> (III.iv.203, 206–07)

It is always exciting when craft meets equal craftiness in a battle of wits. But there is peculiar satisfaction in watching, when vaunted cleverness overreaches itself. The comic formula of the cheater cheated, *Wily Beguiled*, is transmuted into the imagery of siege and explosion, as Hamlet conspires with himself to blow his enemies at the moon. The actual conspiracy, when it happens, will be literary rather than military; it will consist of forging a royal mandate, so that Rosencrantz and Guildenstern will be executed in Hamlet's place; and this will be retrospectively disclosed by Hamlet to Horatio, with rhetorical flourishes parodying the style of Claudius. Thus the episode has been somewhat glossed over, particularly the incidental deaths of the schoolfellows; but it had been a conspicuous feature of the primitive legend; and its elements, widely diffused in folklore, persist through the *motif* of a lucky youth with an ill-fated letter. Hamlet's prototype is the unsuspecting hero, sent on a journey bearing his own death warrant; jolted into some realization of the hazards confronting him, he finally turns adversity into advantage.

Another element in the archaic tale has proved susceptible of endless refinement. This was the spectacle of a cunning hero forced to wear a mask of stupidity, which originally lent Hamlet his oafish name. In dissembling, in counterfeiting madness, in playing his antic part, he exemplifies the humanistic tradition of the wise fool. In his wayward fashion, he pursues the wisdom of Socrates, which characteristically masqueraded as ignorance. Hamlet's behavior has been characterized by a student of Shakespeare's wit and humor, John Weiss, as a "sustained gesture of irony." It is that gesture which enables the questioner to reject seeming for being, which helps the doubter to distinguish between appearance and reality. In the dual role of an ironist, Hamlet can remain his tragic self while presenting a quasicomic front. The dissembler of Aristophanic comedy, the *eiron*, had shrewdly exposed the impostor or *alazon*. Neoclassicists like Voltaire were historically warranted in associating the ironic with the comic and deeming it inappropriate for tragedy. The concept was broadly extended by Bishop Thirlwall's essay "On the Irony of Sophocles." If the Greek tragedians had been ironists, it was not because they mocked at their fellow men, but because they concerned themselves with the mockery of fate. Oedipus is the engineer of his own downfall; and his blinding is a requital for taunting the blind Tiresias, as well as an expiation of his trespasses. Human agency seems to confound itself through the workings of some cosmic design. So it seems to the Play-King:

Our wills and fates do so contrary run
That our devices still are overthrown
(III.ii.221–22)

That overthrow is made ironic by the perception of counterdevices, by the aptness with which fates are matched against wills. The outcome must belie the expectation, the disappointment must become concrete, through some logical connection or personal association. This correspondence between device and counterdevice takes its most obvious form in the equivocal oracle. The riddling prophecies that cajole and betray Macbeth are the merest plays upon words, which are carried out by charades on the part of Birnam Wood and Macduff. In *King Lear* the irony is classical when the gods are said to have justly taken Cornwall's life for Gloucester's sight; it is more problematic when Gloucester accuses them of treating mortals as wanton boys treat flies. Poetic justice, which prevails in *Macbeth*, miscarries in *King Lear*, where the ways of providence are as unfathomable as in *Hamlet.*

With *Hamlet*, as we have seen, we are involved in two sets of complementary problems. One set is speculative: why? wherefore? who is the Ghost? and what is the ultimate mystery that it prefigures? The other is practical: what shall we do? how should Hamlet bear himself amid these unexampled difficulties? and how should he accomplish his unsought vocation, revenge? Shakespearean tragedy is deeply concerned with the individual as he faces opportunity, responsibility, and moral choice. It is equally preoccupied with the pattern of events, and whether this is determined by casual accident, fatal necessity, or divine intervention. Given the motive, one must await one's cue. The interplay between these preoccupations is the source of innumerable ironies, both conscious and unconscious, some of them attached to the hero's viewpoint, others detached in a reminiscent overview. "Hamlet has no plan, but *Hamlet* has," as Goethe observed, with a fellow dramatist's understanding. The play has a plot; and so, in another sense, has the Prince; but he cannot foresee the fulfilment of his intentions; he can only test them against hugger-mugger conditions. Yet, as producer of "The Murder of Gonzago," he can take charge of a miniature drama which exerts an effect on the drama at large; he can play god and look down on his creation, in the self-conscious mood of romantic irony. Whereas in *Hamlet* itself, he is no more than a leading actor, whose body will be placed "on a stage"—on a funeral bier which may likewise be viewed as a theatrical platform— among the other corpses at the end. It will then become Horatio's function to play the commentator, and to report upon the ironic upshot of the whole story: "purposes mistook/Fall'n on th' inventors' heads" (V.ii.389, 395–96).

Hamlet points the analogy himself when he addresses the surviving onlookers as "audience to this act" (346). The verb "to act" is synonymous with "to do," in the patient explanation of the Gravedigger, but also with the ambiguous "to perform." "The name of action" has further branches for Hamlet; it often takes on this theatrical inflection, as when he declares that the customs of mourning are "actions that a man might play" (I.ii.84). Conversely, he is pleading for sincerity, when he tells the Players: "Suit the action to the word, the word to the action" (III.ii.19–20). The noun "act" conveys a sexual innuendo, when it is bandied back and forth between Hamlet and Gertrude in the Closet Scene. Some of these ambiguities might be clarified in the light of God's law, if not of man's; for above us "the action lies/In his true nature," as Claudius confesses to himself (III.iii.61–62). Here below, deeds may be obfuscated by words, as they have been in his own case; or else they may be retarded by thoughts, as they are in Hamlet's.

> I do not know
> Why yet I live to say "This thing's to do,"
> Sith I have cause, and will, and strength, and means
> To do't.
>
> (IV.iv.43–46)

Again and again he reproaches himself in his tone; but self-reproach is a sign of conscientiousness rather than cowardice. The Ghost reappears, at an awkward moment, to whet Hamlet's "almost blunted purpose"; but ghosts, after all, are notorious for nagging, especially on the Elizabethan stage (III.iv.111). It takes no less than five of them to rouse Chapman's Senecal hero to *The Revenge of Bussy D'Ambois;* and yet his bravery is widely and loudly attested. Because we are privileged to overhear Hamlet's moments of self-questioning, or to glimpse his incertitude before psychic phenomena, we should not make the mistake of considering him a weak or passive figure. [That his native disposition is active and resolute, though it has been temporarily sicklied over with the pale cast of melancholy— such an impression is fully confirmed by objective testimony from the other characters. / "*Hamlet* is not a drama of weakness," its Russian transla- tor, Boris Pasternak, has clairvoyantly noted, "but of duty and self-denial."

The critical sentimentalization of Hamlet's personality has leaned heavily on the expression, *Gedankenschauspiel*, wrenched from its context in A. W. Schlegel's lectures and mistranslated as "tragedy of thought." This has encouraged the obscurantist conclusion that thought is Hamlet's tragedy; Hamlet is the man who thinks too much, ineffectual because he is intellectual; his nemesis is a failure of nerve, a nervous prostration. Schlegel wanted merely to underline the well-taken point that *Hamlet* was, above all, a drama of ideas, a dramatization of man's intellectual curiosity. By the canons of the humanists, the highest virtue was knowledge put into action. But how to know what to do? That was the question; there was the rub. Hamlet's plight is magnified by the tension between the stream of his highly skeptical consciousness and the undercurrents of murky superstition and swirling paganism. Hence he stands as the very archetype of character at odds with destiny, of the incompatibility between will and fate.

There may be other Shakespearean characters who are just as memorable, and other plots which are no less impressive; but nowhere else has the outlook of the individual in a dilemma been so profoundly realized; and a dilemma, by definition, is an all but unresolvable choice between evils. Rather than with calculation or casuistry, it should be met with the virtue of readiness; sooner or later it will have to be grasped by one or the other of its horns. These, in their broadest terms, have been—for Hamlet, as we interpret him—the problem of what to believe and the problem of how to act. Hamlet is unwittingly compelled to act as if life were a duel, with unbated swords and against a series of furtive assailants. He is unwillingly led to believe that death comes as a cup, filled with poisonous wine and containing a flawless pearl. His doom is generalized in Fulke Greville's chorus:

> Oh, wearisome condition of humanity,
> Born under one law, to another bound . . .

Irony cannot solve the incalculable contradictions between the personal life and the nature of things. Yet it can teach us to live with them; and that is no mean achievement; for Hamlet's knowledge was not idle reflection, according to Nietzsche. It was an insight which hindered action by stripping the veil of illusion from the terrible truth, the terror or the absurdity of existence. This would be intolerable, were it not for the transformations of art, which asserts man's conquest over his fears, and which thereby allays his vexation of spirit. Thus Hamlet's limited victory commences with the play-within-the-play, a working model of the play itself, which repeats the lesson in mastery on a larger scale within our minds. From its very commencement, after the stroke of midnight, we are brought face to face with the supernatural. Volleys of gunfire augment and accelerate the sound effects until, at the conclusion of the dead march, "*a peal of ordnance*" signalizes a battle lost and won.

A. P. ROSSITER

"Troilus and Cressida"

How does a man give a 'popular lecture' on a play undeniably unpopular; which is (with *Timon*) the least liked of Shakespeare's mature works; and which (unlike *Andronicus* and *1 Henry VI*) cannot even be said to have been 'a popular success in its own day'? How can you expect to interest a theatre-going audience in what even its admirers admit to be a bad stage-play: a play whose twenty-four scenes (in modern editions)—you can reduce them to fifteen or sixteen by imagining it in an Elizabethan theatre—include at most a mere *four* that can be called 'dramatic'?

We have reason to believe that *Troilus and Cressida* was written for a specific time and for a special audience: the time, between *Henry V* and *Julius Caesar* (1599) and early 1601; the audience, young intellectuals, many of them law-students from the Inns of Court—young, critical, discontented minds who were attracted by the new poetry of Donne, the newish 'snarling-satire' of Hall, Donne and Marston: attracted by the challenge of deliberate and wanton obscurity—*and* obscenity, also deliberate and wanton: minds trained in logic and rhetoric, swift to grasp the general principles behind an argument and to distinguish the sound from the specious: trained and habituated to debate and therefore prepared to look beyond the mere immediate action (even of a stage-play and ostensibly about love), and to extract and consider the moral, ethical or legal points at issue—seeking to relate them to their own times, about which their late-Elizabethan heads were troubled.

They were troubled (by and large) because old traditional standards

From *Angel With Horns*, edited by Graham Storey. Copyright © 1961 by Longman Group Ltd.

seemed to be failing; 'new Philosophy' put 'all in doubt'; the succession to
the throne was unsettled, the Queen old, and her death might be the signal
for a civil war; the country was weary of the wars with Spain, the rebels
in Ireland; there were uneasy rumours about the ambitions of the Earl of
Essex; and (to come nearest home) Donne and the satirists were demon-
strating that neither life nor love was what it had been supposed to be.

The evidence for this is the play's style—the intellectual demands
it makes; and, with that, the strange address to the reader attached to one
of the two impressions of the 1609 quarto: where it is stressed that 'you
have heere a new play neuer stal'd with the Stage, neuer clapper-clawd
with the palmes of the vulger . . . not . . . sullied with the smoaky breath
of the multitude'. It is patent that (whether from the seven books of
Homer translated by Chapman in 1598 or from some other source) the
audience is expected to know who everybody is; and even more obvious
that a knowledge of Chaucer's story is assumed (e.g., Calchas in III. iii. 1
ff: never named till l. 31, at that). This knowledge makes a *kind* of
Sophoclean irony possible; and, again, a particular sort of deflation of the
heroic (the chivalric, *not* the Homeric of Homer: for Homer had no more
heard of Troilus and Cressida than he had of Aristotle). It is *not* an
assertion that the Homeric or heroic story was 'really only like that' (flat,
unheroic, rather sordid or absurd). That is Shaw's method in *Caesar and
Cleopatra* (a more amusing play, in that kind). The Troilus and Cressida
story is medieval and chivalric, and it is this which is deflated. Much of
the effect of the play depends on expecting what you do not get.

That is why there are only two proper costumes: either the 'modern dress' of 1600 or the modern dress of the 1938 Westminster production
(when it achieved fame for the first time). *Troilus and Cressida* never was a
play about Ancient Greeks, and it should not look like one; that only
substitutes a banal, Samuel-Butler-like debunking for something more
unsettling: the expectation of certain courtly and noble (chivalric) standards in war and love which are found not to apply to life as it 'really is' in
these modern times. The names, so to speak, need to look a little
désorientés in their dresses.

For one essence of this sort of Elizabethan play is that it invited a
kind of 'application': i.e. evoked in the minds of the judicious stimulating
and disturbing reflections, which revealed the world as it is—not *was*,
more than several centuries B.C. At any rate, that is my basic assumption;
as it would be with the Vienna of *Measure for Measure* and the *ancien
régime* of *All's Well*: that all three are more about 'this-here' than any
'that-there'; and all 'modernist' plays full of vexing questions and perplex-
ing riddles of the human mind, of feeling, conduct, *value*. That is how I
shall examine *Troilus and Cressida*, which (*pace* W. W. Lawrence and Dr.

E. M. W. Tillyard) is *not* 'chronicle-history' any more than *All's Well* is 'only a Fairy-Tale'. Its very appearance ought to have made the well-read Elizabethan ready for a neat pair of lines from Seneca: '*Hic Troia non est*' (Agamemnon to Cassandra); and the rejoinder, '*Ubi Helena est, Troiam puto*' (*Agamemnon*, 795).

If you consider only the main plot by itself and follow it to its climax (V. ii.), you feel that it belongs to a play with a false bottom. Another layer opens below the love-story, and if you see into it, you find Shakespeare 'importing' something different from what his title has declared. But even the opening of the play shows that anything in the nature of *Romeo and Juliet* would be a mistaken expectation. The Prologue leads off with military-heroical rhetoric, like that of the *Henry V* choruses, proclaiming an epic occasion. The first scene presents a languid, lovelorn young man, too amorous to fight; and to emphasize that hint of a let-down, all his poetically impassioned rhapsodizing is made somewhat absurd by the presence—and the comments—of a buffoonish old Pandarus who is simply a go-between, a mere broker of sexual stock. Chaucer (who invented the middle-aged Pandare) has been perverted: humorous sophistication has been turned to a trick of blatantly flat-footed comment—a knack of saying the wrong thing—which reminds me of Groucho Marx. Troilus's passionate hyperbole is jarred against by what turns the whole scene into a pattern of ridicule. We laugh at Pandarus, but the very aptness of his better ineptitudes makes the amorous-literary frenzies absurd. Throughout the love-scenes, Pandarus is never entirely out of the way. More than once he is utterly *in* it. An ambiguity of attitude towards Troilus's love is introduced before we even glimpse Cressida.

The second scene introduces her—mainly with Pandarus—and it is immediately plain that Troilus's idealized queen of courtly romance is not there. She is a chatty, vulgar little piece, and in the rhyming soliloquy at the end (where she speaks what she takes for her mind), the principles of the loftily chaste heroines of *amour courtois* are brought down exactly to the level of Mrs. Peachum's advice in *The Beggar's Opera*:

> O Polly, you might have toy'd and kissed,
> By keeping men off you keep them on;

and

> The wiles of men we should resist,
> Be wooed at length but never won.

'Things won are done; joy's soul lies in the doing.' This suggestion runs throughout the play. Sexual doings are soon over; and, as Ulysses tells Achilles, deeds in war soon forgotten. Up to a point, we all, doubtless, know that. Beyond that point, it becomes a principle of canny selfishness, and creates the woman who uses sexual attraction for power. The scene (III. ii.) where Cressida declares her love shows her still clinging to her mean ideal—and fearing to give herself: 'Let me go,' she says, 'my own company offends me.' 'You cannot shun yourself,' says Troilus. And she:

> Let me go and try.
> I have a kind of self resides with you;
> But an unkind self, that it self will leave
> To be another's fool . . .
> (III.ii. 143–46)

i.e. the 'self' which would give herself seems to her 'unkind' (unnatural), because it would put her entirely in his power. The character-item is important, for it explains her seduction by Diomedes in the crucial scene before Calchas's tent. Diomedes pretends to be walking out on her in a huff; only one thing will stop him quitting; and as she *must* have power and (as she thinks) make every man dance to her tune, he gets all he wants. As she is highly-sexed by nature, yielding is the easier; and, hiding from the betraying torch-light, Troilus mutters to Ulysses his horrified version of *Cosi fan tutte*:

> Let it not be believ'd for womanhood.
> Think, we had mothers . . .
> (V. ii. 127–28)

Ulysses does not in the least understand: the Cressida whom *he* has encountered, kissing the Greek generals all round as soon as she meets them, was one of the 'sluttish spoils of opportunity, And daughters of the game'. Shakespeare underlined that verdict with one of his wickedest puns. Ulysses has barely finished speaking when a flourish sounds from Troy (for Hector's entry); and all the Greek generals exclaim in chorus: 'The Troyans' trumpet'. A knavish piece of work. Despite this, the Ulyssean word on her is not final. Cressida is *not* simply a little harlot; and, though admittedly 'designing', is too frail to stick to her design. Her passion is quite genuine (so far as that goes); so is her grief at her separation from Troilus. Only nothing is deep-rooted in her. She drops short of all her intentions in a way that is common enough in this play of 'fools on both sides'. '*Vorrei e non vorrei*' labels her throughout, and she makes her final exit trying to say just that, through the obscurity of more Shakespearian verbiage (V. ii. 104–09). Thersites has the last word on her; but she is only the feminine of the rest of them. They *all* fancy or pretend they are being or doing one thing, whereas they are shown up as something quite different: something which egoism, or lack of moral insight, prevents their recognizing. This is true of Achilles and Ajax from the start: it is shown to be true of Hector and Troilus—even of Ulysses. It is the final verdict on the whole war, as I shall try to demonstrate when I deal with the other plots.

Pandarus is not present at the betrayal-scene before Calchas's tent. The harsh croak of Thersites is adequate comment on those who 'war for a placket'. Anyone who believes that the medieval story has not been degraded and defiled should pay attention to the residue of Pandarus. He appears twice more: to be cast off by Troilus (after lamenting various symptoms of disease which no Elizabethan could fail to identify), and to conclude with a lamentation for bawds in his thoroughly venereal Epilogue. I shall touch on this (discreetly) in a moment.

The splendid but difficult lines spoken by Troilus at the revelation of Cressida's faithlessness hold one of the springs of the play's 'double bottom'. On the face of it, the unhappy lover is trying to hold on to his illusion, to bully himself out of the evidence of his own eyes (as Thersites says). But in so doing, he repeats a movement of thought which is noticeable all through the play: the sudden shift from some particular question to an appeal to, or discussion of, the widest and most universal principles.

> This she? No; this is Diomed's Cressida.
> If beauty have a soul, this is not she;
> If souls guide vows, if vows be sanctimonies,
> If sanctimony be the gods' delight,
> If there be rule in unity itself,
> This was not she. O madness of discourse,
> That cause sets up with and against itself!
> Bifold authority! where reason can revolt
> Without perdition, and loss assume all reason
> Without revolt: this is, and is not, Cressid.
> (V. ii. 135–44)

The key is 'If there be rule in unity itself'. He is not simply saying, 'There ought to be one and one only Cressida, and she the image in my heart and mind' (though that is included in the sense). He is being made to think philosophically by Shakespeare, and his assumptions are those of Ulysses in his speech about 'Degree' in the Greek war-council in Act I. The assumption is that the universe *ought* to be an integral whole, in which everything has its proper status in a divinely-ordained hierarchical order, and therefore an absolute value, an absolute integrity. To recognize this ordered universe is right reason: its principle at the terrestrial level is Natural Law. But what Troilus has seen appears to him as the refutation of those principles. '*If* beauty have a soul . . . *if* souls guide vows, *if* vows be sanctimonies . . . this was *not* she.' Those *ifs* turn into negative propositions. For since this *is* she, there *is* no 'rule in unity itself', no principle of integrity. He can only try to think that he is insane. What seemed to him right reason in loving Cressid now seems madness, though he cannot believe he is mad; and the 'loss' of his reason (for loving) comes with all the sane authority of reason, though the result is rational insanity—alienation. 'Bifold authority', as he calls it, sets up 'cause' (a logical legal case) with and against the same propositions; and one apparently integral being, his love, 'a thing inseparate/Divides more wider than the sky and earth', though he can find no pin-point to mark off the one from the other of the irreconcilable contraries. He, certainly, is in the 'chaos, when degree is suffocate'; or, rather, he *is* it, it he.

If you like to look at it through twentieth-century eyes, this remarkable scene is a thoroughly Existentialist performance on Shakespeare's part. Troilus represents a mind which thinks in terms of the traditional (Platonic) absolute values, confronted with an *existence*: a phenomenon undeniably his, yet with all the sickening insolence of brute fact. For this is not 'Diomed's Cressida': the existence whose being agonizes him is solely his own. As if to invite this kind of examination, Shakespeare makes it utterly clear that for every participant in the scene there is a phenomenon called 'Cressida': Thersites' is no more Ulysses' (though both think her a mere flirt) than Diomed's is Troilus'; nor is Cressida's Cressida like any of these. In each, the individual consciousness spontaneously generates its own norms, and enjoys complete freedom in 'making its own existence.' But this is the same as showing that there are *no* norms, in the sense in which traditional philosophy assumes them. The absolutes are myths. The supposed 'rule in unity itself' is only a fallacious attempt to stifle my awareness that I am I, and (whichever I may be: Ulysses or Thersites or Troilus) that my 'her' is for me the only 'she'. This is the consciousness which Troilus struggles to evade. M. Sartre would tell him that his anguish was the index of awareness of existence come alive for the first time; and, simultaneously, a demonstration of his 'responsibility' for the Trojan War (which is about something called 'Helen').

Troilus has a mind incapable of irony. 'Irony', as Patrick Cruttwell puts it, 'implies the ability to see and to feel more than one thing at once, and to feel one's own self as multiple. The single- and the simple-minded cannot achieve it.' He adds that this 'sense of a multiple and divided personality . . . is also a vital part, deep and widespread, of the new spirit of the age. Civil war—war inside the individual—is a favourite image' (used, e.g., by Shakespeare in *Sonnet 35*, 'Such civil war is in my love and hate'). *Sonnet 137*, 'Thou blind fool, Love . . .', marks the essential difference between this consciousness and Troilus's character and cast of mind. Troilus is *in* an ironic situation, but its tortured victim, incapable of commanding it; the sonnet-writer is capable of the shrewdest ironies.

Before you dismiss all this as far-fetched, wait till I have gone back from this climax of the play to the other plot-threads which are nothing to do with the love-theme; or are only the mechanisms which part the lovers (*via* the exchange of prisoners—Antenor for Cressida).

There are two other plots: one Greek, one Trojan. The Greek (I. iii, II. i, II. iii, etc.) is about the insubordinate and disorderly conduct of the proud Achilles and the plot hatched by Ulysses and old Nestor to give him a snub: by rigging the lottery so that Ajax becomes the champion for a single-combat with Hector. Achilles will then feel that he is no longer the Greeks' unquestioned supreme warrior, and he will come out and drive the Trojans all over the field. It is also about the general principle of order; for Achilles' example has infected the conceited and stupid Ajax, and the morale of the whole army is bad.

As a plot, the scheme is a fiasco. It generates two swollen-headed military nuisances instead of one; and though Achilles does come out and fight, it is only because his catamite Patroclus is killed: he then flies into a barbarous rage and has Hector slaughtered, unarmed and against odds, while he stands by like a gangster watching his gang do his work. Shakespeare did not invent this: it is in Lydgate's *Troy Book*. It would be none the less shocking to Elizabethan standards of fair combat.

The treatment of Achilles is one of several points which prevent my agreeing with the American view—from J. S. P. Tatlock and H. E. Rollins through W. W. Lawrence to Alfred Harbage—that there is no deflation of the classical heroes here: that this is merely a 'chronicle-history'. Another point is the transformation of Ajax. Steevens pointed out that in Lydgate Ajax was one who 'learning did adore' and 'hated pride and flattery'. I fail to see how these American critics reconcile his treatment in the play with their contention that Shakespeare is merely keeping to the traditional lines of the story—as transmitted by the Middle Ages. Again, the treatment of Menelaus as the contemptible Cornuto is purely Elizabethan. Finally, the degradation of Pandarus, with the syphilitic emphasis (pox as a brutal joke), is totally different from the austere—and cruel—handling of the leprosy in Henryson. Nor is there any suggestion of a curse of disease on Cressida.

Through the snub to Achilles, this plot throws up an excursus on *honour*: in a discussion between Achilles and Ulysses (III. iii). And the whole Greek plot is accompanied, as chorus, by the scurrilous abuse of

Thersites, to whom warmongering and whoremongery are as indivisible as anything in the Athanasian Creed: therefore all deserve boils, blains, scabs, bone-aches and every other symptom which the Elizabethans associated with venereal disease. One cannot just dismiss this as 'nasty'. Caroline Spurgeon shows that the play has a dominant image of disease in the body-politic. Disease is the result of imbalance of 'humours'; and the humour in excess is here 'blood'—the essential principle at once of *lust* and *pride*. When I was a boy, country people still thought that boils and eruptions were caused by 'richness of the blood'.

There are, furthermore, *social* considerations about the Elizabethan realization of syphilis, into which I do not propose to enter. I believe, on Charles Sherrington's authority, that it was a 'new' disease (perhaps a mutant?), certainly generated in America and brought to Europe by Columbus. Its existence was one of the 'disturbing new ideas' of the later sixteenth century. Myxomatosis is not a good analogy; but if you imagine a thinking rabbit trying to order its notions of Nature, then you may go on to understand why certain parts of Jacobean thought are 'pathological'.

Now this Greek plot shows exactly that same shift of attention from particulars to wide generalities I have already called your attention to. I assume that Ulysses's 'Degree' speech is familiar. It has been suggested that 'Commentators have been perhaps too much impressed by this piece of rhetoric.' Maybe. But nothing hints we should not take it in earnest (though no one would question Professor Knights' view that Shakespeare is most deeply engaged at the *end*). It is a 'star' piece, yes; but quite untouched by the uncertainties one has about the exact degree of caricature in the orations of Agamemnon and Nestor. Both these certainly tend towards the comic: the first in pomposity (saying little, and that trite, as if it were much), the second in old politicians' prolixity. I am content myself to see both as *fully* intended caricatures of public men: or even as types of Mr. Huxley's third category of intelligence (as classified in the encyclopaedia—human, animal, military). But even on this extreme, view, the proper dramatic effect is to produce a complete change of tone as soon as Ulysses speaks: i.e. to get the audience to attend by amusing them, and then to make use of that attention to carry them through a big, sweeping rhetorical unit, with an intensely important climax as its peroration.

In a weighty rhetorical address, meant to be followed with the concentration due to a legal argument, Ulysses shows how all order—in the heavens, the State, the human microcosm—depends on hierarchical subordination, or 'degree'. Observation of degree means that everything has its right place, and value is determined by that place. Thus when degree is 'vizarded,/Th'unworthiest shows as fairly in the mask': i.e. 'seemings' cannot be distinguished from 'beings'—which is Troilus's dilemma over 'Cressid'. Later on, it is Achilles' problem about his value and Ajax's.

Ulysses goes on to speak of 'the unity and married calm of states', which is rent and deracinated by loss of order; and from that turns his argument to generalizations which apply with equal force to human society *and* to the individual man or mind:

> Take but degree away, untune that string,
> And hark what discord follows! . . .
> Force should be right; or, rather, right and wrong—
> Between whose endless jar justice resides—
> Should lose their names, and so should justice too.
> Then everything includes itself in power,
> Power into will, will into appetite;
> And appetite, an universal wolf,
> So doubly seconded with will and power,
> Must make perforce an universal prey,
> And last eat up himself. Great Agamemnon,
> This chaos, when degree is suffocate,
> Follows the choking.
>
> (I. iii. 109–26)

With that he comes to the particular case: Achilles deriding the Supreme Command; and the next scene shows us Achilles and Ajax in—inaction (just as Cressida was shown to us, to follow Troilus's rhapsodies and the practicalities of Pandarus).

But I must pause there to call attention to two remarkable echoes of those closing lines. The first is in II. iii., when the Generals go to call on Achilles. Ulysses (having been in and seen him) returns to say that Achilles will not fight—makes no excuses—merely goes his own way

> Without observance or respect of any,
> In will peculiar and in self-admission.

Further:

> possess'd he is with greatness,
> . . . . Imagin'd worth
> Holds in his blood such swol'n and hot discourse
> That 'twixt his mental and his active parts
> Kingdom'd Achilles in commotion rages,
> And batters down himself.
>
> (II. iii. 160–61; 165–71)

The falling rhythm insistently recalls 'and last eat up himself', even if we do not realize that Achilles' wilful *pride* was the *point d'appui* of Ulysses' oration on degree. 'In will peculiar' and 'imagin'd worth' have echoes elsewhere, as you will see when I come to Troy and the other plot. This same phrase of Ulysses' comes a second time, quaintly echoed by Thersites during the battle. He has sought everywhere for 'the wenching rogues', Troilus and Diomed, cannot find them, and concludes they have eaten each other like the Kilkenny cats: 'I would laugh at that miracle. Yet, in a sort, lechery eats itself' (V. iv. 34–36).

I need hardly remind you that one meaning of the word *will* in Elizabethan English was 'lust', as is more than adequately shown by the surprising games Shakespeare plays with it in *Sonnet 135*:

> Whoever hath her wish, thou hast thy Will,
> And Will to boot, and Will in over-plus. . . .
> Wilt thou, whose will is large and spacious,
> Not once vouchsafe to hide my will in thine?
> Shall will in others seem right gracious,
> And in my will no fair acceptance shine?

With that borne in mind, I can leave the Achilles-Ajax or 'Pride' theme (one sort of 'imagin'd worth'), and turn to the third strand of plot-material: that about Troy and Hector.

This begins with the middle scene of Act II, where there is a council of war, and a debate, on the question of whether Helen shall be returned to the Greeks. Hector says 'Let Helen go'. Immediately Troilus shows his contempt for 'reason', arguing that honour demands that they do not so lower themselves. When Hector insist 'she is not worth what she doth cost the keeping', the discussion plunges abruptly downwards into the question of the nature of values. For Troilus the subjective is all: 'What's aught but as 'tis valued?' To this Hector replies:

> But value dwells not in particular will:
> It holds his estimate and dignity
> As well wherein 'tis precious of itself
> As in the prizer. . . .
>
> (II. ii. 53–56)

That is: 'The wilful inclination of an individual cannot of itself confer value: it depends on intrinsic merit, as well as on being precious to someone. " 'Tis mad idolatry / To make the service greater than the god"; and the will which ascribes value to what attracts it (and infectiously) is a *doting* will, if it sees imaginary excellences in the object of its affection.' (I have paraphrased the whole of Hector's answer. The lines are extremely difficult, and a convincing example of the close critical attention that

Shakespeare expected from his audience for this play—whoever they may have been).

The importance of the thought in this speech is evident as soon as we see that it draws a distinction which applies to all the main characters. 'Particular will' gives the valuation of the impassioned, wilful and egoistic man who is deaf to reason—and therefore blind to Natural Law. This point is made explicitly. Hector tells Paris and Troilus that they argue like youths incapable of moral philosophy (precisely following Ulysses' argument already quoted):

> The reasons you allege do more conduce
> To the hot passion of distemp'red blood
> Than to make up a free determination
> 'Twixt right and wrong.
>
> (II. ii. 168–71)

He follows this with a direct appeal to Natural Law, by which wife belongs to husband (Helen to Menelaus), thus making nonsense of Troilus's argument that you cannot take and marry a woman and then send her back like clothes on approval (any more than you can buy clothes and return them).

I remark again how Shakespeare seems to be writing for a legal-minded and acutely attentive audience. Troilus's argument was quite specious and self-deluding—rape confers no rights—but critics have been taken in by his 'chivalrous passion' and never noticed that his argument is nonsense, and *meant to be seen to be nonsense*. Carrying off Helen established no contract: the analogy of marriage is therefore totally spurious. Hector replies very justly: 'Statute law exists to curb wilful people who are as blind to right and wrong as you are.'

Now this obfuscation by 'particular will'—and the resulting self-delusion—explains the false estimates that Troilus makes of both Helen and Cressida. He 'idealizes' both: both are 'pearls'; but the idealization is not respectable (that alone totally marks off this love-story from *Romeo and Juliet*). Troilus is, indeed, equated with Paris—whose will to keep Helen is merely desire or lust. Helen is to Troy as Cressida is to Troilus; but the whole Trojan destruction is not women, but *will*.

Shakespeare conscientiously produces Helen in III. i., suitably accompanied by Pandarus (who accompanies himself with an obscene little song); and she is silly and empty, with some of Cressida's tricks of playing the men up prettily. To leave the true valuation in no doubt, he blasts her later through the mouth of Diomed:

> She's bitter to her country . . .
> For every false drop in her bawdy veins
> A Grecian's life hath sunk; for every scruple
> Of her contaminated carrion weight
> A Troyan hath been slain.
>
> (IV. i. 70–74)

The Trojans have good reason to fear 'bad success in a bad cause'; but at the end of this scene of close debate, Hector commits an inexplicable volte-face, and swings over to the side of Paris and Troilus against his own reasoning. That switch is his death-warrant. In V. iii. he rejects all the pleadings of Andromache and the inspired ravings of the prophetess Cassandra, goes out to fight because he has said he would and 'honour' (he insists) demands that he keeps his word: and so meets his end, and Troy with him. Both are victims to Troilus's style of 'thinking'.

Such is the very sketchy and attenuated Trojan plot. But now clues can be carried back to the Greeks. 'Particular will' offers the same diagnosis as 'imagin'd worth'. Just as Troilus is infatuated with a false image of love, so is Achilles with an image of self-love. Ajax, when swollen with flattery, is at once a monstrous balloon of conceit *and* a caricature of Achilles. On a final analysis, the *love*-theme, the *pride*-themes, and the *fall-of-Troy*-theme (for Helen and honour), presents a single core of thought. The play is a comedy of ideas, and coherent on no other assumption.

Its special technique (like that of *Henry IV*) is that the scenes and episodes cast changing lights on one another: as 'cutting' achieves in film-production. This can be shown by the long scene (III. iii.), where Achilles is slighted by the off-hand manner of the Generals, then left to be played on by Ulysses. As intrigue, it is only another attempt to persuade him to fight; but as thought, it belongs to the over-all debate on values. 'What is honour?' is Achilles' problem: 'Am I no longer what I was, because these men slight me?' To this wavering in 'imagin'd worth' Ulysses arrives with ready answers. The measure of worth is recognized effectiveness in the world of action:

> . . . no man is the lord of anything,
> Though in and of him there be much consisting,
> Till he communicate his parts to others;
> Nor doth he of himself know them for aught
> Till he behold them formed in th' applause
> Where th'are extended.
>
> (III. iii. 115–20)

He develops this in the famous lines about Time's wallet (in which good deeds are done and dropped and lost); and thus to

> Perseverance, dear my lord,
> Keeps honour bright. To have done is to hang
> Quite out of fashion, like a rusty nail
> In monumental mock'ry.
>
> (III. iii. 150–53)

Consequently:

> O, let not virtue seek
> Remuneration for the thing it was;
> For beauty, wit,
> High birth, vigour of bone, desert in service,
> Love, friendship, charity, are subjects all
> To envious and calumniating Time.
>
> (III. iii. 169–74)

'One touch of nature makes the whole world kin': that is, immediate and transitory appeal wins their praise (as Samuel Butler said, it might better be 'One touch of *ill*-nature').

Ulysses is disingenuous; but though I recognize his intention to fool Achilles into action, his real 'fooling' is much more serious. He has turned his back on all the absolute values implicit in his 'Degree' oration; is telling Achilles in effect that there are *no* absolute values: that 'honour' is the dividend in a ceaseless business of self-advertisment. Look critically at what he says, and how does the thought differ from the reflections of another experienced practical philosopher on the same subject?

> What is honour? A word. What is in that word? Honour. What is that honour? Air. A trim reckoning! Who hath it? He that died o' Wednesday. Doth he feel it? No. Doth he hear it? No. 'Tis insensible, then? Yea, to the dead. But will it not live with the living? No. Why? Detraction will not suffer it. Therefore I'll none of it. Honour is a mere scutcheon. And so ends my catechism.
>
> (I. *Hy. IV*. V. i. 132 ff.)

It sounds very different in blank verse and Greek costume. Yet the 'rusty mail in monumental mock'ry' *is* 'a mere scutcheon'. In practice, Ulysses shows nothing but a glib and oily art, and denies the 'estimate and dignity' of intrinsic merit. The 'Degree' thinking asserts universal, eternal values: this practical, 'realist' argument denies them. But the *motif* of *Time*, which from this point pervades the love-scenes, cannot be dismissed as a politician's cynicism. Time *is* love's remorseless enemy. Time is the theme of those tragic Sonnets which seem to have the closest connections with some of the deepest feelings in this play. In the agony of separation Troilus is made to catch up Ulysses' image of Time with a wallet; only now as the hurried burglar:

> Injurious time now with a robber's haste
> Crams his rich thievery up, he knows not how.
> (IV. iv. 41–42)

There is keener feeling in these time-references than in anything else; and, for all that, and simultaneously, the implied verdicts of time add their weight to the general riddling and exposure of seemings and appearances. It is not merely Cressida who is 'inconstant': inconstancy is the quality of everyone.

There is no such thing as true honour (based on genuine values) on either side, Trojan or Greek. All the high thinking comes to nothing: ceases to apply the moment men have to act. It is *doing* that counts; and whether in war or love the effects are brief, soon over and forgotten. Moreover, it is passion that leads to the act; and the impassioned will (lustful or furious) is impervious to right reason. Achilles fights, not because order and integrity have been re-established, but from personal rage. Troilus also. I know that Dr. Tillyard says Troilus has effected a 'self-cure', and found 'vent in action' for a new 'fierce and resolute temper'. But what Shakespeare shows me is that he has exchanged one mad passion for another: his rebuking Hector for his magnanimous habit of not striking men when they are down marks the chaos in his mind (if chivalry is old-fashioned folly and 'total war' laudable, what is wrong with Achilles' method of disposing of Hector?).

If the battle-scenes at the end *have* any intended meaning, it is that the whole universe of discourse has become chaotic. As Cassandra says,

> Behold distraction, frenzy, and amazement,
> Like witless antics, one another meet.
> (V. iii. 85–86)

Witness the whole battlefield croaked over by Thersites, like a moral vulture, feeding his mind's eye on carrion. But these later scenes are so incoherent—with so many undeveloped hints in them—that I am not at all sure that Shakespeare was not simply using stuff from some older play (cf. the hasty, ineffectual, careless ends of the two plays of 1599, *Henry V* and *Julius Caesar*).

I can now make an attempt to pull the results of my examination of the different plot-strands together. The play has been called 'a comedy of disillusion' (Dowden), 'a wry-mouthed comedy' (Ridley), a satire (Ulrici, Boas, O. J. Campbell), a piece of propaganda (Dover Wilson and G. B. Harrison), a morality, and (of course) a Problem play. I call it an *'inquisition'*. It has been forgotten that c. 1850 the German critic Gervinus made some very shrewd comments which seem apt for its appearance on the stage: 'It is very remarkable, but every reader will confess that this piece creates throughout no real effect on the mind' (the context shows he means no *emotional* or *sympathetic* effect. This is the final answer to those who would try to see the play as a tragedy).

> We feel throughout the play a wider bearing, a more remote object, and this alone prevents the immediate effect of the subject represented from appearing. The understanding is required to seek out this further aim of our comedy, and the sympathy of the heart is cooled. Here, as in Aristophanes, the action turns not upon the emotions of the soul, but upon the views of the understanding, and accordingly the personages acting occupy the mind as symbols rather than the heart.

He also remarked that we feel no ready engagement with any of the characters, 'not even in the affair of Troilus and Cressida, which speaks to the heart more than any other incident'. He might have backed this strongly, if he had noticed how, from the very beginning, a romantic, indulging self-identification with Troilus is checked by the implicit derision of Pandarus's very existence. There is, again, that queer, totally unrealistic ending of III. ii. (where the lovers are brought together), when each in turn steps right out of character and speaks as if the end of the story were already known: as to the audience it *was*. Troilus says (in effect), 'Let "True as Troilus" become a proverb'; Cressida, 'If I am false, then let "False as Cressid" become one too'; and Pandarus, 'Good; and if that is so, all go-betweens shall be panders'. He ends with a bawdy joke directed at the audience—but never mind that. The important thing is that all the genuine notes of passion come in the *next* scenes: and we (knowing our Chaucer) have been ironically inhibited from taking them at full face-value. At the same time, the verdict of *Time* has been thrust on us—underminingly.

   This rather uncomfortable detachment characterizes the play. We see codes of conduct, standards of values, ethical principles and passions, all standing on trial; and the conclusion appears to be that while the system of thought expounded by Ulysses and relied on by Hector *ought* to be the measure of human conduct, the proper calculus of right and wrong, it simply does not apply to realistically observed human conduct in war or love or diplomacy. This is what has given some the impression of a 'disillusioned Shakespeare', a man embittered by the Sonnet-story, etc.; and others the impression of a satire (where everyone's conduct is measured against Medieval principle, and shown to be wrong—and contemptible).

I do not accept either alternative. I can see this as nothing but a Jacobean play, concerned with the questioning of values in the new and sceptical atmosphere generated from the decay of the worlds of Spenser and the Petrarchan sonneteers: a world in which the perplexities (rather than the triumphs) of Renaissance individualism occupy the attention; where the dismissing of the old stable Medieval universals leaves thoughtful minds with the distressing discovery that if every individual thinks freely for himself and follows his own will, then chaos results, in which all order is lost. Donne plotted the position on the map of the contemporary climate of opinion quite adequately. In *An Anatomie of the World* (1612), having sketched the current devolution-theory (that the world has been in steady decline since the Fall), he turns to his own times:

> And now the Springs and Sommers which we see,
> Like sonnes of women after fiftie bee.
> And new Philosophy calls all in doubt,
> The Element of fire is quite put out;
> The sun is lost, and th'earth, and no mans wit
> Can well direct him where to looke for it.
> And freely men confesse that this world's spent.
> When in the Planets, and the Firmament
> They seeke so many new; they see that this
> Is crumbled out againe to his Atomies.
>
> (203–12)

So much, on the disturbing ideas generated by the 'new' Science. Then he turns to the changes in men's attitudes towards themselves:

> 'Tis all in peeces, all cohaerence gone;
> All just supply, and all Relation:
> Prince, Subject, Father, Sonne, are things forgot,
> For every man alone thinkes he hath got
> To be a Phoenix, and that then can bee
> None of that kinde, of which he is, but hee.
>
> (213–18)

In *Troilus and Cressida* such Phoenixes are only too frequent.

You notice how Donne explicitly refers to 'Degree' in 'Prince, Subject, Father, Sonne', and contrasts that with a 'modern' attitude of self-assertion, self-centredness—'will peculiar and self-admission'. The 'will peculiar and self-admission' of Achilles, the 'particular will' of Troilus, the blatant selfishness of Cressida, Paris, Diomed, Ajax: all seem to belong to this world of 'all cohaerence gone'. So too do the three quite distinct cynicisms of the three commentators: Pandarus (who defames love), Ulysses (a Machiavellian puppet-master, as shrewd as unprincipled), and Thersites (who defiles everything).

This last is unmistakably the Jacobean malcontent: the self-advertising moral critic whose avid curiosity about life brings him only a raging misery at its meanness and meaninglessness, and a self-tormented rage which spits itself out in railing, contempt and abuse (the filthier the better). Whether or not this play had anything to do with the 'War of the theatres' (the Poetomachia, that stage-lampooning-match of 1599–1602, which was really Jonson *versus* the rest), there is much John Marston in Thersites. But despite that (quite irrelevant) 'character' of Ajax in I. ii. (Alexander to Cressida), which sounds like a caricature of Jonson, I cannot be convinced that this is the 'purge' which Shakespeare is said to have administered to him. None the less, it has *resemblances* to the Poetomachia plays. It is a debating-piece, where the Greek and Trojan setting means no more than Rome in *The Poetaster* or Rufus's England in *Satiromastix*; and much of it is tuned to the carping notes which appealed to the active young discontents of the Court and the Inns of Court. As you know, Shakespeare never staged his own times: his settings are historic, exotic, fairytale; he never touched the 'realistic' modern-life, satirical-comedy field worked by Jonson, Chapman, Marston and Middleton. Maybe this is the nearest he came to it: a debating-play on moral and philosophical values, in which (as with Marston's *Antonio and Mellida*, etc. and Chapman's *Bussy D'Ambois*) the *ideas* mattered immeasurably more than the action. It can be called 'somewhat un-Shakespearian' in its refusal to engage our sympathies; yet there is a resembling aloofness about *All's Well* and, it seems to me, *Measure for Measure*, in which sexuality appears in an unlovely light and the old stable values have dissolved into a chaotic confusion of seemings.

Yet *Troilus and Cressida* shows even stronger Shakespearian continuities. It stands between the *Henry IV* plays (which are about honour and action, rule and order) and *Othello*, which I agree with Dr. Leavis in regarding as the tragedy not of perfect idealist love, but of the overwhelming of reason and self-knowledge by passion and self-love, in a self-glorifying egoist—'naturally jealous' (for all that Othello himself or Coleridge or Bradley may say). Human egocentricity and a wincing at human degradation mark, for me, these middle-period plays. The tone begins with *2 Henry IV*, and if I were compelled to illustrate it in a single phrase, it would be from the exchange of the two French Lords in *All's Well* on Bertram's seduction of Diana.

Beyond doubt, the exposure of self-treachery goes further in *Troilus and Cressida* than elsewhere. Go through the play, and who is there left unscathed? The old are old fools, the young either young fools or thriving young cads. All the high talk comes down to Troilus's contemptuous dismissal of Cressida's letter: 'Words, words, mere words, no matter from the heart.' It perplexes me that Shakespeare did not make an overt symbol of the 'one in sumptuous armour' whom Hector kills and strips (V. vi. and viii); only to find him somehow disgustingly diseased—'Most putrified core so fair without . . .'

One character alone comes out of it without a scratch: Antenor. When I used to be told, long ago, to write essays on 'The character in Shakespeare (or fiction) you would most like to have met', I had never heard of Antenor. Now, he would be my man. But perhaps you have not noticed him? Never mind, you will next time you read the play. Five times he enters for certain (it may even be six), and five times he goes out as noncommittally as he came. Pandarus sums him up at I. ii. 182f.: 'He has a shrewd wit, I can tell you; and he's a man good enough; he's one o' th' soundest judgments in Troy, whosoever, and a proper man of person.' But even when the exchange of prisoners is afoot, they speak of him as if he was not there and he does not mind. He never speaks a line; he never utters a word. I see in him the prophetic outline of the average man of good will involved in war: never knowing why he is there nor what is really going on: as muddled as Fabrizio at Waterloo in *La Chartreuse de Parme*, but less scandalized—and, most certainly, Shakespeare's one strong silent man.

ALVIN B. KERNAN

"Othello": An Introduction

W hen Shakespeare wrote *Othello*, about
1604, his knowledge of human nature and his ability to dramatize it
in language and action were at their height. The play offers, even in its
minor characters, a number of unusually full and profound studies of
humanity: Brabantio, the sophisticated, civilized Venetian senator, unable
to comprehend that his delicate daughter could love and marry a Moor,
speaking excitedly of black magic and spells to account for what his mind
cannot understand; Cassio, the gentleman-soldier, polished in manners
and gracious in bearing, wildly drunk and revealing a deeply rooted pride
in his ramblings about senior officers being saved before their juniors;
Emilia, the sensible and conventional waiting woman, making small talk
about love and suddenly remarking that though she believes adultery to be
wrong, still if the price were high enough she would sell—and so, she
believes, would most women. The vision of human nature which the play
offers is one of ancient terrors and primal drives—fear of the unknown,
pride, greed, lust—underlying smooth, civilized surfaces—the noble senator, the competent and well-mannered lieutenant, the conventional
gentlewoman.

The contrast between surface manner and inner nature is even
more pronounced in two of the major characters. "Honest Iago" conceals
beneath his exterior of the plain soldier and blunt, practical man of the
world a diabolism so intense as to defy rational explanation—it must be
taken like lust or pride as simply a given part of human nature, an anti-life
spirit which seeks the destruction of everything outside the self. Othello

From *The Tragedy of Othello*, edited by Alvin B. Kernan. Copyright © 1963 by Alvin
Kernan. Copyright © by Sylvan Barnet. New American Library.

appears in the opening acts as the very personification of self-control, of the man with so secure a sense of his own worth that nothing can ruffle the consequent calmness of mind and manner. But the man who has roamed the wild and savage world unmoved by its terrors, who has not changed countenance when the cannon killed his brother standing beside him, this man is still capable of believing his wife a whore on the slightest of evidence and committing murders to revenge himself. In Desdemona alone do the heart and the hand go together: she is what she seems to be. Ironically, she alone is accused of pretending to be what she is not. Her very openness and honesty make her suspect in a world where few men are what they appear, and her chastity is inevitably brought into question in a world where every other major character is in some degree touched with sexual corruption.

Most criticism of *Othello* has concerned itself with exploring the depths of these characters and tracing the intricate, mysterious operations of their minds. I should like, however, to leave this work to the individual reader . . . in order to discuss, briefly, what might be called the "gross mechanics" of the play, the larger patterns in which events and characters are arranged. These patterns are the context within which the individual characters are defined, just as the pattern of a sentence is the context which defines the exact meaning of the individual words within it.

Othello is probably the most neatly, the most formally constructed of Shakespeare's plays. Every character is, for example, balanced by another similar or contrasting character. Desdemona is balanced by her opposite, Iago; love and concern for others at one end of the scale, hatred and concern for self at the other. The true and loyal soldier Cassio balances the false and traitorous soldier Iago. These balances and contrasts throw into relief the essential qualities of the characters. Desdemona's love, for example, shows up a good deal more clearly in contrast to Iago's hate, and vice versa. The values of contrast are increased and the full range of human nature displayed by extending these simple contrasts into developing series. The essential purity of Desdemona stands in contrast to the more "practical" view of chastity held by Emilia, and her view in turn is illuminated by the workaday view of sensuality held by the courtesan Bianca, who treats love, ordinarily, as commodity. Or, to take another example, Iago's success in fooling Othello is but the culmination of a series of such betrayals that includes the duping of Roderigo, Brabantio, and Cassio. Each duping is the explanatory image of the other, for in every case Iago's method and end are the same: he plays on and teases to life some hitherto controlled and concealed dark passion in his victim. In each case he seeks in some way the same end, the symbolic murder of

Desdemona, the destruction in some form of the life principle of which she is the major embodiment.

These various contrasts and parallelisms ultimately blend into a larger, more general pattern that is the central movement of the play. We can begin to see this pattern in the "symbolic geography" of the play. Every play, or work of art, creates its own particular image of space and time, its own symbolic world. The outer limits of the world of *Othello* are defined by the Turks—the infidels, the unbelievers, the "general enemy" as the play calls them—who, just over the horizon, sail back and forth trying to confuse and trick the Christians in order to invade their domin-ions and destroy them. Out beyond the horizon, reported but unseen, are also those "anters vast and deserts idle" of which Othello speaks. Out there is a land of "rough quarries, rocks, and hills whose heads touch heaven" inhabited by "cannibals that each other eat" and monstrous forms of men "whose heads grow beneath their shoulders." On the edges of this land is the raging ocean with its "high seas, and howling winds," its "guttered rocks and congregated sands" hidden beneath the waters to "enclog the guiltless keel."

Within the circle formed by barbarism, monstrosity, sterility, and the brute power of nature lie the two Christian strongholds of Venice and Cyprus. Renaissance Venice was known for its wealth acquired by trade, its political cunning, and its courtesans; but Shakespeare, while reminding us of the tradition of the "supersubtle Venetian," makes Venice over into a form of *The City*, the ageless image of government, of reason, of law, and of social concord. Here, when Brabantio's strong passions and irrational fears threaten to create riot and injustice, his grievances are examined by a court of law, judged by reason, and the verdict enforced by civic power. Here, the clear mind of the Senate probes the actions of the Turks, penetrates through their pretenses to their true purposes, makes sense of the frantic and fearful contradictory messages which pour in from the fleet, and arranges the necessary defense. Act I, Scene iii—the Senate scene—focuses on the magnificent speeches of Othello and Desdemona as they declare their love and explain it, but the lovers are surrounded, guarded, by the assembled, ranked governors of Venice, who control passions that otherwise would have led to a bloody street brawl and bring justice out of what otherwise would have been riot. The solemn presence and ordering power of the Senate would be most powerfully realized in a stage production, where the senators would appear in their rich robes, with all their symbols of office, seated in ranks around several excited individuals expressing such primal passions as pride of race, fear of dark powers, and violent love. In a play where so much of the language is magnificent, rich, and of heroic proportions, simpler statements come to seem more forceful; and the meaning of *The City* is perhaps nowhere more completely realized than in Brabantio's brief, secure answer to the first fearful cries of theft and talk of copulating animals that Iago and Roderigo send up from the darkness below his window:

> What tell'st thou me of robbing? This is Venice;
> My house is not a grange.

> (I.i.102–03)

Here then are the major reference points on a map of the world of *Othello:* out at the far edge are the Turks, barbarism, disorder, and amoral destructive powers; closer and more familiar is Venice, *The City*, order, law, and reason. Cyprus, standing on the frontier between barbarism and *The City*, is not the secure fortress of civilization that Venice is. It is rather an outpost, weakly defended and far out in the raging ocean, close to the "general enemy" and the immediate object of his attack. It is a "town of war yet wild" where the "people's hearts [are] brimful of fear." Here passions are more explosive and closer to the surface than in Venice, and here, instead of the ancient order and established government of *The City*, there is only one man to control violence and defend civilization— the Moor Othello, himself of savage origins and a converted Christian.

The movement of the play is from Venice to Cyprus, from *The City* to the outpost, from organized society to a condition much closer to raw nature, and from collective life to the life of the solitary individual. This movement is a characteristic pattern in Shakespeare's plays, both comedies and tragedies: in *A Midsummer Night's Dream* the lovers and players go from the civilized, daylight world of Athens to the irrational, magical wood outside Athens and the primal powers of life represented by the elves and fairies; Lear moves from his palace and secure identity to the savage world of the heath where all values and all identities come into question; and everyone in *The Tempest* is shipwrecked at some time on Prospero's magic island, where life seen from a new perspective assumes strange and fantastic shapes. At the other end of this journey there is always some kind of return to *The City*, to the palace, and to old relationships, but the nature of this return differs widely in Shakespeare's plays. In *Othello* the movement at the end of the play is back toward Venice, the Turk defeated; but Desdemona, Othello, Emilia, and Roderigo do not return. Their deaths are the price paid for the return.

This passage from Venice to Cyprus to fight the Turk and encounter the forces of barbarism is the geographical form of an action that occurs on the social and psychological levels as well. That is, there are social and mental conditions that correspond to Venice and Cyprus, and there are forces at work in society and in man that correspond to the Turks, the raging seas, and "cannibals that each other eat."

The exposure to danger, the breakdown and the ultimate reestablishment of society—the parallel on the social level to the action on the geographical level—is quickly traced. We have already noted that the Venetian Senate embodies order, reason, justice, and concord, the binding forces that hold *The City* together. In Venice the ancient laws and the established customs of society work to control violent men and violent passions to ensure the safety and well-being of the individual and the group. But there are anarchic forces at work in the city, which threaten traditional social forms and relationships, and all these forces center in Iago. His discontent with his own rank and his determination to displace Cassio endanger the orderly military hierarchy in which the junior serves his senior. He endangers marriage, the traditional form for ordering male and female relationships, by his own unfounded suspicions of his wife and by his efforts to destroy Othello's marriage by fanning to life the darker, anarchic passions of Brabantio and Roderigo. He tries to subvert the operation of law and justice by first stirring up Brabantio to gather his followers and seek revenge in the streets; and then when the two warlike forces are met, Iago begins a quarrel with Roderigo in hopes of starting a brawl. The nature of the antisocial forces that Iago represents are focused in the imagery of his advice to Roderigo on how to call out to her father the news of Desdemona's marriage. Call, he says,

> with like timorous [frightening] accent and dire yell
> As when, by night and negligence, the fire
> Is spied in populous cities.

(I.i.72–74)

Fire, panic, darkness, neglect of duty—these are the natural and human forces that destroy great cities and turn their citizens to mobs.

In Venice, Iago's attempts to create civic chaos are frustrated by Othello's calm management of himself and the orderly legal proceedings of the Senate. In Cyprus, however, society is less secure—even as the island is more exposed to the Turks—and Othello alone is responsible for finding truth and maintaining order. Here Iago's poison begins to work, and he succeeds at once in manufacturing the riot that he failed to create in Venice. Seen on stage, the fight on the watch between Cassio and Montano is chaos come again: two drunken officers, charged with the defense of the town, trying to kill each other like savage animals, a bedlam of voices and shouts, broken, disordered furniture, and above all this the discordant clamor of the "dreadful" alarm bell—used to signal attacks and fire. This success is but the prologue for other more serious disruptions of society and of the various human relationships that it fosters. The General is set against his officer, husband against wife, Christian against Christian, servant against master. Justice becomes a travesty of itself as Othello—using legal terms such as "It is the *cause*" —assumes the offices of accuser, judge, jury, and executioner of his wife. Manners disappear as the Moor strikes his wife publicly and treats her maid as a procuress. The brightly lighted Senate chamber is now replaced with a dark Cyprus street where Venetians cut one another down and men are murdered from behind. This anarchy finally gives way in the last scene, when Desdemona's faith is proven, to a restoration of order and an execution of justice on the two major criminals.

What we have followed so far is a movement expressed in geographical and social symbols from Venice to a Cyprus exposed to attack, from *The City* to barbarism, from Christendom to the domain of the Turks, from order to riot, from justice to wild revenge and murder, from truth to falsehood. It now remains to see just what this movement means on the level of the individual in the heart and mind of man. Of the three major characters, Desdemona, Othello, and Iago, the first and the last do not change their natures or their attitudes toward life during the course of the play. These two are polar opposites, the antitheses of each other. To speak in the most general terms, Desdemona expresses in her language and actions an innocent, unselfish love and concern for others. Othello catches her very essence when he speaks of her miraculous love, which transcended their differences in age, color, beauty, and culture:

> She loved me for the dangers I had passed,
> And I loved her that she did pity them.
> (I.iii.166–67)

This love in its various forms finds expression not only in her absolute commitment of herself to Othello, but in her gentleness, her kindness to others, her innocent trust in all men, her pleas for Cassio's restoration to Othello's favor; and it endures even past death at her husband's hands, for she comes back to life for a moment to answer Emilia's question, "who hath done this deed?" with the unbelievable words,

> Nobody—I myself. Farewell.
> Commend me to my kind lord. O, farewell!
> (V.ii.123–24)

Iago is her opposite in every way. Where she is open and guileless, he is never what he seems to be; where she thinks the best of everyone, he thinks the worst, usually turning to imagery of animals and physical functions to express his low opinion of human nature; where she seeks to serve and love others, he uses others to further his own dark aims and satisfy his hatred of mankind; where she is emotional and idealistic, he is icily logical and cynical. Desdemona and Iago are much more complicated than this, but perhaps enough has been said to suggest the nature of these two moral poles of the play. One is a life force that strives for order, community, growth, and light. The other is an anti-life force that seeks anarchy, death, and darkness. One is the foundation of all that men have built in the world, including *The City*; the other leads back toward ancient chaos and barbarism.

Othello, like most men, is a combination of the forces of love and hate, which are isolated in impossibly pure states in Desdemona and Iago. His psychic voyage from Venice to Cyprus is a passage of the soul and the will from the values of one of these characters to those of the other. This passage is charted by his acceptance and rejection of one or the other. He begins by refusing to have Iago as his lieutenant, choosing the more "theoretical" though less experienced Cassio. He marries Desdemona. Though he is not aware that he does so, he expresses the full meaning of this choice when he speaks of her in such suggestive terms as "my soul's joy" and refers to her even as he is about to kill her, as "Promethean heat," the vital fire that gives life to the world. Similarly, he comes to know that all that is valuable in life depends on her love, and in the magnificent speech beginning, "O now, forever / Farewell the tranquil mind" (III.iii.344–45), he details the emptiness of all human activity if Desdemona be proved false. But Iago, taking advantage of latent "Iagolike" feelings and thoughts in Othello, persuades him that Desdemona is only common clay. Othello then gives himself over to Iago at the end of III.iii, where they kneel together to plan the revenge, and Othello says. "Now art thou my lieutenant." To which Iago responds with blood-chilling simplicity, "I am your own forever." The full meaning of this choice is expressed, again unconsciously, by Othello when he says of Desdemona,

> Perdition catch my soul
> But I do love thee! and when I love thee not,
> Chaos is come again.
>
> (III.iii.90–92)

The murder of Desdemona acts out the final destruction in Othello himself of all the ordering powers of love, of trust, of the bond between human beings.

Desdemona and Iago then represent two states of mind, two

understandings of life, and Othello's movement from one to the other is the movement on the level of character and psychology from Venice to Cyprus, from *The City* to anarchy. His return to *The City* and the defeat of the Turk is effected, at the expense of his own life, when he learns *what* he has killed and executes himself as the only fitting judgment on his act. His willingness to speak of what he has done—in contrast to Iago's sullen silence—is a willingness to recognize the meaning of Desdemona's faith and chastity, to acknowledge that innocence and love do exist, and that therefore *The City* can stand, though his life is required to validate the truth and justice on which it is built.

Othello offers a variety of interrelated symbols that locate and define in historical, natural, social, moral, and human terms those qualities of being and universal forces that are forever at war in the universe and between which tragic man is always in movement. On one side there are Turks, cannibals, barbarism, monstrous deformities of nature, the brute force of the sea, riot, mobs, darkness, Iago, hatred, lust, concern for the self only, and cynicism. On the other side there are Venice, *The City*, law, senates, amity, hierarchy, Desdemona, love, concern for others, and innocent trust. As the characters of the play act and speak, they bring together, by means of parallelism and metaphor, the various forms of the different ways of life. There is, for example, a meaningful similarity in the underhanded way Iago works and the ruse by which the Turks try to fool the Venetians into thinking they are bound for Rhodes when their object is Cyprus. Or, there is again a flash of identification when we hear that the reefs and shoals that threaten ships are "ensteeped," that is, hidden under the surface of the sea, as Iago is hidden under the surface of his "honesty." But Shakespeare binds the various levels of being more closely together by the use of imagery that compares things on one level of action with things on another. For example, when Iago swears that his low judgment of all female virtue "is true, or else I am a Turk" (II.i.113), logic demands, since one woman, Desdemona, *is* true and chaste, that we account him "a Turk." He is thus identified with the unbelievers, the Ottoman Turks, and that Asiatic power, which for centuries threatened Christendom, is shown to have its social and psychological equivalent in Iago's particular attitude toward life. Similarly, when Othello sees the drunken brawl on the watchtower, he exclaims,

> Are we turned Turks, and to ourselves do that
> Which heaven hath forbid the Ottomites?
> (II.iii.169–70)

At the very time when the historical enemy has been defeated, his fleet providentially routed by the great storm, his characteristics—drunken loss of control, brawling over honor, disorder—begin to conquer the island only so recently and fortuitously saved. The conquest continues, and the defender of the island, Othello, convinced of Desdemona's guilt, compares his determination to revenge himself to "the Pontic Sea, / Whose icy current and compulsive course / Nev'r keeps retiring ebb" (III.iii.450–52). The comparison tells us that in his rage and hatred he has become one with the savage seas and the brute, amoral powers of nature that are displayed in the storm scene at the beginning of Act II. But most important is Othello's identification of himself at the end of the play as the "base Judean" who "threw a pearl away richer than all his tribe." The more familiar Quarto reading is "base Indian," but both words point toward the barbarian who fails to recognize value and beauty when he possesses it—the primitive savage who picks up a pearl and throws it away not knowing its worth; or the Jews (Judas may be specifically meant) who denied and crucified another great figure of love, thinking they were dealing with only a troublesome rabble-rouser. A few lines further on Othello proceeds to the final and absolute identification of himself with the infidel. He speaks of a "malignant and a turbaned Turk" who "beat a Venetian and traduced the state," and he then acknowledges that he is that Turk by stabbing himself, even as he once stabbed the other unbeliever. So he ends as both the Turk and the destroyer of the Turk, the infidel and the defender of the faith.

When Iago's schemes are at last exposed, Othello, finding it impossible for a moment to believe that a *man* could have contrived such evil, stares at Iago's feet and then says sadly, "but that's a fable." What he hopes to find when he looks down are the cloven hoofs of the devil, and had they been there he would have been an actor in a morality play, tempted beyond his strength, like many a man before him, by a supernatural power outside himself. In some ways I have schematized *Othello* as just such a morality play, offering an allergorical journey between heaven and hell on a stage filled with purely symbolic figures. This is the kind of abtraction of art toward which criticism inevitably moves, and in this case the allegorical framework is very solidly there. But Othello does not see the cloven hoofs when he looks down; he sees a pair of human feet at the end of a very human body; and he is forced to realize that far from living in some simplified, "fabulous" world where evil is a metaphysical power raiding human life from without, he dwells where evil is somehow inextricably woven with good into man himself. On his stage the good angel does not return to heaven when defeated, but is murdered, and her body remains on the bed, "cold, cold." He lives where good intentions, past services, psychic weaknesses, and an inability to see through evil cannot excuse an act, as they might in some simpler world where more perfect justice existed. In short, Othello is forced to recognize that he lives in a tragic world, and he pays the price for having been great enough to inhabit it.

Here is the essence of Shakespeare's art, an ability to create immediate, full, and total life as men actually live and experience it; and yet at the same time to arrange this reality so that it gives substance to and derives shape from a formal vision of all life that comprehends and reaches back from man and nature through society and history to cosmic powers that operate through all time and space. His plays are both allegorical and realistic at once; his characters both recognizable men and at the same time devils, demigods, and forces in nature. I have discussed only the more allegorical elements in *Othello*, the skeleton of ideas and formal patterns within which the characters must necessarily be understood. But it is equally true that the exact qualities of the abstract moral values and ideas, their full reality, exist only in the characters. It is necessary to know that Desdemona represents one particular human value, love or charity, in order to avoid making such mistakes as searching for some tragic flaw in her which would justify her death. But at the same time, if we would know what love and charity *are* in all their fullness, then our definition can only be the actions, the language, the emotions of the character Desdemona. She is Shakespeare's word for love. If we wish to know not just the obvious fact that men choose evil over good, but *why* they do so, then we must look both analytically and feelingly at all the evidence that the world offers for believing that Desdemona is false and at all the biases in Othello's mind that predispose him to believe such evidence. Othello's passage from Venice to Cyprus, from absolute love for Desdemona to extinguishing the light in her bedchamber, and to the execution of himself, these are Shakespeare's words for tragic man.

KENNETH BURKE

"Coriolanus" and the Delights of Faction

This chapter is to involve one of my experiments with the safest and surest kind of prophecy; namely: prophecy after the event. Our job will be to ask how Shakespeare's grotesque tragedy, *Coriolanus*, "ought to be." And we can check on the correctness of our prophecies by consulting the text.

We begin with these assumptions: Since the work is a tragedy, it will require some kind of symbolic action in which some notable form of victimage is imitated, for the purgation, or edification of an audience. The character that is to be sacrificed must be fit for his role as victim; and everything must so fit together that the audience will find the sacrifice plausible and acceptable (thereby furtively participating in the judgment against the victim, and thus even willing the victimage). The expectations and desires of the audience will be shaped by conditions within the play. But the topics exploited for persuasive purposes *within* the play will also have strategic relevance to kinds of "values" and "tensions" that prevail *outside* the play.

There is a benign perversity operating here. In one sense, the aesthetic and the ethical coincide, since a way of life gives rise to a moral code, and the dramatist can exploit this moral code for poetic effects by building up characters that variously exemplify the system of vices and virtues to which the code explicitly or implicitly subscribes. But in another sense the aesthetic and the ethical are at odds, since the dramatist

From *Hudson Review* 2, vol. 19 (Summer 1966). Copyright © 1966 by University of California Press.

can transform our moral problems into sources of poetic entertainment. Any ethical "thou shalt not" sets up the conditions for an author to engage an audience by depicting characters that variously violate or threaten to violate the "thou shalt not." And many motivational conflicts that might distress us in real life can be transformed into kinds of poetic imitation that engross us. Thus in the realm of the aesthetic we may be delighted by accounts of distress and corruption that would make the moralist quite miserable.

The moral problem, or social tension, that is here to be exploited for the production of the "tragic pleasure" is purely and simply a kind of discord intrinsic to the distinction between upper classes and lower classes. However, a certain "distance" could be got in Shakespeare's day by treating the problem in terms not of contemporary London but of ancient Rome. A somewhat analogous situation is to be seen in Euripides' tragedy of *The Trojan Women*, which appeared some months after the Athenians had destroyed the little island of Melos, though on its face the play was concerned with the Trojan war, the theme of *The Iliad*. When *Coriolanus* appeared there had been considerable rioting due to the Enclosure Acts by which many tenants had been dispossessed of their traditional rights to the land, and were suffering great hardships. Both of these plays may, in their way, have gained strictly contemporary relevance from the allusive exploiting of a "timely topic." But in any case, each was dealing with a distress of much longer duration, in Euripides' case the horrors of war, and in Shakespeare's case the *malaise* of the conflict between the privileged and the underprivileged, as stated in terms of a struggle between the patricians and plebeians of old Rome.

If we are going to "dramatize" such a tension, we shall want first of all a kind of character who in some way helps *intensify* the tension. Where there are any marked differences in social status, in the situation itself there is a kind of "built-in pride," no matter how carefully one might try to mitigate such contrasts. And despite polite attempts to gloss things over, the unresolved situation is intrinsically there. By the nature of the case, it involves *exclusions*.

But for our purposes the main consideration is this: Whereas a hostess, or a diplomat, or an ingratiating politician, or a public relations counsel might go as far as possible towards *toning down* such situations, the dramatist must work his cures by a quite different method. He must find ways to *play them up*. In some respects, therefore, this play will require a kind of character who is designed to help aggravate the uneasiness of the relationship between nobles and commoners.

For this aspect of his role, our chosen victim is obviously a perfect fit. In contrast with the suave Menenius, who has been addressing the mutinous citizens with such a cautious mixture of gravity and humor, our chosen victim's first words to the people are: "What's the matter, you dissentious rogues, / That, rubbing the poor itch of your opinion, / Make yourselves scabs?" Thereafter, again and again, his gruff (or if you will, arrogant) manner of speaking is designed to point up (for the audience) the conflict intrinsic to the class distinctions with which the play is "drastically" concerned. (It's well to recall here that, in earlier medical usage, a "drastic" was the name for the strongest kind of "cathartic." Also, the word derives etymologically from the same root as "drama.")

The Greek word *hubris* sometimes translates best as "pride," sometimes as "excess." And in Athenian law *hubris* was also used to designate a civil offense, an insulting air of superiority, deemed punishable by death. When you note how neatly all three meanings come together in the role of Coriolanus, I think you will realize at least one reason why I find the play so fascinating. The grotesque hero is *excessively* downright, forthright, outright (and even, after his fashion, upright), in his unquestioned assumption that the common people are intrinsically inferior to the nobility. Indeed, though the word "noble" suggests to most of us *either* moral *or* social connotations, Coriolanus takes it for granted that only the *socially* noble can have nobility of any sort. (The word appears about seventy-six times in the play. In half of these contexts it is applied to Coriolanus himself. And, to my knowledge, it is never used ironically, as with Mark Antony's transformations of the word "honourable.") Coriolanus is excessive in ways that prepare the audience to relinquish him for his role as scapegoat, in accentuating a trait that the audience also shares with him, though seldom so avowedly.

More "prophesying after the event" is still to be done. But first, perhaps we should pause to give a generalized outline of the plot, having in mind the kind of tension (or factional malaise) that the drama would transform into terms of purgative appeal:

> After having gained popular acclaim through prowess in war, a courageous but arrogant patrician, who had been left fatherless when young and was raised by his mother, is persuaded by his mother to sue for high political office. In campaigning, he alienates the plebeians who, goaded by his political rivals, condemn him to exile. When in exile, making an alliance with the commander of the armies he had conquered, he leads a force against his own country. But before the decisive battle, during a visit by his closest relatives, his mother persuades him not to attack. In so doing, she unintentionally sets in motion the conditions whereby the allied commander, whom he had formerly vanquished and who envies his fame, successfully plots his assassination.

It is impressive how perfectly the chosen victim's virtues and vices work together, in fitting him for his sacrificial function. The several scenes in the first act that build up his prowess as a soldier not only endow him with a sufficient measure of the heroics necessary for tragic dignification. They also serve to make it clear why, when he returns to Rome and, against his will, consents to seek the office of consul, he is bound to be a misfit. Shakespeare himself usually gives us the formula for such matters. It is stated by the Tribune, Brutus, in Act III, scene iii: Get him angry, for

> . . . He hath been us'd
> Ever to conquer, and to have his worth
> Of contradiction. Being once chaf'd, he cannot
> Be rein'd again to temperance; then he speaks
> What's in his heart, and that is there which looks
> With us to break his neck.

He is not the "war games" kind of military man, not the "computer mentality"; thus we spontaneously accept it that his valiant though somewhat swashbuckling ways as a warrior will make him incompetent in the wiles of peaceful persuasion, which the wily Shakespeare so persuasively puts in a bad light, *within* the conditions of the play, by his treatment of the Tribunes. Though Shakespeare's theater is, from start to finish, a masterful enterprise in the arts of persuasion, high among his resources is the building of characters who are weak in such devices. Indeed, considered from this point of view, Coriolanus' bluntness is in the same class with Cordelia's fatal inability to flatter Lear. Later we shall find other reasons to think of Lear in connection with Coriolanus' railings. Meanwhile, note how the Tribunes' skill at petition is portrayed as not much better than mere cunning, even though somewhat justified by our highborn goat's arrogance in his dealings with the commoners. He finds it impossible even to simulate an attitude of deference. And once we have his number, when he sets out to supplicate, armed with the slogan "The word is 'mildly,' " the resources of dramatic irony have already prepared us for the furious outbursts that will get the impetuous war-hero banished from Rome, a climax capped perfectly by his quick rejoinder, "I banish you!" As a fearless fighter, he is trained to give commands and to risk his life, not to supplicate. And the better to build him up, in the role of the Tribunes Shakespeare makes the art of political supplication seem quite unsavory.

All told, Coriolanus' courage and outspokenness make him a sufficiently "noble" character to dignify a play by the sacrificing of him. And excessive ways of constantly reaffirming his assumption that only the *social* nobility can be *morally* noble indicts him for sacrifice. But more than this is needed to make him effectively yieldable.

For one thing, always in drama we encounter a variation on the theme of what I would call the "paradox of substance." A character cannot "be himself" unless many others among the dramatis personae contribute to this end, so that the very essence of a character's nature is in a large measure defined, or determined, by the other characters who variously assist or oppose him. The most obvious instance of what I mean is the role of Aufidius. If it is an integral part of Coriolanus' role to be slain, there must be a slayer. And in this sense Aufidius is "derived from" the character of Coriolanus. The conditions of the play set up Coriolanus as a gerundive, a "to be killed," and Aufidius is to be the primary instrument in the killing. As is typical of a Shakespearean play, just before the close of the first act Aufidius points the arrows of the audience's expectations by announcing to a soldier (and thus to the audience) that he will destroy Coriolanus in whatever way possible. Even so, it's always good if a man speaks with high respect of a slain rival; accordingly, though Aufidius must be plotter enough to fulfill his role in Coriolanus' death, he must be of sufficient dignity so that his final tribute to the "noble memory" of Coriolanus will serve to give the audience a parting reassurance that they have participated in the symbolic sacrifice of a victim worth the killing. The assurance was made doubly necessary by the fact that, just before the slaying, there had been a kind of last-moment revelation, when Aufidius called the bold warrior a "boy of tears," thus propounding a final formula for Coriolanus' relationship to his mother. Aufidius' claims as a worthy opponent (despite his unsavory traits) are established in Coriolanus' first reference to him, such as, "I sin in envying his nobility," and "He is a lion/That I am proud to hunt."

This relationship we should dwell on. For it best illustrates just what we mean by "prophesying after the event" in order to "derive" the play in terms of poetics. If the characters are viewed simply as "people," we should treat the relationship between Coriolanus and Volumnia much as Plutarch did, in the "Life" from which Shakespeare borrowed so much of his plot. Coriolanus would thus be interpreted as the offspring of a bellicose, overbearing mother, who sought to compensate for the death of his father by being both mother and father to him. There is one change worth noting. Whereas Plutarch attributes Coriolanus' resultant irritability to womanishness, Shakespeare seems to have settled for a mere failure to outgrow boyishness. But our main point is this: Along the lines of poetic principles, the derivation should be reversed; and instead of viewing

Coriolanus as an offspring of his mother, we view her role as a function contributory to his.

Thus, in an early scene, she is portrayed as a pugnacious virago of whom the son became a responsive masculine copy. This portrait of her prepares us to accept it as "natural" that, when he returns from the battlefields, *she* can persuade him, against his wishes, to stand for consul. And thus, later in the play, we will accept it that *she* can persuade him not to attack Rome—and (quite unintentionally on her part) this decision sets up the conditions responsible for his death. In brief, when using her to account for Coriolanus' character in the first place, Shakespeare is preparing her to serve as plausible explanation for two crucial moments in the *plot*: a nonpolitical man's ventures into politics, and a fighting man's failure to join in battle when success was certain. In brief, her relation to Coriolanus motivates for us two decisions of his that are basically necessary, to make the *turns* in the tragedy seem plausible.

I say "turns," having in mind the Aristotelian word, "peripety," to name the striking moment, near the center of a complex plot, when some significant reversal takes place. But I might here pause to note that this is a play of many such reversals. In Act I, there are the many scenes that might in general be entitled the "Tides of Battle," including the one where Coriolanus—or at that time, Caius Marcius, since he has not yet received his new name from the city he conquered—is thought to be lost, through having single-handedly pursued the enemy within the gate of Corioli, fighting alone where Plutarch less theatrically had reported him as but leader of a small band. At the end of Act II, the commoners are persuaded by the Tribunes to retract their intention of voting for Coriolanus as consul. The big peripety is, as one might expect, in Act III, the hero's fatal bursts of rage having been prepared for ironically by his decision to be mild. In this act, there is a kind of peripety-atop-peripety, when Coriolanus retorts to his banishers, "I banish you!"

In Act IV, scene v, there is a neat turn when Aufidius' servingmen, who would treat Coriolanus shabbily when he first appears, abruptly change their tune after he has talked with Aufidius, and the compact against Rome has been agreed on. Besides being one of the few comic spots in the play. this scene is also useful in preparing for the last fatal reversal, since it brings out the fact that, even if Coriolanus and Aufidius are to become allies, Coriolanus' reputation is a threat to Aufidius. Another reversal, in scene vi, occurs when, just after the Tribunes and citizens have been congratulating themselves on the conditions of peace resulting from Coriolanus' banishment, they are startled by the news that Coriolanus is marching on Rome.

In Act V, there is a fatal peripety, when Coriolanus is persuaded by his mother to give up his intention of attacking Rome. This leads to another peripety, the ironic twist whereby, soon after Menenius has explained to one of the Tribunes that Coriolanus will never yield ("There is no more mercy in him than there is milk in a male tiger"), they learn that Coriolanus has begun to withdraw. And even though the arrows of our expectations were clearly pointing in this direction, there is a final peripety in the hero's slaying.

Coriolanus' wife, Virgilia, is quickly "derivable." In contrast with his continual bluster, she is his "gracious silence." Contrasting with his blood-thirsty mother, she faints at the very mention of blood. In her sensitiveness and devotion, she is by implication a vote for Coriolanus. There's a skillful touch, in Act IV, scene ii, where she flares up for a moment against the Tribunes, and boasts of her husband as a fighter: "He'ld make an end of thy posterity." There's a different twist, but surely conceived in the spirit of the same theater, when the young son (who is a chip off the old block, and loved to rip apart a butterfly) flares up at his father. The most notable thing about Valeria, from the standpoint of Shakespearean dramaturgy, is the fact that, though this friend of the family serves well for handling the relation between mother-in-law and daughter, she has a much less active role in the play than she does in Plutarch. For in Plutarch, *she* suggests that the women go to plead with Coriolanus and dissuade him from attacking Rome, whereas the whole musculature of Shakespeare's play requires maximum stress upon his mother's role in this development. The two Generals (Titus Lartius and Cominius) are "derivable" from Coriolanus in the sense that, both being men of high repute, their constant respect for him speaks for him. Also, his loyalty to them serves to establish that he is not avid for dictatorial power, but genuinely represents an integral conflict between patricians and plebeians. (Shakespeare's formula for Coriolanus' treatment of the commoners had been summed up by a minor character thus: "He seeks their hate with greater devotion than they can render it him.") The citizens have the mixture of distress, resentment, and instability that enables them to help Coriolanus get into the kind of quandaries necessary for him to enact his role. As for the Tribunes, besides their function in making Coriolanus' bluster look admirable in comparison with their scheming, they serve to carry the play forward by goading him into the rage that leads to his banishment, and thus eventually (as one thing leads to another) to his death. All told, in being the kind of characters they are, the other figures help Coriolanus be the kind of character he is; and by their actions at precisely the times when they do act, they help lead the appointed (or stylistically anointed) victim to the decision required, by the logic of the plot, for his downfall. He must turn the army away from Rome, and under conditions that lead step by step to the sacrifice that will permit the purging of the audience.

But we have not yet considered the remarkable function of Menenius. At first glance, one could "derive" him from Coriolanus only in the sense that he serves as the ideal link between the patrician and plebeian factions. In this role, along with his loyalty to Coriolanus, he serves particularly well for shaping the audience's sympathies. For though he is a patrician, and frankly shares the prejudices of his class, the commoners (and the audience) like him. His use in this regard is of crucial importance to the play when, in Act IV, scene vi, a messenger brings the news that Coriolanus is leading an army against Rome. To the extent that Rome allusively stood for England, it was not easy to keep the audience sympathetic with a man whose conduct at this point was so close to out-and-out treason (particularly since at so many points in the play he irritates us). But Menenius picks up Cominius' line, placing the blame upon the Tribunes and the people ("O, you have made good work!")—and when two characters of such high repute take this stand, it helps crowd the audience a bit by shifting the emphasis from the *hero's treason* to his *enemies' provocation* (with the bad effects of the provocation being stressed, while the considerations that would justify it were here left unmentioned). The trick was to show the Tribunes and the people regretting their decision to banish Coriolanus rather than to let them review their grounds for the banishment. This is excellent dramaturgic maneuvering—for Shakespeare, as is typical of him, is here working with more complex motives than an audience's simplest responses to patriot and traitor.

But Menenius' "derivation" as a function of Coriolanus' sacrifice contains other notable ingredients. Despite the great contrast between the diplomatic eloquence of the self-styled "humorous patrician" (who is Coriolanus' godfather) and the heavy-footed, grotesquely heroic mouthings of the formally inevitable victim (for one is mellow where the other is raw), Menenius applies almost the same formula to them both. Of himself he says, "What I think, I utter, and spend my malice in my breath." The same readiness with the word he attributes to Coriolanus thus: "His heart's his mouth./What his breast forges, that his tongue must vent." (War itself, elsewhere in the play, is called "sprightly, waking, audible, and full of vent," an expression that could serve also to describe Coriolanus' invective.)

But whereas Menenius shares Coriolanus' belief in the intrinsic superiority of the patricians, and makes no secret of the fact even when addressing the commoners, his function will be to uphold circumspectly, "reasonably," much the same position that Coriolanus must represent exorbitantly. (I say "must" because his excessiveness is a formal require-ment of his role as victim.) Menenius is the only character in the play (except Aufidius' servants) charged with the responsibilities of putting some aspects of this solemn bluster in a comical light.

His early speech likening the body politic to the human body (one of the many themes Shakespeare found in Plutarch, though it was also a standard notion of the times) serves not only to present the attitude of the patricians in the best light (as Coriolanus must present it in the worst). It also sets the conditions for much body imagery throughout the play, particularly images of bodily disease, such as go well with the fact that the body politic is in great disarray. What more relevant than an imagery of bodily diseases in a play dealing with disorders of the body politic? Similarly, since the people are starving, images to do with devouring serve to keep thought of such conditions hovering about the edges of our consciousness. And the many references to animals are so treated as to reinforce the vigorous animality of the underlying situation.

The question of imagery, I submit, should be "derived" thus late in the enterprise. With works of a preponderantly imagistic cast (as in much modern poetry), one might properly *begin* with questions of imagery. But in a drama of this sort, one can most profitably begin with considerations of action and character, afterwards deducing the logic of the imagery from these prior considerations, rather than using imagery as the "way-in."

II

Fundamentally, then, the play exploits to the ends of dramatic entertain-ment, with corresponding catharsis, the tension intrinsic to a kind of social division, or divisiveness, particularly characteristic of complex soci-eties, but present to some degree in even the simplest modes of living. (I take it that the presence of a priesthood or similar functionaries dealing with things of this world in terms of a "beyond," is on its face evidence that a society is marked by some degree of social differentiation, with corresponding conflicts of interest. And at the very least, even tribes that come closest to a homogeneous way of life are marked by differentiation between the work of men and women or between youth and age.)

This malaise, which affects us all but which in varying degrees and under varying circumstances we attempt to mitigate, is here made insult-ingly unforgettable. Coriolanus' *hubris* (whether you choose to translate it as "pride" or as "excessiveness") aggravates the situation constantly. And when he dies (after a change of heart that enables us to pity him even while we resent his exaggerated ways of representing our own less admirable susceptibilities, with their corresponding "bad conscience"), he dies as one who has taken on the responsibility and has been appropriately punished. Thereby, we are cleansed, thanks to his overstating of our case.

Along with this tension, which is of long duration in societies, we considered the likelihood that, when the play originally appeared, it also exploited a "timely topic," the unrest caused by the Enclosure Acts, when new men of means took over for sheepraising much land that had traditionally been available to small farmers, and these "legally" dispossessed tenants were in a state of great frustration. Many were starving while the monopolists were being made into patricians. It was a time when many *nouveaux-riches* were being knighted—and as Aristotle points out, it is *new* fortunes that people particularly resent.

An ironic turn of history has endowed this play with a new kind of "timely topic," owing to the vagaries of current dictatorships. But I would incline to contend that this "new immediacy" is more apparent than real. In the first place, Coriolanus isn't a good fit for the contemporary pattern because the frankness of his dislike for the common people would make him wholly incompetent as a rabble-rouser. A modern demagogue might secretly share Coriolanus' prejudices—but he certainly would not advertise the fact as Coriolanus did. His public heart would bleed for the poor, even while he was secretly shipping state funds to a Swiss bank, against the day when his empire would collapse, and he would flee the country, hoping to spend his last years in luxurious retirement on the Riviera. Presumably our nations is always in danger of pouring considerable funds down such rat-holes. Thus, I feel that the attempt to present *Coriolanus* in the light of modern conditions can never quite succeed, since these conditions tend rather to conceal than to point up the cultural trends underlying its purgative use of the tension between upper and lower classes. Or should we call it a "tension behind the tension"? I have in mind a situation of this sort:

The Renaissance was particularly exercised by Machiavelli because he so accurately represented the transvaluation of values involved in the rise of nationalism. A transvaluation was called for, because *religion* aimed at *universal* virtues, whereas the virtues of *nationalism* would necessarily be *factional*, insofar as they pitted nation against nation. Conduct viewed as vice from the standpoint of universal religious values might readily be viewed as admirable if it helped some interests prevail over others. This twist greatly exercised Machiavelli. But though (from the universal point of view) nations confront one another as factions, from the standpoint of any one nation factionalism is conceived in a narrower sense, with nationalism itself taking over the role of the universal.

In Shakespeare's day, as so many of his plays indicate, the kind of *family* factionalism that went with feudal relationships was being transformed into the kind of *class* factionalism that would attain its "perfection" (if we may apply that term to so turbulent a development) in the rise of nationalism, with its drive towards the building of the British Empire. And here Shakespeare tackled this particular tangle of motives in a remarkably direct manner, except of course for the kind of "distance" (with corresponding protection) the play got by treating the subject in terms of ancient Rome rather than his contemporary London.

All told, the motivation split into four overlapping loci: nation, class, family, individual. And in *Coriolanus* we witness a remarkably complex simplification of these issues, dramatically translated into terms of action and character.

Individualism may come and go, but there is a compelling sense in which the individual is always basic. The centrality of the nervous system is such that each of us is unique (each man's steak and his particular toothache being his own and no one else's). And even those who are killed *en masse* nonetheless die one by one. Symbolicity (by assigning proper names and attesting to the rights of private ownership) strongly punctuates this physical kind of individuality. And Shakespeare adds his momentous contribution by building so many plays on the "star" system, with a titular role. I think it is safe to say that *Coriolanus* most thoroughly meets this description. Think of such lines as: "O, me alone! Make you a sword of me?" (I, vi); "Alone I fought in your Corioles walls" (I, vii); "Alone I did it." (V, vi)—or his resolve to stand "As if a man were author of himself" (V, iii)—or a Tribune's grudging tribute to him: "He has no equal" (I, i)—or his own mother's formula: "You are too absolute" (III, ii). And the play backs up such statements by incessantly making him the center of our attention whether he is on the stage or off.

Yet even his name is not his own, but derives from the sacking of a city. And when he is threatening to lead an army against Rome, he does not know himself; and the sympathetic Cominius tells us (V, i) that he "forbade all names./He was a kind of nothing, titleless,/Till he had forged himself a name o' th' fire / of burning Rome"—and that's precisely what, in obedience to his mother's pleadings, he did not do. Incidentally, the longer one works with this text, the more ingenious Shakespeare's invention seems when, just before Coriolanus is killed, he *apologizes* because he had fallen into a rage: "Pardon me, lords, 'tis the first time ever/I was forced to scold." But he is addressing the *lords* of Antium, not the commoners. Shortly thereafter the Conspirators will shout, "Kill, kill, kill, kill, kill him!" thereby as they slay modifying poor impotent Lear's line, "Then, kill, kill, kill, kill, kill, kill!" (IV, vi, 192).

But such considerations bring us to the next locus of motives, the *familial*, which the play brings to a focus in the "mother, wife, child" formula, used variously by Menenius (V, i, 28–29), himself (V, ii, 78), and Volumnia (V, iii, 101), hers being the most effective, when she bewails the sight of him for "Making the mother, wife, and child to see/The son, the husband, and the father tearing/His country's bowels out." Yet to say as much is to move us almost as quickly into the realm of *class* and *nation*, since his family identity was so intensely that of a *patrician*, and his individualistic ways of being a patrician had brought him into conflict with all Rome.

Here you confront the true poignancy of his predicament, the formula being: individualistic prowess, made haughty towards the people by mother's training, and naturally unfit for the ways of peaceful persuasion with regard to the citizenry as a whole. The *class* motive comes to a focus terministically in the manipulations that have to do with the key word, "noble." But the *nation* as motive gets its forceful poignancy when the play so sets things up that Coriolanus maneuvers himself and is maneuvered into a situation whereby this individualistic mother-motivated patrician patriot is all set to attack his own country, which at the beginning of the play he had defended with such signal valor, despite his invective against the commoners. As Granville-Barker has well said: "Play and character become truly tragic only when Marcius, to be traitor to Rome, must turn traitor to himself."

Yet, so far as I can see, the treatment of this motivational tangle (individual-family-class-nation) is not in itself "cathartic," unless one uses the term in the Crocean sense rather than the Aristotelian. (That is, I have in mind the kind of relief that results purely from the well-ordered presentation of an entanglement. Such a complexity just *is*. But Shakespeare transforms this motionless knot into terms of an irreversible narrative sequence, the "cure" here residing not in a sacrifice as such, but rather in the feeling of "getting somewhere" by the sheer act of expression, even though the scene centered in conditions when Coriolanus was totally immobilized, a quite unusual state for so outgoing a character.) My soundest evidence for catharsis of this sort (whereby the sheer unfolding of expression can impart a kind of relief to our kind of animal, that lives by locomotion) is the nursery rhyme:

> The grand old Duke of York
> He had ten thousand men

He marched them up to the top of the hill
Then he marched them down again.
And when they were up they were up
And when they were down they were down
And when they were only halfway up
They were neither up nor down.

III

I'm among the company of those who would call *Coriolanus* a "grotesque" tragedy. So our final problem is to make clear just wherein its grotesqueness resides, and how this quality might also contribute to its nature as medicinal.

Obviously, in contrast with the typical sacrificial victims of Greek tragedy, Coriolanus rather resembles a character in a satyr play. He is almost like a throwback to the kind of scurrilities that Aristotle associates with the origins of the tragic iamb, in relation to the traditional meter of lampoons. (See Poetics IV) So some critics have called it a "satiric" tragedy. But "grotesque" seems closer, since Coriolanus is *not* being satirized. The clearest evidence that he is being presented as a *bona fide* hero is the fact that *every* person of good standing in the play admires him or loves him and is loyal to him, despite his excesses. What does all this mean?

Still considering the problem from the standpoint of *tensions* and their exploitation for dramatic effects (that is to say, poetic delight), can we not find another kind of tension exploited here for medicinal purposes? It concerns the function of Coriolanus as a "railer," a master of vituperation. Dramaturgically, such a figure is, at the very least, of service in the sense that, by keeping things stirred up, he enables the dramatist to fish in troubled waters. When a cantankerous character like Coriolanus is on the stage (and Shakespeare turns up many such), there is a categorical guaranty that things will keep on the move. Yet, beyond that sheerly technical convenience (whereby Coriolanus does in one way what Iago does in another, towards keeping a play in motion), there is the possibility that such a role in itself may be curative, as a symbolic remedy for one particular kind of repression typical of most societies.

I might best make my point by quoting some remarks I made elsewhere about another scurrilous tragic victim, Shakespeare's Timon of Athens. There, however, the cut is different. Coriolanus throughout is respectful to the patricians and directs his insults only to the plebeians. But Timon, beginning as a great lover of mankind, ends as a total misanthrope. These paragraphs from my essay on *Timon of Athens* bear upon Timon's possible appeal as vilifier in the absolute.

> *Invective,* I submit, is a primary "freedom of speech," rooted extralinguistically in the helpless rage of an infant that states its attitude by utterances wholly unbridled. In this sense, no mode of expression could be more "radical," unless it be the closely allied motive of sheer *lamentation,* undirected wailing. And perhaps the sounds of contentment which an infant makes, when nursing or when being bedded or fondled, mark the pre-articulate origins of a third basic "freedom," *praise.*
>
> Among these three, if rage is the infantile prototype of invective, it is a kind of "freedom" that must soon be subjected to control, once articulacy develops. For though even praise can get one into trouble (for instance, when one happens to praise A's enemy in the presence of A, who happens also to be both powerful and rancorous); and though lamentation can on occasion be equally embarrassing (if one is heard to lament a situation among persons who favor it), invective most directly invites pugnacity, since it is itself a species of pugnacity.
>
> Obviously, the Shakespearean theater lends itself perfectly to the effects of invective. Coriolanus is an excellent case in point. Even a reader who might loathe his politics cannot but be engrossed by this man's mouthings. Lear also has a strong measure of such appeal, with his impotent senile maledictions that come quite close to the state of man's equally powerless infantile beginnings. . . . And that delightfully run-down aristocrat, Falstaff, delights us by making a game of such exercises.

Though one has heard much about the repression of sexual motives, in our average dealings invective is the mode of expression most thoroughly repressed. This state of affairs probably contributes considerably to such "cultural" manifestations as the excessive violence on television, and the popular consumption of crude political oratory. Some primitive tribes set aside a special place where an aggrieved party can go and curse the king without fear of punishment (though if our society had such an accommodation, I'm sure there'd be a secret agent hiding behind every bush). In earlier days the gifted railer was considered invaluable by reason of his expert skill at cursing the forces deemed dangerous to the welfare of the tribe (see on this point some interesting data in Robert C. Elliott's book, *The Power of Satire: Magic, Ritual, Art,* and above all his suggestive and entertaining Appendix on "The Curse"). At the very least, in figures such as Coriolanus we get much of such expressiveness, without the rationale of magic, but under the "controlled conditions" of a drama about political unrest. And if he dies of being so forthright, downright and outright (if not exactly upright), it's what he "deserved." For as regards the *categorical* appeal of invective, it resides not so much in the particular objects inveighed against, but in the sheer process of inveighing. And Coriolanus, like Timon, has given vent with fatal overthoroughness to untoward tendencies which, in our "second nature," we have "naturally" learned to repress.

IV

In conclusion, then, where are we? We have been considering Coriolanus' qualifications as a scapegoat, whose symbolic sacrifice is designed to afford an audience pleasure. We have suggested: (1) His primary role as a cathartic vessel resides in the excessiveness with which he forces us to confront the discriminatory motives intrinsic to society as we know it. (2) There is a sheerly "expressive" kind of catharsis in his way of giving form to the complexities of *family*, *class*, and *national* motives as they come to a focus in the self-conflicts of an *individual*. (3) There is the "curative" function of invective as such, when thus released under controlled conditions that transform the repressed into the expressed, yet do us no damage. (4) The attempt has been made to consider the "paradox of substance" whereby the chosen scapegoat can "be himself" and arrive at the end "proper to his nature" only if many events and other persons "conspire" to this end, the persons by being exactly the kind of persons they are, and the events by developing in the exact order in which they do develop. To sum it all up, then, in a final formula for tragic catharsis (a formula I wrote with such a play as *Coriolanus* in mind, though it could be applied *mutatis mutandis* to other texts):

> Take some pervasive unresolved tension typical of a given social order (or of life in general). While maintaining the "thought" of it in its overall importance, reduce it to terms of personal conflict (conflict between friends, or members of the same family). Feature some prominent figure who, in keeping with his character, though possessing admirable qualities, carries this conflict to excess. Put him in a situation that points up the conflict. Surround him with a cluster of characters whose relations to him and to one another help motivate and accentuate his excesses. So arrange the plot that, after a logically motivated turn, his excesses lead necessarily to his downfall. Finally, suggest that his misfortune will be followed by a promise of general peace.

COMMENTS

Our reference to the Enclosure Acts requires a gloss. Though the private enclosing of public land ("commons") had begun in the thirteenth century, its effects were still being felt at the time when Shakespeare wrote, and indeed much later (as cf. Goldsmith). Indeed, when we read of one churchman's lament, "Where there have been many householders and inhabitants, there is now but a shepherd and his dog," we suddenly get a closer glimpse into the aristocratic connotations of pastoral poetry. It is the shepherd who, among the lowly, would be identified with the big new landowners (who made their money by "legally" dispossessing small farmers of their traditional rights and turning over the land to sheepgrazing, connected with the higher profits in wool).

Professor William Frost, at the University of California, Santa Barbara, has suggested that the tension should be located rather as anticipatory of the later Civil Wars than as reminiscent of earlier disturbances (that had their epitomizing in the Wars of the Roses). Thus he would see a symbol of crown vs. parliament rather than of landowners vs. peasants. I think that both interpretations would fit here. In its possible relation to a "timely topic" (recent rioting) it could be reflecting the result of enclosures that were still "progressively" driving dispossessed peasants to the towns. It would also be reflecting emergent disorders that would come to a focus in Cromwell's time. But essentially, over the long stretch, it would be exploiting the tension intrinsic to differences of status.

As for the food imagery (talk of devouring, etc.): Though its relation to the theme of starving rioters obviously accounts for its presence, students who approach the play from an overly psychoanalytic point of view are likely to become so interested in food imagery as the possible deflection of a sexual motive they completely neglect the primary rational explanation, in terms of the people's economic distress.

Most often, perhaps, the tragic principle operates as follows: The hero acts; in the course of acting, he organizes an opposition; then, in the course of suffering the opposition (or seeing "in terms of" it) he transcends his earlier position—and the audience, by identification with him, undergoes a similar "cathartic" transformation.

But in the case of Coriolanus the process seems somewhat different. The hero never really matures. His killer formulates the victim's plight in the formula, "thou boy of tears" (a summarizing "revelation," we might say, which the audience is prepared to receive just before the end of the play). And the ultimate insight is in the audience's own developments rather than in their sympathetic duplication of a higher vision on the part of sacrificed hero.

Many kinds of works involve variants of this process. In the case of

Richard Wright's *Native Son*, for instance, Bigger was not the sort of character who could (while remaining in character) arrive at a conceptually mature statement of his difficulties. But such a statement could properly be made by a lawyer who, in defending him, could present the sheer *theory* of the case. This is probably one reason why, where plots hinge about characters of limited insight, the device of a concluding court trial is especially serviceable. Another resource is the use of an emotionally imagistic solution, as in James Baldwin's *Go Tell It On the Mountain*, where the Negro problem is merged with a religious conversion that ambiguously suggests homosexual connotations.

Coriolanus is to Menenius as raw adolescence is to ripe old age. Lear is sick old age that falls into infantile tantrums, a Coriolanus without the physical power. And I dare repeat: It is tremendously interesting to see how, for all their superficial differences, Cordelia and Coriolanus both exemplify variants of a forthrightness that is essential to the advancing of the plot. If Lear, Cordelia, and Coriolanus were like Menenius, neither of these tragedies would be possible.

Though the names are taken over literally from Plutarch, it is remarkable how tonally suggestive some of them are, from the standpoint of their roles in this English play. "Volumnia" suggests the voluminous—and often, on students' papers, I have seen the name spelled "Volumina." "Virgilia" suggests "virginal." "Aufidius" suggests "perfidious." And in the light of Freudian theories concerning the fecal nature of invective, the last two syllables of the hero's name are so "right," people now often seek to dodge the issue by altering the traditional pronunciation (making the *a* broad instead of long).

This article should be a summing-up in three ways:

First, its stress upon the Dramatistic principle of victimage (the "sacrificial" motive) provides a logological analogue of the issue at which Friedrich Nietzsche grew wroth in his *Birth of Tragedy*. Its concern with dramatic catharsis modifies the version of dialectical (Platonic) transcendence featured in the third of these essays.

Second, it is designed to show by specific example how our theory of symbolic action in general can be tied down to considerations of poetics in particular.

Third, it should serve to point up the difference between an approach to a text in terms of poetics ("intrinsically") and an approach to it ("extrinsically") from the sociological point of view. And above all, the distinction should be made in a *nonindividious way*, both approaches being needed for the full treatment of symbolic action. Besides using beliefs (what Aristotle's *Rhetoric* would call "topics," or "places") to give characters and situations the appeal of verisimilitude (to make an imitation seem "natural" or "lifelike" even while we remain aware that it is an artifact), a work uses beliefs to arouse states of tension, by pitting some beliefs (or "equations") against others. Or, to put the case in sociological terms, we could say that a given society is characterized by a scheme of "values" that variously reinforce one another or conflict with one another in given situations and that authors variously embody such "values" in constructing characters and plots. In this sense, the *Rhetoric* can serve as a bridge between sociology and literary criticism (except insofar as sociologists and literary critics fail to ask how the *Rhetoric* can be applied even to their own field).

Thinking along such lines, in lectures I have at times placed more emphasis upon this area of overlap. For instance, Talcott Parsons' collection of essays, *Social Structure and Personality*, serves as a convenient point of entry for a treatment of the play in terms of "Social Structure and Poetics." But his concern with the interweaving of sociological and psychological coordinates is paralleled by a different but analogous interweaving of poetics and the sociological-psychological.

After noting the recurrence of the term "expectation" in the Parsons volume, one can discuss the similarity between the role of expectation in classical form and the place of expectations in men's notions of current reality and in threats and promises regarding the future. The kind of "values" and "expectations" that a sociologist deals with can be shown to figure also in the structure of a literary work, as enjoyed for its own sake (so that practical problems are transcended by being transformed into sources of artistic enjoyment). And by the same token, the role of "values" can be shown to figure prominently in the "equations" that are either implicit or explicit in a given work. But, of course, the reverse kind of "derivation" which we would consider central to Poetics (as when "deriving" Volumnia from Coriolanus) would be wholly alien to either sociology or psychology. And whereas Plutarch, viewed as biography, would be judged by tests of "truth," or "factuality," the play should be judged by tests of "verisimilitude," or "plausibility." However, the symmetry of the case is impaired by the fact that Plutarch was not by any means a biographer in the sheerly "factual" sense; and his method of writing encouraged kinds of "identification" that go with poetic appeal.

*　　*　　*

Finally, though I dare hope that one can distinguish between dialectical transcendence and dramatic catharsis at their extremes. . . , I must admit that the realms covered by the two terms considerably overlap. . . . I have sometimes used one of the terms where I might as well have used the other.

We might discern the rudiments of transcendence when an individual dons a uniform. For now he is seen in terms of this "more inclusive whole" (that can also be called *less* inclusive, insofar as it eliminates many of the individual's personal possibilities); and it could be called "cathartic" in the sense that the identification indicated by the uniform is in effect the "sacrifice," or symbolic "slaying," of the individual's nonuniformed identity. In story, as in history, a situation can undergo a rudimentary kind of transcendence by the sheer process of moving on to other matters.

The rudiments of catharsis are present in that most readily available resource of symbolism: substitution. For implicit in the possibilities of substitution there is the possibility of vicarious victimage.

There is a further process not reducible to terms of either "transcendence" or "catharsis". . . . It involves analogues of unburdening or cleansing, in the sheerly physiological sense (as with the *explicit* use of fecal imagery in Aristophanic comedy or Swiftian satire, and the "dignified" devices for *implicitly* transforming bathos into pathos).

The relation to victimage is revealed in the "fecal" nature of invective. But this "problematic" element can also impinge upon a realm of motives that, while honorifically related in one respect to the hierarchal mysteries of courtliness, in another respect would seem to be rooted in infantile "equations" that *precede* the notions of "propriety" inculcated by toilet training. In his *Psychology of the Unconscious*, Jung offers some excellent instances of "reverence" as so conceived.

NORTHROP FRYE

My Father As He Slept: The Tragedy of Order

The basis of the tragic vision is being in time, the sense of the one-directional quality of life, where everything happens once and for all, where every act brings unavoidable and fateful consequences, and where all experience vanishes, not simply into the past, but into nothingness, annihilation. In the tragic vision death is, not an incident in life, not even the inevitable end of life, but the essential event that gives shape and form to life. Death is what defines the individual, and marks him off from the continuity of life that flows indefinitely between the past and the future. It gives to the individual life a parabola shape, rising from birth to maturity and sinking again, and this parabola movement of rise and fall is also the typical shape of tragedy. The mood of tragedy preserves our ambiguous and paradoxical feeling about death; it is inevitable and always happens, and yet, when it does happen, it carries with it some sense of the unnatural and premature. The naiveté of Marlowe's Tamburlaine, astonished by the fact that *he* should die when he has been wading through other men's blood for years, is an example, and even Shakespeare's Caesar, so thoroughly disciplined in his views of death in general, still finds his actual death a surprise.

Being in time is not the whole of the tragic vision: it is, in itself, the ironic vision. Because it is the basis of the tragic vision, the ironic and the tragic are often confused or identified. The nineteenth-century pessimism which produced the philosophy of Schopenhauer and the novels of

Thomas Hardy seems to me ironic rather than tragic. So does the philosophy and literature of existentialism, which I think of, for reasons that may become clearer later on, as post-tragic. But tragedy, no less than irony, *is* existential: the conceptions that existential thinkers have tried to struggle with, care, dread, nausea, absurdity, authenticity, and the like, are all relevant to the theory of tragedy. Tragedy is also existential in a broader, and perhaps contradictory, sense, in that the experience of the tragic cannot be moralized or contained within any conceptual world-view. A tragic hero is a tragic hero whether he is a good or a bad man; a tragic action is a tragic action whether it seems to us admirable or villainous, inevitable or arbitrary. And while a religious or philosophical system that answers all questions and solves all problems may find a place for tragedy, and so make it a part of a larger and less tragic whole, it can never absorb the kind of experience that tragedy represents. That remains outside of all approaches to being through thought rather than existence. The remark of the dying Hotspur, "Thought's the slave of life," comes out of the heart of the tragic vision.

Tragedy revolves around the primary contract of man and nature, the contract fulfilled by man's death, death being, as we say, the debt he owes to nature. What makes tragedy tragic, and not simply ironic, is the presence in it of a countermovement of being that we call the heroic, a capacity for action or passion, for doing or suffering, which is above ordinary human experience. This heroic energy, glorified by itself as something invincible which bursts the boundaries of normal experience, is the basis of romance. In tragedy the heroic is within the human context, and so is still limited and finite, formed and shaped by death. In Greek tragedy especially, we can see how death is both the punishment of the aggressor and the reward of his victim. This makes tragic sense, if not moral sense. But because the heroic is above the normal limits of experience, it also suggests something infinite imprisoned in the finite. This something infinite may be morally either good or bad, for the worst of men may still be a hero if he is big enough to anger or frighten the gods. Man may be infinite if he is infinite only in his evil desires. The hero is an individual, but being so great an individual he seems constantly on the point of being swept into titanic forces he cannot control. The fact that an infinite energy is driving towards death in tragedy means that the impetus of tragedy is *sacrificial*. Sacrifice expresses the principle that in human life the infinite takes the same direction as the finite.

Tragedy, then, shows us the impact of heroic energy on the human situation. The heroic is normally destroyed in the conflict, and the human situation goes on surviving. "A living dog is better than a dead lion," says the Preacher: whether better or not, the dialectic of tragedy works through to a situation in which the heroic is normally dead and the less heroic is all that can remain alive. Octavius and Aufidius may be shrewder and more prudent men than Mark Antony or Coriolanus, but they are smaller men. Tragedy often ends with the survivors forming, or about to form, a secondary or social contract, a relation among more ordinary men which will achieve enough working justice or equity to minimize further tragedy. In the worlds of Fortinbras and Malcolm fewer ghosts will walk; after the deaths of Romeo and Juliet there will be less lethal feuding in Verona.

Sometimes the social contract that forms at the end of a tragedy is of great depth and significance, as it is in the *Oresteia*; sometimes, in Greek tragedy, it exists only in the final comments of the chorus; sometimes, as often in Shakespeare, it is merely an exhausted and demoralized huddle. Whatever it is, it usually expresses some limiting or falling away of perspective after the great heroic voices have been silenced. This comes out clearly in the last two lines of *King Lear*:

> The oldest hath borne most: we that are young
> Shall never see so much, nor live so long.

The basis of irony is the independence of the way things are from the way we want them to be; in tragedy a heroic effort against this independence is made and fails; we then come to terms with irony by reducing our wants. In tragedy the ironic vision survives the heroic one, but the heroic vision is the one we remember, and the tragedy is for its sake. The more ironic the tragedy, the fewer the central characters who die. In *Troilus and Cressida*, though the setting is a battlefield where men die like flies every day, none of the central characters dies except the greatest of all, Hector; in *Timon of Athens* nobody dies except the only noble character, Timon. Our first tentative conclusion about the feelings roused in us by the tragic experience, therefore, is something like this: the heroic and the infinite have been; the human and finite are.

In Greek tragedy, the gods have the function of enforcing what we have called the primary contract of man and nature. The gods are to human society what the warrior aristocracy is to the workers within human society itself. Like aristocrats, they act toward their inferiors with a kind of rough justice, but they are by no means infallible, and we often glimpse their underlying panic about the danger that men will become too powerful. Man has certain duties toward the gods, and he expects, without having the right to claim, certain benefits in return. But as long as the gods are there, man is limited in his scope, ambitions, and powers. Men in Greek tragedy are *brotoi*, "dying ones," a word with a concrete force in it that our word "mortals" hardly conveys.

Such a view is by no means original with the Greeks: much earlier, for example, the Gilgamesh epic in Mesopotamia had portrayed the gods in a similar aristocratic role. There, the gods found that they could not continue to live without having to work: this being beneath their dignity, they created men to do the work for them. The epic then goes on to describe how man attempts and fails to achieve immortality. It is a very ironic story, but if we compare it with the Iliad we feel that the heroic, or distinctively tragic, component is missing. The intense interest that the gods in the Iliad take in the conflict going on below them is their response to the infinite quality in human heroism. They watch it, not with a detached ironic amusement, but with a tragic sense of engagement. For one thing, some of the heroes are their own progeny. The only moral check on their desire to seduce human women is the slave-owner's check, the fact that all children born of such a union will be lost in the lower society. We are occasionally reminded in the Iliad that the Olympian gods, no less than the Christian God, are losing their own sons in the human struggle, and, unlike the Christian God, they are compelled to leave their sons' souls in Hades.

As for the heroes themselves, their life sustains a continuous illusion. Nothing that is *done* in a heroic conflict has anything except death for its form, and the *klea andron* that Homer celebrates, the brave deeds of men, consist only in spilling and destroying life. In Sarpedon's speech to Glaucus in the Iliad there is one terrible instant of awareness in which Sarpedon says that if he could think of himself as ageless and immortal, like the gods, he would walk out of the battle at once. But, being a man, his life *is* death, and there is nowhere in life that is not a battlefield. Unlike his counterpart Arjuna in the *Bhagavadgita*, he can hope for no further illumination on that battlefield. The Greek heroes belong to a leisure class remote from our ordinary preoccupations; this gives them more time, not for enjoying life, but for doing what the unheroic cannot do: looking steadily and constantly into the abyss of death and nothingness. The Greek gods respect this, just as the Christian God respects the corresponding contemplative attitude, the *contemptus mundi*, on the part of the saint.

There are two kinds of death in Greek tragedy: ordinary death, which happens to everybody, and heroic death, which may be directly caused by the gods out of fear or anger, or, if not, has at any rate some peculiar significance, a marking out of a victim. Death may thus be seen as caused by the impersonal force of fate or by the will of the gods.

Sometimes, as in the fall of Oedipus, an oracle or prophecy is being fulfilled, and this combines the two themes of divine will and natural event. Gods and fate both represent an order or balance in the scheme of things, the way things are. If this order is disturbed by human pride, boastfulness, or insatiable ambition, a personal divine force reacts to it, after which the pattern of ordinary fate reappears in human life. This reappearance is called nemesis. Death in itself is a natural event; a death brought about by the gods forcibly assimilates human life to nature. Thus the gods, however harsh in their wrath or jealousy, manifest by their actions a social and moral force in human life itself, the principle of stability, or living in the face of death, which in the soul is called temperance (*sophrosyne*) and in society justice.

The individual gods, like individual men, may be partial and passionate: Greek poets and philosophers, like their successors, could never quite solve the problem of how a being can be an individual and yet not ultimately finite. But even in Homer we can see how conflicts among the gods are contained within a single divine order, the will of Zeus. This single divine order corresponds to the order of temperance or stability among the conflicting impulses of the human mind. The Hippolytus of Euripides is a chaste and virtuous youth: in other words he is a worshipper of Artemis. He is eventually justified by his faith in Artemis, but he is so aggressively chaste and virtuous that he provokes the anger of Aphrodite and comes to grief. In relation to the whole group of Olympian gods, his chastity is excessive and unbalanced. But temperance and stability do not provide a static order; they are an ordering of powers and forces. Pentheus in *The Bacchae* tries to keep a tight grip on himself when confronted with Dionysus, and is swept out of the way like a leaf in a hurricane.

In *The Birth of Tragedy* Nietzsche describes the Greek sense of the limited and finite as the "Apollonian" side of Greek culture. This is the sense that comes out particularly in the exquisite Greek feeling for plastic form, and which, in the verbal arts, ranges from the profoundest conceptions in Greek thought, Plato's *idea* and Aristotle's *telos*, to cautionary proverbs of the "nothing too much" type. The sense of infinite heroic energy Nietzsche identifies with the "Dionysian," where the individual is not defined and assigned a place in the scheme of things, but released by being dissolved into the drunken and frenzied group of worshippers. Nietzsche's Apollonian–Dionysian distinction is one of those central insights into critical theory that critics must sooner or later come to terms with, though coming to terms with it means, first of all, deciding whether the particular historical projection given to the insight is the best one. I use it because I find it illuminating for Shakespeare: I am quite prepared to believe that it may be less so for the Greeks, where Nietzsche's argument seems greatly weakened by what appears to me a preposterous view of Euripides. Nietzsche is on much sounder ground in saying that the spirit of tragedy was destroyed by a spirit he identifies with Socrates and associates with comedy and irony. Tragedy is existential: Socrates, with his conception of militant knowledge, begins an essentialist tradition in human thought. His disciple Plato is the greatest of all the essentialist philosophers, of those who have approached reality through thought rather than experience, and Plato's literary affinities are clearly with the comic poets, not the tragic ones.

We next meet tragedy in Seneca, whose tragedies are Greek subjects recollected in tranquillity. Or relative tranquillity: there are melodramatic qualities in Elizabethan drama that are popularly thought of as Senecan—ghosts screaming for revenge, an action full of horrors and with lots and lots of blood—but these are mainly generalizations from one Senecan play, *Thyestes*. In this play Atreus revenges himself on his brother by inviting him to dinner and serving him his children in a pie—an incident which reappears in *Titus Andronicus*—but even this is an authentic Greek theme. Seneca is, again, an essentialist philosopher, a Stoic, and for him the two contracts we have mentioned, the primary contract with gods and nature which is natural law, and the secondary social contract which is moral law, are identical. He tends to think of his characters as heroic in proportion to the extent to which they identify themselves with this law. They are heroic in endurance rather than in action, in their capacity to surmount suffering rather than in the power of their wills.

Hence rhetoric, the ability to express an articulate awareness of what is happening, has a function in Seneca that is quite different from its function in the three great Greeks. In the Greek plays the action is presented by the characters and represented by the chorus: the chorus has a role of response to the action that, like the music in an opera, puts the audience's emotion into focus. Seneca retains the chorus, but he has much less need for it: the rhetorical speeches take over most of the chorus's real dramatic functions. Even action, in Seneca, is constantly dominated by consciousness. To know is a higher destiny than to experience, and by virtue of his consciousness man may rank himself with the gods, in fact may even outgrow them. In Euripides' *Heracles* the hero's feat of entering hell and carrying off Cerberus is a physical feat so astounding that the goddess Hera promptly sends madness upon him. Otherwise, man will become too big for his breeches. The important thing is not whether Heracles' madness is internal or external in origin: the important thing is that his madness is the kind of thing that inevitably happens when the power of the gods is threatened. Seneca's Juno is equally anxious to set limits to human power, but the madness is, to a much greater extent, a weakness in Hercules himself which she exploits. Seneca thinks of Hercules' feat as a harrowing of hell, an allegory of the kind of power in man that may eventually deliver him from the power of the gods, unless, as Juno says, the gods can succeed in setting man to war with himself. The source of the conflict, to use Greek terms, is *praxis* in Euripides, a conflict in the dramatic action; it is *theoria* in Seneca, a conflict of mental attitudes.

The early Elizabethan tragic dramatists, like Seneca, developed a highly rhetorical texture, and had even less need of a chorus. Again, gods are essential to the Greek conception of tragedy, but they are not really essential to Senecan tragedy. A later play in the Senecan tradition, *Octavia*, which introduces the Emperor Nero and Seneca himself as characters, has a ghost, but no gods, and indicates that if Roman tragedy had survived it would have gone in the direction of historical rather than mythical themes, the direction from which the Elizabethans started. The Elizabethans had little place for the gods either, which they regarded as personifications of natural forces. This means that social and political situations have a much more important place in Elizabethan than in Greek tragedy. In Greek tragedy catastrophe is referred primarily to the gods: crimes are offences against them, which is why purely ritual themes, such as leaving a body unburied, are so prominent. Royal figures are certainly important, but their subordination to the gods is always emphasized. Elizabethan tragedy not only had no gods, but was also a secular form avoiding the explicit use of Christian conceptions of deity. In contrast to the miracle plays, it used relatively few subjects from the Bible; in contrast to the morality plays, especially *Everyman*, it gave the teachings of the church a minor role. The figure of the proud cardinal, whose crimson robes make him a natural dramatic focus, is a popular symbol of the subordination of church to state. For the Elizabethans, the royal figure or human ruler tended to become the mythical centre of the action, and the relations of the ruler and his people take the place of the relations of gods and men.

The organizing conceptions of Elizabethan tragedy are the order of nature and the wheel of fortune. Nature as an order, though an order permeated with sin and death as a result of the fall of man, is the conception in Elizabethan drama corresponding to what we have called the ironic vision or being in time—Nietzsche's "Apollonian" vision. Fortune as a wheel rotated by the energy and ambition of man, which, however gigantic, can never get above a certain point, and consequently has to sink again, is the "Dionysian" or heroic vision which complements it. The order of nature provides the *data* of the human situation, the conditions man accepts by getting born. The wheel of fortune supplies the *facta*, what he contributes by his own energy and will.

But nature and fortune are not an antithesis: they interpenetrate in a very complex way. In the first place, there are two levels of nature. Man lives in a lower nature, the physical world or world of the four elements which moves in cycles. This is particularly the Dionysian world of energy, and it is, for practical purposes, identical with the wheel of fortune. A state of aggressiveness, or what we now call the law of the jungle, is "natural" to man, but natural only on this lower level of nature. Above this world is a world of specifically human nature, the world represented by the Christian paradise and the Classical Golden Age, and symbolized by the starry spheres with their heavenly music. Man lost this world with the fall of Adam, but everything that is good for man, law, virtue, education, religion, helps to raise him toward it again. It is therefore also natural to man, on the higher level of nature, to be civilized and in a state of social discipline. The king or ruler symbolizes the invisible ideals of social discipline, and the respect paid to him derives from those ideals. But while he symbolizes them he does not incarnate them. No earthly king is clear of the wheel of fortune, or independent of the aggressive energy of the lower nature. He must know how to wage war, how to punish, how to out-manœuvre the over-ambitious. In *Richard II* the kingdom is symbolized by a garden, and the garden, which is a state of art and a state of nature at the same time, represents the upper human level of nature. The gardener is addressed as "old Adam's likeness." But the garden is not the garden of Eden; it is the garden that "old" Adam was forced to cultivate after his fall, a garden requiring constant effort and vigilance.

In contrast to most of his contemporaries (Chapman is the chief exception), Shakespeare's sense of tragedy is deeply rooted in history. *Richard II* and *Richard III* are nearly identical with tragedy in form, and even when a history-play ends on a strong major chord it is never a comedy. The difference is chiefly that tragedy rounds off its action and history suggests a continuous story. We may compare the Greek dramatic tragedies with the Iliad, which, though complete in itself, is part of an epic cycle that keeps on going. As complete in itself, it is a tragedy, the tragedy of Hector; as part of the epic cycle, its central figure is Achilles, who does not die in the Iliad, but leaves us with a powerful intimation of mortality. Sometimes the continuity of history gives a cadence to a history-play that tragedy cannot achieve. *Henry V* ends with the conquest of France, just before Henry died and all his achievements began to vanish; *Henry VIII* ends with the triumph of Cranmer, Cromwell, and Anne Boleyn, along with the audience's knowledge of what soon happened to them. In other words, the history-play is more explicitly attached to the rotation of the wheel of fortune than the tragedy. But the difference is only one of degree: Fortinbras, Malcolm, perhaps Edgar, all provide some sense of "historical" continuity for their tragedies; we know what happens to Troy after the conclusion of *Troilus and Cressida*; Athens comes to terms with Alcibiades after the death of Timon, and the Roman plays are episodes of the continuing story of Rome.

The easiest way to get at the structure of Elizabethan tragedy is to think of it as a reversal of the structure of comedy. Comedy exhibits a type of action that I have elsewhere called a drive towards identity. This identity is of three kinds. There is plural or social identity, when a new social group crystallizes around the marriage of the hero and heroine in the final moments of the comedy. There is dual or erotic identity, when the hero and heroine get married. And there is individual identity, when a character comes to know himself in a way that he did not before, like Parolles, Angelo, or Katherina the shrew. Translating this division into tragic terms, there are three main kinds of tragic structure in Shakespeare and his contemporaries. There is, first, a social tragedy, with its roots in history, concerned with the fall of princes. There is, second, a tragedy that deals with the separation of lovers, the conflict of duty and passion, or the conflict of social and personal (sexual or family) interests. And there is, third, a tragedy in which the hero is removed from his social context, and is compelled to search for a purely individual identity. In Greek drama, these tragic structures might be called the Agamemnon type, the Antigone type, and the Oedipus type. In terms closer to Christianity, they might be called the tragedy of the killing of the father, the tragedy of the sacrifice of the son, and the tragedy of the isolation of the spirit. A critic who had learned his critical categories from Blake, like the present writer, would most naturally think of them as, respectively, tragedies of Urizen, tragedies of Luvah, and tragedies of Tharmas. In Shakespeare, we have a group of tragedies of order, *Julius Caesar, Macbeth*, and *Hamlet*; a group of tragedies of passion, *Romeo and Juliet, Antony and Cleopatra, Troilus and Cressida*, and *Coriolanus*; and a group of tragedies of isolation, *King Lear, Othello*, and *Timon of Athens*. These are not pigeonholes, only different areas of emphasis; most of the plays have aspects that link them to all three groups. What seems a rather odd placing of *Othello* and *Coriolanus* should become clearer as we go on; *Titus Andronicus* belongs mainly to the first group. As passion or strong interest always conflicts either with another passion or with some externalized force, the passion-tragedy could also be called the dilemma-tragedy, as the example of *Antigone* indicates.

In each of Shakespeare's three social tragedies, *Julius Caesar, Macbeth*, and *Hamlet*, we have a tragic action based on three main character-groups. First is the order-figure: Julius Caesar in that play; Duncan in *Macbeth*; Hamlet's father. He is killed by a rebel-figure or usurper: Brutus and the other conspirators; Macbeth; Claudius. Third comes a nemesis-figure or nemesis-group: Antony and Octavius; Malcolm and Macduff; Hamlet. It is sometimes assumed that the hero, the character with the title-role, is always at the centre of the play, and that all plays are to be related in the same way to the hero; but each of the heroes of these three tragedies belongs to a different aspect of the total action. The nemesis-figure is partly a revenger and partly an avenger. He is primarily obsessed with killing the rebel-figure, but he has a secondary function of restoring something of the previous order.

The Elizabethan social or historical tragedy shows, much more clearly than the other two kinds, the impact of heroic energy on the human condition, the wheel of fortune creaking against the greater wheel of nature. Central to the form is an Elizabethan assumption about society, which is simple but takes some historical imagination to grasp. Society to the Elizabethans was a structure of personal authority, with the ruler at its head, and a personal chain of authority extending from the ruler down. Everybody had a superior, and this fact, negatively, emphasized the limited and finite nature of the human situation. Positively, the fact that the ruler was an individual with a personality was what enabled his subjects to be individuals and to have personalities too. The man who possesses the secret and invisible virtues of human nature is the man with the quiet mind, so celebrated in Elizabethan lyric poetry. But such a man is dependent on the ceaseless vigilance of the ruler for his peace.

The view of social order, with its stress on the limited, the finite, and the individual, corresponds, as indicated above, to Nietzsche's Apollonian vision in Greek culture. That makes it hard for us to understand it. We ourselves live in a Dionysian society, with mass movements sweeping across it, leaders rising and falling, and constantly taking the risk of being dissolved into a featureless tyranny where all sense of the individual disappears. We even live on a Dionysian earth, staggering drunkenly around the sun. The treatment of the citizens in *Julius Caesar* and *Coriolanus* puzzles us: we are apt to feel that Shakespeare's attitude is anti-democratic, instead of recognizing that the situation itself is pre-democratic. In my own graduate-student days during the nineteen-thirties, there appeared an

Orson Welles adaptation of *Julius Caesar* which required the hero to wear a fascist uniform and pop his eyes like Mussolini, and among students there was a good deal of discussion about whether Shakespeare's portrayal of, say, Coriolanus showed "fascist tendencies" or not. But fascism is a disease of democracy: the fascist leader is a demagogue, and a demagogue is precisely what Coriolanus is not. The demagogues in that play are the tribunes whom the people have chosen as their own managers. The people in Shakespeare constitute a "Dionysian" energy in society: that is, they represent nothing but a potentiality of response to leadership. We are apt to assume, like Brutus, that leadership and freedom threaten one another, but, for us as for Shakespeare, there is no freedom without the sense of the individual, and in the tragic vision, at least, the leader or hero is the primary and original individual. The good leader individualizes his follow-ers; the tyrant or bad leader intensifies mass energy into a mob. Shake-speare has grasped the ambiguous nature of Dionysus in a way that Nietzsche (like D. H. Lawrence later) misses. In no period of history does Dionysus have anything to do with freedom; his function is to release us from the burden of freedom. The last thing the mob says in both *Julius Caesar* and *Coriolanus* is pure Dionysus: "Tear him to pieces."

Two contemporary plays, much simpler in their construction than any of Shakespeare's, illustrate the impact of the *facta* of fortune on the *data* of nature. At one extreme we have Marlowe's Tamburlaine, who is the Dionysian energy of fortune incarnate. Tamburlaine is a "scourge of God," conquering one demoralized society after another with nothing in the order of nature to stop him: nothing, that is, except death itself. He is a portent of the kind of limitless ferocity that would get loose if the alliance of social and natural order represented by the strong ruler were to break down. At the opposite extreme (perhaps designed to be that) we have Chapman's double play on the conspiracy and tragedy of Byron. Here the central figure is an idealized Henry IV of France, a firm, wise, patient ruler who has to deal with the excessive ambition and egotism of one of his subjects. He gives Byron every chance to fit into the social order, and only when forbearance becomes obviously impossible does he reluctantly consent to Byron's execution. One scene consists of a reported speech by Elizabeth I, and Essex is mentioned more than once in the dialogue, so it is clear that Henry IV is not the only ideal monarch in Europe. Henry and Elizabeth are what we have called order-figures, rulers whose personalities give form and shape to their kingdoms. Byron, along with Tamburlaine, is a rebel-figure: whatever his moral status he is a genuine hero, and everything about him suggests the unbounded and infinite, just as everything about the order-figure suggests law, finiteness, and the principle of individuality.

In Shakespeare's day there had been no permanently successful example of popular sovereignty. Machiavelli had drawn the conclusion that there were two forms of government: popular governments, which were unstable, and principalities, or what we should call dictatorships, the stability of which depended on the force and cunning of the prince. This analysis, of course, horrified the idealists of the sixteenth century who were trying to rationalize the government of the prince with arguments about the "general good," and so Machiavelli became, by way of the attacks on him, a conventional bogey of Elizabethan drama. From the point of view of tragic structure, what Machiavelli was doing was destroying the integrity of tragedy by obliterating the difference between the order-figure and the rebel-figure. Machiavelli comes into Marlowe's *Jew of Malta* to speak the prologue, and there he asks: "What right had Caesar to the empire?"—in itself surely a fair enough question, and one which expresses the central issue in the tragedy of order.

The order-figure, in Shakespeare, holds his position through a subtle combination of *de jure* and *de facto* authority. In the history plays, legitimacy is a factor of great importance: a magical aura surrounds the rightful heir, and the favour of God, or at least the co-operation of nature, seems bound up with preserving the line of succession. It is clear that hereditary succession is regarded as essential to a fully developed social order. Richard II was an impossible king, but Bolingbroke's seizure of the crown was an awful and portentous event, throwing a shadow over the whole Lancastrian line. It does not affect Henry V, apparently, because he succeeded his father in good faith, but it brings disaster as soon as he dies. In the first part of *Henry VI* we are told something which is played down in the later histories: that Bolingbroke not only took the crown from the Lord's anointed, but pushed the person next in line, the Earl of Mortimer, out of the way. In trying to determine the moral boundary between the ruthlessness of Henry V or Henry VIII and the rascality of John or Richard III, the attempts of the latter two to get rid of the heir apparent are clearly decisive. Bolingbroke, though he wanted Richard II murdered, has to dissociate himself from the actual deed by making a scapegoat out of Exton: in *King John* it is insisted that Hubert is "damned" if he really killed Arthur. Still, John, like Richard III and Macbeth, was simply accepting the logic of the *de jure* argument, which implies that anyone who has any claim to the throne at all can acquire the *de jure* aura by murdering everybody who has a better claim. To some extent this is true—that is, it is to some extent accepted by Shakespeare as a dramatic postulate. Once Arthur is dead, the legitimate heir becomes John's son, the young Henry III, and the fortune of England is bound up with recognizing him as such. In plays where leadership does not depend wholly on hereditary succession, as in the Roman plays and *Hamlet*, the choice of a predecessor, including Caesar's preference for Antony and Hamlet's for Fortinbras, has a good deal of moral significance. Enough is said, however, about the merits and services of Coriolanus, Othello, Caesar, Titus, and others to make it obvious that in some social contexts *de jure* authority can be earned as well as inherited.

Richard II was a lawful king, but a mediaeval king was perennially short of money, and if he were extravagant or a poor manager he had to live practically like a brigand in the middle of his own society. In this situation the question of what kind of law the lawful king represents becomes very ambiguous. The success of Bolingbroke's rebellion depends partly on its justice: he makes common cause with those plundered by Richard's favourites. The justice he appeals to is the right of inheriting private property: a dramatist who could write a whole play about King John without mentioning Magna Carta could hardly have cared less about the freedom that broadens through precedents. But Bolingbroke's real success lies in, so to speak, the nature of nature. Richard is the natural head of the state, but has not done a ruler's work, and society's need for a centre of order throws up a natural force in the form of Bolingbroke. One does not feel either that Bolingbroke is a pawn of circumstances or that he is consumed by personal ambition: one feels that he is part of a process too much in accord with nature to be described even by such a mysterious term as fate. Shakespeare presents him rather as Marvell was later to present Oliver Cromwell:

> Nature that hateth emptiness
> Allows of penetration less,
>   And therefore must make room
>   Where greater spirits come.

Richard is king *de jure*; Bolingbroke is the power *de facto*, but at a certain point the *de facto* power acquires the *de jure* attribute as well: this point is represented by York's dramatic transfer of loyalties. We are not dealing in this play with a simple moral issue: Bolingbroke is neither a wicked usurper like Macbeth nor a righteous avenger like Richmond. Both his supporter Northumberland and his opponent Carlisle are right in their attitudes. Julius Caesar has no *de jure* monarch to displace, but he comes to power in the same way, through society's need for a personal leader.

The ruler, we said, represents, though he does not embody, the upper order of nature, the world man was originally intended to live in. The conventional physical symbol of this order is that of the starry spheres with their unheard music. The music is that of the Apollonian world, for Apollo was the god of music, at least of the music that suggests "harmony," order, and stability. Nietzsche's Dionysian conception of music belongs to the age of Wagner. Metaphors of harmony are seldom far away from any discussion of social order, and the passing of such an order is regularly symbolized by music. This is true even of the fall of Catherine of Aragon in *Henry VIII*. The deposed Richard II is poet, actor, and musician, and when he hears music and remarks,

> How sour sweet music is
> When time is broke and no proportion kept!

he goes on to make it clear that the words "time" and "proportion" link music and social order together.

Closely allied to this use of music is the suggestion of the supernatural. Ghosts, omens, portents, oracles, magic, witchcraft do not enter tragedy primarily as marvels: they are not there to be exhilarating, in the way that they are in romance. As things experienced, they threaten our sense of reality with madness: as things conceived, they show up the limited and finite nature of the human perspective, especially in thought. Thus they emphasize the existential irony in tragedy by showing that there are always more things to be experienced in heaven and earth than philosophy can digest. The authority of the order-figure is attached to a mysterious and invisible nature of which we know little except that it has authority, and, in Shakespearean tragedy, it is usually only the ruler's ghost that walks. Except for the episode of Hercules leaving Antony, where mysterious music is again heard, there is nothing really supernatural in Shakespeare's tragedies that is not connected with the murder of the order-figures. In *Macbeth* we have Banquo's ghost instead of Duncan's, partly because of the emphasis on the repose that Duncan has gained by getting murdered, and partly because the line of the reigning monarch descends from Banquo. The scene in which Duncan makes Malcolm Prince of Cumberland in front of Macbeth is oddly anticipatory of the scene in *Paradise Lost* in which God the Father arouses the jealousy of Satan by displaying his Son, and it is interesting that Milton considered writing a *Macbeth* which would include the ghost of Duncan. . . . The physical symbol of order is that of the stars in their courses: rebellion is symbolized by comets, thunder and lightning, "exhalations," and similar aspects of meteorology unusual enough to be called unnatural, because they interrupt the sense of nature as predictable.

Elizabethan tragedy, while it may in some respects be Senecan, is certainly not Stoic. The Stoic's primary loyalty is a loyalty of conviction to the universal law of nature and to humanity as a whole. In Shakespeare and his contemporaries what commands loyalty is a specific social order embodied in a specific person. In the histories there is no conception of any loyalty broader than England, and even when Shakespeare's subject is the Roman Empire in which Stoicism grew up, loyalties are still concrete and personal. It is a *comitatus* group that gathers around both Caesar and Antony. In the tragedies, as in the comedies, Shakespeare's settings are deliberately archaic. The form of society in them is closer to that of the Iliad, or of *Beowulf*, than it is to ours—or to his own. The social unit involved may be a great kingdom—England or France or the Roman Empire—but its head and eyes, to use images very frequently employed, are the ruler and his small select band of personal followers. Warfare, again, continually breaks down into the warfare of the Iliad: physical prowess by individual heroes fighting in pairs. Coriolanus has no sense whatever of what Ulysses calls "the still and mental parts" of battle: he simply dashes in and fights with his own hands. The histories ignore the more realistic side of mediaeval warfare, the side that was essentially a ransom racket. The collapse of this sense of personal heroism, as in Achilles' murder of Hector or Octavius' contemptuous refusal of Antony's challenge, indicates the subsiding of the tragic into the ironic vision. The role of religion also is Homeric. Prayer in Homer consists mainly of reminding the gods pointedly that they have been well fed by a hero's sacrifices, and that victory in battle is the obvious way of making sure that the supply does not fail. Similarly, the God of Shakespeare's histories ignores the pleas of the afflicted, but appears to respond eagerly to Henry's suggestion that he will do "more" than the two chantries he has already built for King Richard's soul if he wins Agincourt.

Brutus in *Julius Caesar* is something of a Stoic, even though it is Cassius who calls himself one, and Brutus is one of the few characters in Shakespeare capable of an impersonal loyalty. But Brutus is utterly lost in the Elizabethan Rome that Shakespeare depicts. He assumes that the process of leadership looks after itself, and that his only task is to remove the danger of tyranny. Consequently he is helpless in the face of Antony, who understands the principle of personal leadership. Cassius, in contrast, is motivated in his hatred of Caesar by personal feelings; because they are personal they are concrete, and because they are concrete he can see clearly what has to be done to consolidate power. But he is emotionally dependent on Brutus: that is, his loyalties, like his resentments, are personal, and Brutus is the one man for whom personal loyalties are inappropriate. Enobarbus in *Antony and Cleopatra* shows the existential nature of tragedy even more clearly. He attempts a kind of intellectual detachment that would rationalize his leaving a losing cause and joining one that seems more in accord with the laws of nature and the general good of humanity. After all, nobody can think of Mark Antony as the Lord's anointed. But Enobarbus' own nature and humanity are bound up with his personal loyalty to Antony and to Cleopatra—for it is only when Cleopatra seems about to betray Antony that he gives in to his impulse to desert. Once he has exchanged a loyalty of experience for a loyalty of rational conviction, however, and compares his detachment with Antony's generosity, he is too numbed even to feel like a traitor. He feels simply that he is no longer alive, and he does not have to kill himself: he merely lies down and dies.

An equally instructive figure outside Shakespeare is Clermont, the hero of Chapman's second Bussy play. Clermont believes himself to be a Stoic hero, invulnerable to the blows of fate, his soul in accord with the laws of nature, an indestructible centre for his own universe. He holds forth on these subjects at considerable length to anyone who will listen, and as a good many people are compelled to listen, the play develops into quite a Stoical harangue. Clermont, however, is a protégé of the Duke of Guise, hence his loyalties, and therefore his real existence, are bound up with that Duke, whom he supports to the point of defending the St. Bartholomew Day massacre in front of an Elizabethan audience that was at least half Protestant. When the Duke is assassinated, Clermont commits suicide, describing himself as the Duke's "creature" after having all but convinced us that he is a creature of universal law. True, an exalted notion of friendship is a central aspect of that law, but what the action really shows us is a philosophy blown to pieces by the existential facts of murder, irrational loyalty, and revenge.

A loyalty like this brings us very close to the spirit of the real Machiavelli, who found the source of social stability in a ruling personality and who recognized that the qualities of leadership were not moral. In Shakespeare there are, in practice, certain moral limits to leadership: an undying loyalty to Macbeth or Richard III would be quixotic. But theoretically there are no limits. Bosola in Webster's *Duchess of Malfi* reminds us of this when he remarks that it is no harm to die in so good a quarrel, after he had wiped out practically the whole cast as a result of being the loyal "creature" of two desperately wicked men. The strength of personal loyalty accounts not only for so many suicides in Elizabethan tragedy, or attempted suicides like Horatio's, but also for the irresistible power of the motivation for revenge. Brutus predicts that as Antony is Julius Caesar's creature, he cannot survive Caesar's death as an effective force. This is typical of the way that Brutus misinterprets political facts: Antony's single-minded desire to revenge Caesar makes him immensely stronger than Brutus.

One of the most familiar facts of Elizabethan tragedy is that revenge is so often presented as a duty, a moral imperative, the very call of conscience itself, and may still be so even if the avenger is a ferocious sadist who thoroughly enjoys what he is doing. The sanctions of religion often endorse the revenge, and the audience is usually assumed to be sympathetic to it. If Desdemona had been sleeping with Cassio, we (that is, most people in most audiences including Shakespeare's) might still think that Othello's murder of her was wrong, but certainly Othello would not have thought so, and the other characters would have taken, not our view, but the view of the tragic convention. Hamlet believes that "heaven was ordinant" in seeing to it that Rosencrantz and Guildenstern were killed without "shriving-time allowed." They were merely serving the king whom they had every reason to believe was the rightful king, but this time the convention is pulling in the opposite direction. Hamlet, again, is less remorseful about killing Polonius than annoyed with Polonius for not being Claudius, and seems genuinely bewildered that Laertes should be hostile to him. He can only realize, by an effort of which he is rather proud, that Laertes too might want to avenge a father's murder:

> For, by the image of my cause, I see
> The portraiture of his.

We should say that Hamlet at this point was completely paranoid, and in fact Hamlet also blames his madness when apologizing to Laertes for having exterminated his family. But the sanctity of the greater revenge atones for everything: Laertes dies full of remorse for his own treachery and flights of angels sing Hamlet to his rest.

In Shakespearean tragedy, man is not really man until he has entered what is called a social contract, when he ceases to be a "subject" in the philosophical sense and becomes a subject in the political one, essentially related to his society. The ordered society in Shakespeare is, to use Heidegger's term, ecstatic: its members are outside themselves, at work in the world, and their being is their function. As we saw, the vital thread of Enobarbus' life was the tie that bound him to Antony, not anything inside himself. What Falstaff sardonically notes of the relation of Shallow to his servants could in other contexts be quite seriously true: "Their spirits are so married in conjunction with the participation of society that they flock together in consent, like so many wild-geese." In the first part of *Henry VI*, Talbot, the hero of the play, is kidnapped by a French Countess, who says to him:

> Long time thy shadow hath been thrall to me,
> For in my gallery thy picture hangs:
> But now the substance shall endure the like,
> And I will chain these legs and arms of thine.

Talbot tells her that in seizing him she still has only the shadow, for "his substance, sinews, arms and strength" consist of the soldiers who follow him.

It follows that, for the leader, there is no difference between reality and appearance, between what he is and what he seems to be. His reality is his appearance, and what he does is what he is. Machiavelli remarks that it is not important that a prince should be virtuous, only that he should seem so. Until we stop to think about it, it is difficult to realize how far this principle goes in Shakespeare. Edward IV was the first to stab Prince Edward on the field of Tewkesbury, and he condemned his brother Clarence to death out of a superstitious fear of his name, influenced by his mistress. Yet, had it not been for the villainy of Gloucester, Edward would have got away with what is practically a saint's death, mourned by his faithful queen. The piety of Henry VI, on the other hand, was genuine, and therefore contemptible, because it prevented him from being a sufficiently ruthless ruler.

The prince is a *dramatic* figure: like the actor, he is required not so much to be as to appear, to put on a show. The conception of reputation in Shakespeare is bound up with the emphasis on appearance. It seems selfish for Hamlet to prevent Horatio's suicide, not because he cares about Horatio's life, but because he wants somebody to survive to tell his story properly. It seems weak in Othello, as Eliot says, to beg that a story of his killing an anti-Venetian Turk should be told about him. It seems cowardly for Cleopatra to be motivated to suicide, and Macbeth to his final hopeless fight with Macduff, out of a fear of being publicly ridiculed. But for successful rulers, how they appear in society is their real existence, and it is natural that a sense of an original function should appear like a mirage to these tragic figures in the last moments of their isolation and failure. At the end of *Hamlet* we get a strong feeling that the play we are watching is, in a sense, Horatio's story, and this feeling links together the two conceptions of reputation as the real personality and of the actor as the real man.

The good ruler is not, clearly, the ruler who performs good acts, but the ruler who does what has to be done at the time. The word "time" is very important here, and we shall return to it. Ruling involves a good deal of killing and executing, assaulting other countries when they are in a weak spot, committing minor injustices for the sake of greater ends. *De jure* authority is of little importance without *de facto* power, and the basis of *de facto* power is the ordeal by battle, the symbol of which appears at the beginning of *Richard II* in connection with Bolingbroke. The good ruler, in short, is the ruler who wins his battles. *Henry V* is a very complex play, but all its complexities do not eliminate from it the simple-minded glorification of the victory of Agincourt, and the conquest of France. It is in the exhilaration of this victory that England, in all its history, comes nearest to feeling its social identity. The feeling seems to depend on two elements to be found only on a battlefield: the presence of death and the inspiring power of enmity. In contrast to hatred, which is divisive, enmity is a socially unifying force. Two servants in *Coriolanus* agree that while war creates enmity, it is peace that breeds hatred, because then "men have less need of one another," and one thinks of Falstaff's chilling phrase about the men he recruits: "the cankers of a calm world and a long peace." The leader who has the authority to expose his followers to death is the leader who commands loyalty. Timon tries to build up a peaceful society on a basis of equality, generosity, and mutual friendship, and sees it instantly disintegrate in front of him.

In the Folio text of *Julius Caesar*, Caesar makes a vague boast that he "doth not wrong": what he originally said, according to Ben Jonson, was: "Caesar did never wrong, but with just cause." Jonson thought this ridiculous, but the fact that one may do wrong with just cause is central to the whole paradox of ruling, and it is highly characteristic of Shakespeare's Caesar that he had the insight to see this. For Shakespeare's Caesar was in a position to answer Machiavelli's question in Marlowe about his right to the empire. The answer is not the simple one that might is right, but still less is it the idealistic one that might imitates right. The ruler is not, like the judge, a mere incarnation of law: he is a personality, and in tragedy the personality takes precedence over whatever is conceptual or moral. If we start with the view that the head of the state should be an instrument of law or a philosopher-king, we shall end with disillusioned reflections about the little wisdom with which the world is governed. In Shakespeare's histories and tragedies the world is not governed by wisdom at all, but by personal will. For Shakespeare's order-figures it would be more accurate to say that right imitates might. The process of holding power, however ruthless, is primary; whatever order and justice and stability there may be follow after that.

It is easy to infer from all this that Shakespeare was a great "believer" in personal rule, and wanted his audience to believe in it too: that he idealized strong rulers and minimized their faults, glorified the successful military leader and admired ruthlessness and hardness. The Roman leaders are much more attractive in him than they are in Plutarch. One could quote a good deal in support of this thesis and still misinterpret the poet. The poet presents a vision of society: the critic, in trying to interpret the vision, is almost compelled to translate it into a conception or theory of society. As a theory of society, what we have been expounding sounds rather childish, especially to people who, like ourselves, live in a post-tragic age. For us, to put a personal loyalty above a loyalty of principle, as the Nazis did, is culturally regressive: it begins in hysteria and ends in psychosis. But Shakespeare has no theory of society: what he has is a vision of society, and that vision is so powerfully convincing that we accept it without question. We often think of Shakespeare's tragedies as reflecting the social facts of his own age, but, as already indicated, they do this only to a very limited extent. The settings of King Lear, Macbeth, Hamlet, Coriolanus are primitive by Elizabethan standards too, and because they are primitive they are archetypal, reflecting the immutable facts of passion and power and loyalty and absurdity that are always present in human life. The vision in Shakespeare's tragedies is, quite simply, a tragic vision, a vision in which death is the end of all action, and in which the actions that lead most directly to death are the strongest ones. The wise man, says Socrates the philosopher, will live by the laws of the just state whatever state he is living in. Every man, says the tragic dramatist, lives, or would like to live, by the self-destroying passions that are most clearly revealed in the archaic settings of Shakespeare's tragedies.

In the three plays that are typically tragedies of order, the order-figure is murdered fairly soon. Hamlet's father is killed before the play begins; Duncan just as he is about to enjoy some of the fruits of victory; Caesar just before he accepts the kingship and enters into his de jure heritage. No actual ruler is outside the operation of the wheel of fortune, and no triumph therefore can be without its reminders of death. The Ides of March come for Caesar; Duncan is saved from the treachery of the Thane of Cawdor by the Thane's more treacherous successor; and on the great day of the senior Hamlet's life, when he won his duel with the King of Norway and Prince Hamlet was born, the first grave-digger entered into his occupation. But the simple irony of fortune's turning wheel is not the real dramatic point of these assassinations. Critics who have noted that Aristotle's word "hamartia" is also the ordinary New Testament word for sin have often assumed that a tragic victim must have a "flaw" or a "proud mind" that will make his death morally intelligible. But the flaw of the murdered ruler is simply to be there, and his proud mind is merely to be what he is. Unlike Edward IV, who imprisoned his brother because his name began with G, Caesar dismisses the warning soothsayer as a "dreamer." Caesar's "flaw," then, is only that he fails to be a superstitious tyrant. As for pride of mind, even Caesar hardly has that in an excessive degree, much less the "meek" Duncan. The fall of the prince may have a moral cause, but the cause is not primary: what is primary is the event. Or rather, not only the event, but the event along with its consequences. The important thing about the order-figure, in short, is not that he gets murdered, but that he *has been* murdered. The essential tragic action starts just after his death. This is also true of the action of *King Lear*, where the order-figure, by abdicating as king, has destroyed his own social context, and has therefore essentially murdered himself.

The pushing back of the murder of the ruler into something pre-tragic is closely connected with a prominent feature in the histories: the tendency to idealize an earlier age. The story of the War of the Roses in *Henry VI* looks back longingly to the great days of Agincourt and laments the premature death of Henry V. But there were conspiracies against Henry V, as well as against his father, which looked back to the deposition of Richard II as the beginning of all social evils. We go back to Richard's time, and find John of Gaunt idealizing an age which ended with Edward III. There is a trace of the same feeling at the opening of *Julius Caesar*, with the tribune's despairing cry: "Knew ye not Pompey?" We are back to the point at which we began. The heroic has been; only the human is. It is the same feeling that gives the lost cause its glamour: the feeling that paints Oliver Cromwell with the wart on his nose and gives Charles I all the Van Dykes. As we continue to study the romantic appeal of the lost cause, it begins to attach itself to the dream of a lost paradise or golden age. For, as Proust tells us, all paradises are paradises that we have lost; all social ideals are ideals that no longer exist; justice itself, considered as an ideal, vanished long ago with Astraea.

Poetry must have an image; drama must have a character, and the feeling of lost social identity is what is expressed in the story of the fallen prince. The fallen prince is the "primal father" of a rather desperate myth of Freud's, which seems to assume a crude notion of a "collective unconscious" that literary criticism, fortunately, does not need. In criticism, the murdered prince, from Agamemnon onwards, stands for the sense of falling away from social unity which is constantly present in every generation. The tragic vision begins with being in time, and time is always time *after*. It is always later than a time when we had a greater allowance of life and could attach more significance in that life to parental figures. Or,

reversing the image, we now watch a heroic action with what is described
by Lewis of France in *King John* as:

> those baby eyes
> That never saw the giant world enraged.

We have frequently mentioned Richard II, and we notice that
Richard uses several phrases linking his deposition to the trial of Christ.
The primary reason for this is that Richard has one of the essential
characteristics of royalty, being a born actor, and Bolingbroke can steal
his crown but not his show. He adopts these parallels, not because he is a
Christ-like character, but because he fancies himself in that role. And yet
his dramatic instinct is sound. As king, Richard has "lost the hearts" of
both nobles and commons, and so for all practical purposes has abdicated
his birthright. As a man, he attracts the same mixture of sympathy and
condemnation as any other man who has muffed a very important job. But
purely as lost cause, as a symbol of man's rejection of the Lord's anointed,
he is entitled to his echoes. Behind the echoes of the rejected Christ are
the echoes of the lost paradise itself, for, as the Queen says in the garden
scene, Richard's fall is "a second fall of cursed man." Every fall of every
ruler is that.

There are, then, two symbolic aspects of the ruler, or what we
have been calling the order-figure, in Shakespeare's tragedies. There is the
deposed or murdered ruler, Caesar, Duncan, Hamlet's father, Richard II,
the abdicating Lear, who, as that, represents a lost social identity: we shall
not look upon his like again, or the like of what he stood for. His
archetype is neither Apollo nor Dionysus, but Keats's hero Hyperion, the
father of the sun-god, to whom Hamlet's father is twice compared. The
other is the ruler conceived as actual ruler, the successful strong man,
Octavius, Henry V, Henry VIII, and Julius Caesar for the first two acts of
his play. Such a figure is both Apollo and Dionysus, lord of both the order
of nature and the heroic energy of fortune. The leader controls a world
where reality is also appearance, and therefore illusion, as well as reality.
Nietzsche points out how the defining of individuality, which is the key to
Apollonian order, is only made possible by continuous illusion. The social
order the leader represents grows by conquest and successful battles; sanity
depends on hysteria; law and stability depend on punishment. His palace
is founded on a prison, as Henry V unconsciously indicates:

> We are no tyrant, but a Christian king;
> Unto whose grace our passion is as subject
> As is our wretches fettered in our prisons.

The strong ruler is in the position that Camus in our day has identified with Sisyphus, forever condemned to roll the stone of time. A ruler who has been killed at the height of his powers, or is thought of as living a long time ago, like the Edward the Confessor of *Macbeth* who could heal the sick, may become a legend of mystery and magic, a dream of glory that is hardly a memory and has ceased to be a hope. His legend becomes, like the ghost of the murdered Caesar to Brutus at Philippi, the symbol of our own evil genius, of our inability to reach our own ideals. Polite fictions about the present, such as the implicit reference to James I in the *Macbeth* passage, or Cranmer's prophecy at the end of *Henry VIII*, turn the tragic vision into something else. The tragic present is always in the intervening rebel state. And so every actual strong ruler, as that, is something of an avenger or nemesis, someone who re-establishes and renews a legendary glory in a spirit of wrath. The more successful he is, the more his order appears to be an emergency order, proved in war, which is, as Henry V says, the vengeance of God. Then the strong ruler in his turn passes into legend and his achievements into nothing.

In the total action of *Hamlet* there are three concentric tragic spheres, each with a murdered father and a nemesis. At the centre is Polonius, murdered by accident and avenged by his son. Around this comes the main action of the play, where Hamlet's father is murdered and avenged by his son. Around this again comes the story of the old and the young Fortinbras of Norway, the father slain by Hamlet's father, the son achieving by accident what a successful revenge would have achieved, the throne of Denmark. Of Fortinbras we know little except that he will fight for anything; so whatever the future of Denmark may be, it is unlikely to be a peaceful future. The story of Polonius, Laertes, and the mad Ophelia is an ironic tragedy of blood. . . . The story of the old and the young Fortinbras gives to the whole action the dimension of being in time, the turning of the wheel of history. In between comes the story of Hamlet, Hamlet whose mind is a complete universe in itself, ranging from hints of a divinity that shapes our ends to a melancholy sense of the unbearable loathsomeness of physical life, and whose actions range from delicate courtesy to shocking brutality. All this magnificent vision of heroic energy is poured out as a sacrifice to a dead father, to a ghost who returns screaming for blood from what is supposed to be a place of purification. Hamlet is forced to strike everything out of his "tables" that represents thought and feeling and observation and awareness, and concentrate solely on hatred and revenge, a violent alteration of his natural mental habits that makes his assuming madness only partly voluntary. It is the paradox of tragedy that he shows us infinitely more than hatred and revenge, that he could never have shown it without the impulse to revenge, and that nothing is left of it except silence for him and the telling of his story for us.

DAVID DAICHES

Imagery and Meaning in "Antony and Cleopatra"

Antony and Cleopatra is at once the most magnificent and the most puzzling of Shakespeare's tragedies. Its magnificence resides in the splendour and amplitude of its poetry, in the apparently effortless brilliance with which language is employed in order to search and illuminate the implications of the action; it puzzles because the action itself seems to be of no moral interest yet it compels a kind of wondering attention which would normally be given only to a play with a profoundly challenging moral pattern. Bradley sensed this paradox when he asked, "Why is it that, although we close the book in a triumph which is more than reconciliation, this is mingled, as we look back on the story, with a sadness so peculiar, almost the sadness of disenchantment?" And he added: "With all our admiration and sympathy for the lovers we do not wish them to gain the world. It is better for the world's sake, and not less for their own, that they should fail and die." This is surely to simplify the problem to the point of distortion, for it is not that Antony and Cleopatra arouse our admiration while doing wrong, so that we thrill to them yet cannot in conscience wish them success. It is rather that in this play Shakespeare seems to be building a moral universe out of non-moral materials. Yet I do not think that we can answer Bradley merely by making a spirited defence of the characters of the hero and heroine, as Dover Wilson does, convincingly enough, if not altogether relevantly.

Shakespeare, taking the familiar story, and many details, from North's

From *More Literary Essays.* Copyright © 1968 by David Daiches. The University of Chicago Press.

Plutarch, turns it into a poetic drama in which the poetry works continuously to give quite new dimensions to the action. In no other tragedy of Shakespeare does the actual story, the summarisable plot, seem at such a distance from the way it emerges in the play. Of course a great work of literature, most of all a great poetic drama, is always very much more than its summarisable plot. But a prose account of the action of *Hamlet* or *Othello* or *Macbeth* would at least give us some faint idea of the kind of tragedy that we are here involved with; certainly it would not lead us in the directly opposite direction and suggest a wholly different kind of play. This, however, is precisely what a prose account of the action of *Antony and Cleopatra* would do: if we read Plutarch's *Life of Antony* without thinking at all of Shakespeare's play (admittedly, this is now difficult for most of us to do) it suggests altogether different kinds of dramatic possibilities. In short, Shakespeare in this play puts poetic imagery to work in order to make the story tell far more than we could have conceived possible of this particular story and to involve it in aspects of the human situation from which the events themselves seem to be at the farthest possible remove. And *this*, I suggest, is what lies at the bottom of Bradley's disquiet—a disquiet which cannot be banished by any defence of the characters' behaviour or by pooh-poohing Bradley's Victorian morality. What strikes us, after we have given ourselves to the play and emerged from it again, is the incredibility of Shakespeare's achievement: it is the wonder of his having succeeded in making this action stretch to this meaning. It is impossible, and yet it happens. Coleridge considered the play "perhaps the most wonderful" of all Shakespeare's, and wonder is indeed one of our many reactions to it. He sticks to history minutely, argued Coleridge, yet in few even of his own plays does he impress "the notion of his giant strength so much, perhaps [there is] none in which he impresses it more strongly". Whether Shakespeare stuck to history as minutely as Coleridge thought is beside the point; Coleridge here puts his finger on a central feature of the play—the wonder of Shakespeare's having made a play with this kind of life and richness and exploratory quality out of the particular tract of history and biography which he used.

Shakespeare's play is not, of course, as Dryden's was to be, about "All for Love, or the World Well Lost", though this is one strand woven into the total fabric. It is—to summarise it crudely—about the different roles that man can play on the various stages which human activity provides for him, and about the relation of these roles to the player's true identity. Shortly before his suicide, when Antony sees events as having cheated him out of his role both of lover and of conqueror, he expresses his sense of the dissolution of identity:

> Sometime we see a cloud that's dragonish,
> A vapour sometime, like a bear, or lion,
> A tower'd citadel, a pendent rock,
> A forked mountain, or blue promontory
> With trees upon 't, that nod unto the world,
> And mock our eyes with air.

He goes on to say that he

> made these wars for Egypt, and the queen,
> Whose heart I thought I had, for she had mine,

and having, as he believes, lost Cleopatra's heart, he no longer has a real identity as lover or as man of action. The melancholy music of the lines rises up to involve us in this sad sense of loss of self. When, however, he is informed by Mardian that Cleopatra has killed herself for love of him, his identity as lover is immediately re-established and he assumes this role again with a new confidence:

> I will o'ertake thee, Cleopatra, and
> Weep for my pardon. So it must be, for now
> All length is torture: since the torch is out,
> Lie down and stray no farther. Now all labour
> Mars what it does: yea, very force entangles
> Itself with strength: seal then, and all is done.
> Eros!—I come, my queen:—Eros!—Stay for me,
> Where souls do couch on flowers, we'll hand in hand,
> And with our sprightly port make the ghosts gaze:
> Dido, and her Aeneas, shall want troops,
> And all the haunt be ours.

At first it seems that the re-establishment of his identity as lover means the abandonment of his identity as soldier—"No more a soldier", he exclaims; but soon it becomes clear that in his resolution to follow Cleopatra to death he is at last adequately uniting both roles. Cleopatra has now assumed the role of conqueror, and he will imitate her:

> I, that with my sword
> Quarter'd the world, and o'er green Neptune's back
> With ships made cities, condemn myself, to lack
> The courage of a woman, less noble mind
> Than she which by her death our Caesar tells
> "I am conqueror of myself."

When he discovers that Cleopatra has not killed herself after all, he does not fall back into his earlier state of disillusion with her; he remains the lover and the loved, ready to act out the last of love's gestures:

> I am dying, Egypt, dying; only
> I here importune death awhile, until
> Of many thousand kisses, the poor last
> I lay upon thy lips.

Finally, at the moment of death, he reassumes the character of conqueror also:

> but please your thoughts
> In feeding them with those my former fortunes
> Wherein I liv'd: the greatest prince o' the world,
> The noblest; and do now not basely die,
> Not cowardly put off my helmet to
> My countryman: a Roman, by a Roman
> Valiantly vanquish'd.

Cleopatra's great cry of grief at his death is the equivalent from her side of Antony's speech about the changing shapes of the clouds: no identities are now left in the world, no distinction between mighty and trivial; she is overwhelmed in a patternless and so meaningless world in which all roles are interchangeable:

> O, wither'd is the garland of the war,
> The soldier's pole is fall'n: young boys and girls
> Are level now with men: the odds is gone,
> And there is nothing left remarkable
> Beneath the visiting moon.

Her love for Antony, we now realise, had been what gave meaning to reality for her; it had been the top in a hierarchy of facts, and when Antony is gone there is no hierarchy, no order, and so no significance in reality. Her own position as queen equally becomes meaningless: she is

> No more but e'en a woman, and commanded
> By such poor passion as the maid that milks,
> And does the meanest chares.

At the end of the play Cleopatra re-establishes order by the culminating role-taking of her death. So Othello, once he has learned that it was Iago's malevolence and not the order-destroying and meaning-destroying fact of Desdemona's faithlessness that produced the appearance of Desdemona's guilt, is enabled to assume again the role of proud warrior: suicide is inevitable for him, as it is for Antony and Cleopatra, yet it is now an act possessing meaning. (I might add, in passing, that it seems to me that there has been much misguided criticism of *Othello* and *Hamlet* in recent years by critics who wrongly assume that, for Shakespeare, charac-

ters who act histrionically are therefore acting immorally. A proper reading of *Antony and Cleopatra* can help us to correct this error.)

Let me go back to the beginning of the play and see if I can trace
some of the ways in which Shakespeare uses poetic imagery to establish his
main patterns of meaning. The opening lines give us with startling
immediacy the stern Roman view of Antony's love for Cleopatra, separat-
ing at once the Roman from the Egyptian word:

> Nay, but this dotage of our general's
> O'erflows the measure: those his goodly eyes,
> That o'er the files and musters of the war
> Have glow'd like plated Mars, now bend, now turn
> The office and devotion of their view
> Upon a tawny front: his captain's heart,
> Which in the scuffles of great fights hath burst
> The buckles on his breast, reneges all temper,
> And is become the bellows and the fan
> To cool a gipsy's lust.

Granville-Barker has well described the quality of the verse:

> This is as ample and virile in substance, as luminous and as consonant in
> its music as anything well could be. One tremendous sentence, the ends
> of the lines not answering to pauses either; these, such as they are, fall
> midway . . . , so that fresh impulse may overleap the formal vision, and
> the force be the force of the whole. Note, too, the placing of the
> dominant "o'erflows the measure" and its complement "reneges all tem-
> per" with the doubled parenthesis between them, and how the "now
> bend, now turn" saves this from slackness; how "files and musters" and
> "office and devotion" strengthen the beat of the verse, with "plated
> Mars" coming like the sudden blare of a trumpet, and "burst the buckles
> on his breast" to sound the exploding indignation which culminates in
> the deadly

> And is become the bellows and the fan
> To cool a gipsy's lust.

Granville-Barker has noted how the force of the imagery here is
carried over to the reader or hearer. But what of the imagery itself? The
word "dotage" strikes hard in the very first line—a damning and degrading
word. But note that it is "this dotage of our general's". Antony is still, to
the Roman onlooker, "our general": there is a shared pride in that word
"our" and a deliberate placing in the hierarchy of command in the word
"general". The general is a general, but his observed behaviour is to be
described by this viewer as dotage. This *viewer*, because when Philo says
"*this* dotage" he is pointing at what he sees, drawing his companion's

attention to the visible paradox, a general, yet in his dotage. Antony is seen by Philo as playing two contrary roles at the same time—and this is not in accordance with the proper proportions of things, it "o'erflows the measure". It would be proportionate for a general to love, but not for him to *dote*. For a general to dote "reneges all temper", that is, it renounces all decent self-restraint, it is disproportionate, an improper placing of a particular kind of behaviour in the hierarchy of human activities and emotions.

A general has his proper "office and devotion", his appropriate service and loyalty. For a general's eyes—"goodly eyes", it is emphasised, that have in the past appropriately and suitably "glowed like plated Mars"—now to turn

> The office and devotion of their view
> Upon a tawny front

is again outrageous indecorum, wild disproportion. This disproportion is emphasised again and brought to a climax with

> his captain's heart,
> Which in the scuffles of great fights hath burst,
> The buckles on his breast, reneges all temper,
> And is become the bellows and the fan
> To cool a gipsy's lust.

What has military glory to do with such domestic objects as a bellows and a fan? The juxtaposition is deliberately outrageous. Similarly, the captain's heart put at the service of a gipsy's lust reiterates the disproportion, the total scrambling of that hierarchy which gives people and objects their proper virtue and their proper meaning. Yet "tawny front" can suggest not only "dusky face" but also a leonine façade, and "gipsy" is etymologically and phonetically linked with the noble adjective "Egyptian". While Philo's language suggests his shocked awareness of a supreme disproportion, it also suggests that this is one man's interpretation. "Egyptian" is wilfully degraded into "gipsy". As the spectacle of the two lovers moves across to the middle of the stage to Philo's cry of "Look, where they come"—the lovers are now before our eyes as well as his—Philo's sense of the disproportion involved becomes agonising:

> Take but good note, and you shall see in him
> The triple pillar of the world transform'd
> Into a strumpet's fool.

And he invites his companion, in biblical-sounding language, to "behold and see".

But it is we, the audience or the reader, who now both see and hear. And what is it that we hear?

CLEOPATRA: If it be love indeed, tell me how much.
ANTONY: There's beggary in love that can be reckon'd.
CLEOPATRA: I'll set a bourn how far to be belov'd.
ANTONY: Then must thou needs find out new heaven, new earth.

We move at once from the Roman soldier's view of Antony's behaviour to the view of the lovers themselves. Here, too, is disproportion, but disproportion of a very different kind from that seen by Philo. Antony declares that there is no limit to his love, that to measure it would involve going beyond the confines of both heaven and earth. This indeed "reneges all temper"—but in glory, not in a shocking confusion of categories. The public entry of Antony and Cleopatra is a posed affair; it is preceded by a flourish of trumpets and accompanied by all the panoply of a royal progress; the lovers are acting out their love. To part of the audience— Philo and Demetrius, the shocked Roman soldiers—the role represents a monstrous confounding of categories; to the actors themselves, it is a glorious extravagance and subsumes everything else; to us who read or watch the play—well, what is it to us? Whose side are we on? We are jolted from Philo's offensively debasing comments to the sight and sound of the two lovers protesting their love. "All the world loves a lover", the proverb goes, and one naturally takes the lovers' side. But with Philo's words ringing in our ears we remain watchful, eager, interested: what is the true identity of this pair?

No pause for speculation is allowed. At once an attendant enters, saying

News, my good lord, from Rome

—from that Rome whose representative has just so devastatingly described Antony's behaviour. The brisk official announcement crashes into the world of amorous extravagance that the lovers' dialogue has been building up. Antony's barked, annoyed response—"Grates me, the sum"—shows him forced suddenly out of one role into another which he is most reluctant to play. At this Cleopatra suddenly changes too, quite unexpectedly yet wholly convincingly, into the playful, teasing mocker of her lover:

Nay, hear them, Antony:
Fulvia perchance is angry; or who knows
If the scarce-bearded Caesar have not sent
His powerful mandate to you, "do this, or this;

> Take in that kingdom, and enfranchise that;
> Perform't, or else we damn thee."

This shocks Antony out of his second role—the lover whose lovemaking is broken into by the claims of business—into yet a third, the surprised and puzzled lover:

> How, my love?

With what wonderful economy does Shakespeare capture this third movement of mind and feeling in Antony. He is surprised out of his annoyance with the interrupter, wondering what Cleopatra is up to. She soon shows him, as she goes on:

> Perchance? nay, and most like:
> You must not stay here longer, your dismission
> Is come from Caesar, therefore hear it, Antony.
> Where's Fulvia's process? Caesar's I would say. Both?
> Call in the messengers. As I am Egypt's queen,
> Thou blushest, Antony, and that blood of thine
> Is Caesar's homager: else so thy cheek pays shame
> When shrill-tongued Fulvia scolds. The messengers!

She ends, note, by brusquely telling him to attend to the messengers: but she has made sure that, for the time being at least, he won't. Her mocking references to Fulvia, Antony's deserted wife—and we remember that Plutarch has described Fulvia as "a woman not so basely minded to spend her time in spinning and housewivery, and was not contented to master her husband at home but would also rule him in his office abroad"—sting Antony into rejection of all that Rome means. In his next speech he confirms Philo's view of the monstrous disproportion of his behaviour in a remarkable outburst which gains our sympathy not by any explicit or implicit moral justification but by its taking in all of human existence by the way and then including and surpassing it:

> Let Rome in Tiber melt, and the wide arch
> Of the rang'd empire fall! Here is my space,
> Kingdoms are clay: our dungy earth alike
> Feeds beast as man; the nobleness of life
> Is to do thus: when such a mutual pair,
> And such a twain can do't, in which I bind,
> On pain of punishment, the world to weet
> We stand up peerless.

When Coleridge, in the passage I have already quoted, referred to Shakespeare's "impressing the notion of giant strength" in this play, he added: "This is owing to the manner in which it is sustained throughout—that he *lives* in and through the play—to the numerous momentary flashes of nature counteracting the historic abstraction, . . ." Here is the living in and through the play, here are the flashes of nature. "Let . . . the wide arch of the rang'd empire fall." This is hyperbole with real content. "Rang'd" suggests "ordered" as well as "widely ranging". The ordered variety of political life, which is how Rome lies in the imagination, must give way to the subsuming of all order and all variety in the oneness of this present experience, which is how the passion of love fills the imagination. It is the obverse of truth that John Donne expressed:

> For love, all love of other sights controules,
> And makes one little roome, an every where.

All nobility of action is subsumed in the embrace of "such a noble pair". If the two poles between which Antony moves are Rome and Egypt, for the moment the Roman pole is annihilated. But Antony has a long way to go before he can find a role which combines his character of man of action and lover, which *justifies* him (not perhaps in a moral sense but in the sense that it accommodates his full *psyche*): the chain of events which finally drives him to suicide is made, in virtue of the poetic imagery in the play, to be the only way in which his various roles can come together in the same action. At this stage, we see him changing parts, but every change is accompanied by some awareness of what is being given up by not participating in other kinds of human action. How compelling and inclusive is the phrase "our dungy earth alike / Feeds beast as man", taking as it does into its purview in one sweep of perception the very basis of human and animal life and their common dependence on this "dungy earth". And how that phrase "dungy earth" stresses the coarse and common, yet rich and life-giving, elements that link the highest with the lowest in any hierarchy. In a sense Antony is not here abandoning everything in the world by his and Cleopatra's mutual love: he is taking it all with him. But only in a sense: as the play moves on Shakespeare develops more and more ways of taking all life with him in presenting the adventures of this couple. Between this speech and the recurrence of the image in a different context in Cleopatra's speech in Act V, scene II, whole worlds of meaning have been established:

> My desolation does begin to make
> A better life: 'tis paltry to be Caesar:
> Not being Fortune, he's but Fortune's knave,
> A minister of her will: and it is great
> To do that thing that ends all other deeds,

> Which shackles accidents, and bolts up change;
> Which sleeps, and never palates more the dung,
> The beggar's nurse, and Caesar's.

Here the search for a timeless identity, "which shackles accidents, and bolts up change", is movingly linked to a profound sense of the common necessities of all human existence. And when the dying Cleopatra, with the aspic at her breast, exclaims

> Peace, peace!
> Dost thou not see my baby at my breast,
> That sucks the nurse asleep?

the imagery takes on yet another new dimension, so that not only does Cleopatra establish herself at the end as combining the roles of mistress and wife, of courtesan and queen, of Egyptian and Roman, of live-giver and life-taker, but this final unification of roles is linked—in ways that go far beyond the actual story—to a compassionate awareness of the sad yet satisfying realities of human needs and human experience.

But to return to the dialogue in Act I, scene I. Antony's moment of abandon to his vision of his and Cleopatra's mutual love cannot be sustained, for it cannot at this stage correspond to all the demands of his and Cleopatra's nature. He again repudiates his Roman business and then, by associating love with pleasure and pleasure with mere sport, modulates rapidly from the lover to the mere hedonist:

> There's not a minute of our lives should stretch
> Without some pleasure now. What sport tonight?

Cleopatra with continuing provocativeness acts the part of his Roman conscience—"Hear the ambassadors" is her only reply to the speech just quoted—but Antony, who has moved from passion to hedonism to joviality, insists on taking this as simply part of her attractive variety:

> Fie, wrangling queen!
> Whom everything becomes, to chide, to laugh,
> To weep: how every passion fully strives
> To make itself, in thee, fair and admired!

This topic of Cleopatra's infinite variety is to sound again and again, in many different ways, throughout the play before the hero and the heroine come to rest in the final and fatal gesture that can make variety into true identity. At this stage in the play Shakespeare deftly moves the royal lovers off the stage to let us hear again the two tough Roman soldiers whose comments had opened the action.

> I am full sorry
> That he approves the common liar, who
> Thus speaks of him at Rome,

says Demetrius, giving another shake to the kaleidoscope so that we now
see Antony neither as the debauched general nor as the passionate lover
but simply as a nasty item in a gossip column.

We move straight from this splendid opening, with its shifting
points of view and provocative contrasts between the former and the
present Antony and between the Roman and the Egyptian view, to be
given what Granville-Barker calls "a taste of the chattering, shiftless,
sensual, credulous Court, with its trulls and wizards and effeminates". The
dialogue is in prose before Cleopatra's entrance, and it is indeed low
chatter, though even here the quiet, almost but not quite embittered,
realism of Enobarbus' speech stands out: "Mine, and most of our fortunes
to-night, shall be—drunk to bed." This, then, it would seem, is the
atmosphere that has bred Cleopatra. The queen enters, seeking Antony,
aware that "A Roman thought hath struck him", and worried. She
prepares her tactics, bidding Enobarbus fetch Antony and then sweeping
out as Antony enters. Antony, when he appears, is purely Roman: the
blank verse he speaks is brisk and business-like, moving in short senten-
ces. The news from Rome shames him. He is shaken into wishing to hear
Cleopatra named "as she is call'd in Rome" and to see himself through
Fulvia's eyes. He has changed roles very thoroughly, and the atmosphere
of the Egyptian Court, to which we have just been exposed, helps to make
us sympathise. When Cleopatra reappears she has already been diminished, not only by the Court atmosphere and by Antony's Roman speech,
but—and most of all—by Enobarbus' sardonic commentary on her behaviour
and motives. Her tricks are all in vain, and after trying out a variety of
moods and responses she is firmly shut up by Antony's Roman "Quarrel no
more, but be prepared to know / The purposes I bear." She then tries the
pathetic—

> Sir, you and I must part, but that's not it:
> Sir, you and I have lov'd, but there's not it;—

and in the end, unable to deflect him from his "Roman thought", she acts
the goddess of Victory and leaves him with the memory of an impressive
parting:

> Upon your sword
> Sit laurel victory, and smooth success
> Be strew'd before your feet!

But Antony has already come to see himself as Philo and Demetrius had seen him at the play's opening; we have heard him repeat Philo's very word, "dotage"—

>These strong Egyptian fetters I must break,
>Or lose myself in dotage.

At this point it looks as though the play is to be a tug-of-war comedy, with Antony being pulled now by Egyptian sensuality, now by Roman duty. And indeed, there is an element of this in the play, and some critics have seen this element as its main theme. But this is surely to take too narrow a view, a view, moreover, which makes nonsense of some of the play's finest features as well as of the responses of most careful readers. Of course one might take a mechanical view of the pattern of action and argue that because in the end Antony plays a Roman part (committing suicide) in Egypt for love of his Egyptian Queen he reconciles Rome and Egypt in his death, while Cleopatra, who similarly dies a Roman death in vindication of her Egyptian grandeur, similarly unites the two worlds. But this misses out so much that it cannot begin to be a proper account of what really goes on in the play. True, the conflict between Rome and Egypt *is* important in the play; it is also true that, as has often been noted, this is the most spacious of the plays, and the whole known Roman world is involved. But any attempt to see the play as merely a balancing of opposites, geographical and psychological, impoverishes it intolerably and also results in the sharpening of the dilemma I described at the beginning. *Antony and Cleopatra* is a play about ways of confronting experience, about variety and identity.

In Act I, scene IV we suddenly see Antony in yet another light, when Octavius Caesar refers to him as "our great competitor", and this is followed by further images of disproportion applied to Antony—"tumble on the bed of Ptolemy", "give a kingdom for a mirth", and so on; yet with these words still in our ears we are brought back to Alexandria to hear Cleopatra, seeing Antony's meaning for her more clearly at a distance, describe him as

>The demi-Atlas of this earth, the arm
>And burgonet of men

—a first foretaste of the grand mythological description she gives of him after his death to Dolabella:

>His legs bestrid the ocean, his rear'd arm
>Crested the world: his voice was propertied
>As all the tuned spheres, and that to friends:

> But when he meant to quail, and shake the orb,
> He was rattling thunder. For his bounty,
> There was no winter in 't: an autumn 'twas
> That grew the more by reaping: his delights
> Were dolphin-like, they show'd his back above
> The element they lived in: in his livery
> Walk'd crowns and crownets: realms and islands were
> As plates dropp'd from his pocket.

These tremendous images of power, benevolence, and sensuality—or of greatness, love, and joy—sum up the different aspects of Antony's identity, which are seen together, as co-existing, at last after his death. In life they interfered with each other, and can only be described separately. Nevertheless, the introduction of the figure of "the demi-Atlas of this earth" so soon after Octavius Caesar's complaints about what Antony has declined to, is deliberate and effective. We should note, too, that even Caesar shows himself fully aware of the heroic Antony, though he sees him as the Antony who was and who may be again, not as the present Antony:

> Antony,
> Leave thy lascivious wassails. When thou once
> Was beaten from Modena, where thou slew'st
> Hirtius and Pansa, consuls, at thy heel
> Did famine follow, whom thou fought'st against,
> Though daintily brought up, with patience more
> Than savages could suffer. Thou didst drink
> The stale of horses, and the gilded puddle
> Which beasts would cough at: thy palate then did deign
> The roughest berry, on the rudest hedge;
> Yea, like the stag, when snow the pasture sheets,
> The barks of trees thou browsed. On the Alps
> It is reported thou didst eat strange flesh,
> Which some did die to look on: and all this—
> It wounds thine honour that I speak it now—
> Was borne so like a soldier, that thy cheek
> So much as lank'd not.

This is not only imagery suggestive of almost super-human heroism: it is also violently anti-sensual imagery. The contrast between "lascivious wassails" and "thy palate then did deign / The roughest berry" is absolute. Victory in Egypt is associated with riotous celebration; in Rome with endurance. Cleopatra at the end of the play combines both these notions in her death, which is both a suffering and a ceremony.

When Caesar and Antony confront each other in Rome, Antony

admits the most important charge—that in Egypt he had not sufficiently known himself:

> And then when poisoned hours had bound me up
> From mine own knowledge.

Caesar, cold and passionless, never has any doubt of his own identity; that is one of the advantages of having such a limited character. Lepidus' character consists in wanting to like and be liked by everybody; he has no real identity at all. Not that Shakespeare presents all this schematically. The presentation teems with life at every point, and some of the situations in which Lepidus is involved are richly comic.

Meanwhile, Antony acts out his re-acquired *persona* of the good Roman leader and dutiful family man. He marries Caesar's sister Octavia, and is all courtesy and affection. But Enobarbus has been with the back-room boys satisfying their eager curiosity about Egypt. It is somewhat reminiscent of late Victorian—or even twentieth century—English businessmen interrogating one of their number who has returned from a visit to Paris. "Is it really true what they say about it? Can you really see this and do that?" "Eight wild boars roasted whole at a breakfast, and but twelve persons there. Is this true?" asks Maecenas: the detail is lifted boldly from Plutarch but Shakespeare puts it to his own use. Enobarbus is being pumped about Egypt, and in replying, this sardonic realist with no illusions tells the simple truth about Cleopatra's irresistible seductiveness. It is into his mouth that Shakespeare puts the magnificent and well-known description of Antony's first meeting with Cleopatra (again from Plutarch, but how transmuted!), thus guaranteeing its truth; it is Enobarbus too who evokes her quintessential sex appeal with the brief but brilliant account of her captivating breathlessness after hopping "forty paces through the public street", and above all it is Enobarbus who replies to Maecenas' "Now Antony must leave her utterly" with

> Never; he will not:
> Age cannot wither her, nor custom stale
> Her infinite variety: other women cloy
> The appetites they feed, but she makes hungry,
> Where most she satisfies. For vilest things
> Become themselves in her, that the holy priests
> Bless her, when she is riggish.

This is not role-taking: it is the considered opinion of a hard-boiled campaigner, and in the light of it we know that Antony has a long way to go before his different *personae* can unite.

If *we* are never allowed to forget Cleopatra, how can Antony? It takes only a casual encounter with an Egyptian soothsayer—whether sent by Cleopatra to weaken Antony's Roman will or not Shakespeare doesn't say—to turn him to Egypt again:

> I will to Egypt;
> And though I make this marriage for my peace,
> I' the east my pleasure lies.

Mere sensuality is drawing him, it appears. Never up to this point has the love theme, as Antony reflects it, seemed so tawdry. It almost seems as though there is an obvious moral pattern emerging, with Rome on the good side and Egypt on the bad. This is further suggested by the following scene in Alexandria showing Cleopatra's reaction to the news of Antony's marriage to Octavia. Yet, after all her tantrums, with her

> Pity me, Charmian,
> But do not speak to me,

a new note of quiet genuineness emerges in Cleopatra's love for Antony. And if we come to feel that the political world of Roman efficiency represents the moral good in this conflict between Rome and Egypt, we are soon brought to the scene in Pompey's galley in which power and politics are reduced to their lowest level. Antony fools the drunken Lepidus by talking meaningless nonsense in reply to Lepidus' questions about Egypt; Menas tries to persuade Pompey to slaughter his guests and so secure the sole rule of the world, and Pompey replies that Menas should have done it first and told him about it afterwards; the reluctant Caesar is persuaded to join in the heavy drinking. Lepidus, "the third part of the world", has already been carried off drunk. And finally Enobarbus persuades Caesar to join in a dance with Antony and Pompey while a boy sings a drinking song. The utter emptiness of this revelry is desolating, and it casts a bleak light on the whole Roman world. When the song and dance are over Caesar says he has had enough:

> What would you more? Pompey, good-night.
> Good brother,
> Let me request you off: our graver business
> Frowns at this levity.

Menas and Enobarbus retire to the former's cabin for more music and drinking.

In the light of this dreary and almost enforced celebration we think of Enobarbus' description of Cleopatra's first welcome to Antony or the later presentation [Act IV, scene VIII] of Antony's response to temporary victory and realise that there is another aspect to Egyptian revelry than the dissolute chatter of Act I, scene II. Egyptian celebration has a humanity and a fullness wholly lacking on Pompey's galley.

> Enter the city, clip your wives, your friends,
> Tell them your feats, whilst they with joyful tears
> Wash the congealment from your wounds, and kiss
> The honour'd gashes whole,

exclaims Antony in genial triumph to his men and, to Cleopatra when she enters:

> My nightingale,
> We have beat them to their beds. What, girl, though grey
> Do something mingle with our younger brown, yet ha' we
> A brain that nourishes our nerves, and can
> Get goal for goal of youth. Behold this man,
> Commend unto his lips thy favouring hand:
> Kiss it, my warrior: he hath fought to-day
> As if a god in hate of mankind had
> Destroy'd in such a shape.

And Antony goes on to proclaim a victory celebration:

> Give me thy hand,
> Through Alexandria make a jolly march,
> Bear our hack'd targets like the men that owe them.
> Had our great palace the capacity
> To camp this host, we all would sup together,
> And drink carouses to the next day's fate,
> Which promises royal peril. Trumpeters,
> With brazen din blast you the city's ear,
> Make mingle with our rattling tabourines,
> That heaven and earth may strike their sounds together,
> Applauding our approach.

Kissing, touching, and shaking of hands are frequent where Antony is the centre of a celebratory scene: it is the human touch, the contact, the insistence on sharing feeling. So against "I' the east my pleasure lies" we must set on the one hand Roman pleasure as symbolised by the scene in Pompey's galley and on the other the warm human responsiveness to environment which Antony evinces in so many of his Egyptian moods. Antony's behaviour in the scene just referred to, when he joyfully celebrates a belated and temporary success which can already be seen as the prelude to almost certain defeat, can be interpreted (and has been interpreted) as the old roué breaking up, losing his grip and his sense of proportion. But surely this is to apply an irrelevant kind of psychologising to the development of the action. Shakespeare's concern here, it seems to

me, is to keep providing Antony with ever changing emotional environ-
ments, to bring out all the weaknesses and strengths of his character, as a
prelude to his finding his integrating identity in death. There is of course
a sense of decline; Antony's power and fortune are shown as waning
together, and the ups and downs in his moods become as a result increasingly violent. But the latter part of the play is not simply a psychological
study of the decline of the sensual man in intellectual and emotional
stability as his fortunes decline (as Granville-Barker, brilliant though his
study of the play is, seems to imply). If it were that, it would be merely
pathetic, and it would be hard to account for the note of triumph that
rises more than once as the play moves to its conclusion. The play is in
fact both triumph and tragedy; Antony, and more especially Cleopatra,
achieve in death what they have been unable to achieve in life: the
triumph lies in the achievement, the tragedy in that the price of the
achievement is death. In the last analysis the play rises above morality to
strike a blow in vindication of the human species. Queen or courtesan or
lover or sensualist, or all of these, Cleopatra in her death does not let
humankind down.

When Antony returns to Egypt, his defection is announced by
Caesar as involving total surrender to oriental perversity and showman-
ship. The scene opens in the middle of his catalogue:

> Contemning Rome he has done all this, and more
> In Alexandria: here's the manner of 't:
> I' the market-place, on a tribunal silver'd,
> Cleopatra and himself in chairs of gold
> Were publicly enthron'd: at the feet sat
> Caesarion, whom they call my father's son,
> And all the unlawful issue that their lust
> Since then hath made between them. Unto her
> He gave the stablishment of Egypt, made her
> Of Lower Syria, Cyprus, Lydia,
> Absolute queen.

Quite apart from the contempt of Caesar which this implies, it offends the
Romans because it is not Caesar's cool use of power but the histrionic
public exhibition of power, acting out a ceremony of power "in the public
eye" (in Maecenas' incredulous phrase). This is an important aspect of
Antony's character: speech and gesture are for him part of action; we
make love partly by talking about it, we enjoy power by announcing it
with proper pageantry. Caesar goes on to report in horror:

> I' the common show-place, where they exercise,
> His sons he there proclaim'd the kings of kings;

> Great Media, Parthia, and Armenia,
> He gave to Alexander; to Ptolemy he assign'd
> Syria, Cilicia, and Phoenicia: she
> In the habiliments of the goddess Isis
> That day appear'd, and oft before gave audience,
> As 'tis reported, so.

This is acting, role-taking. The grandeur of the ceremonies seems to come through even Caesar's repugnant description. He waits, however, for Octavia's arrival to reduce all this at one blow to what seems to him its proper meaning:

> He hath given his empire
> Up to a whore, who now are levying
> The kings o' the earth for war. He hath assembled
> Bocchus, the king of Libya, Archelaus
> Of Cappadocia, Philadelphos, king
> Of Paphlagonia; the Thracian king Adallas;
> King Manchus of Arabia, King of Pont,
> Herod of Jewry; Mithridates, king
> Of Comagene, Polemon and Amyntas,
> The kings of Mede and Lycaonia,
> With a more larger list of sceptres.

The litany of eastern names suggests both exotic power and sinister threat to the familiar Roman world; but the chief force of the speech comes in the shocked association of the words "empire" and "whore". The "kings o' the earth"—how abstractly absolute the phrase is; the largeness and grandeur of the company seem unlimited. For Caesar, a thing is either one thing or another, and everything should belong to its proper place. A whore to whom an empire has been given up is perhaps made by that fact into something else: certainly, there is a transcending of normal categories. And this is the point. The outlandish assembly of the kings of the earth is monstrous enough, but that all this should be done in the name of a whore is an outrageous confounding of categories. One feels that this, rather than Antony's disloyalty, is Caesar's real complaint. It is not that it is totally ridiculous to call Cleopatra a whore. Antony sees her as such on occasion: he uses language much less moderate than Caesar's when he imagines that she has betrayed him. "Triple-turned whore", he calls her. But Antony, even in his moments of highest rage with Cleopatra, is aware that the identity he fastens on her in his abuse of her is but one of her identities—"What's her name, / Since she was Cleopatra?" He can apply to her a term much worse than "whore", employing that contemptuous food imagery which reduces a woman to a mere object to satisfy the appetite:

> I found you as a morsel, cold upon
> Dead Caesar's trencher: nay, you were a fragment
> Of Gnaeus Pompey's, besides what hotter hours,
> Unregister'd in vulgar fame, you have
> Luxuriously pick'd out.

Antony's emotional vagaries in the long movement of his decline exhibit him as beyond the control of any stabilising self; it is almost as though Shakespeare is making the point that in order to gain one's identity one must lose it. Antony is seen by his friend Scarus, whose military advice he rejects as he rejects everybody's except Cleopatra's, as "the noble ruin of her (i.e., Cleopatra's) magic", and Shakespeare makes it clear that this is one aspect of the truth. Antony's military judgment is overborne by Cleopatra's reckless desires and intuitions. Even Enobarbus breaks out of his sardonic acquiescence in whatever goes on, to expostulate with Cleopatra herself in a tone of rising anxiety: notice how effectively Shakespeare uses his urgent repetitions;

> CLEOPATRA: I will be even with thee, doubt it not.
> ENOBARBUS: But why, why, why?
> CLEOPATRA: Thou hast forspoke my being in these wars,
>   And say'st it is not fit.
> ENOBARBUS: Well, is it, is it?

Soldier and lover are here contradictory roles, which must be acted separately. To attempt to act them out simultaneously is to risk ruining both. Shakespeare spares us nothing—the bickering, the infatuate action, the changes of mood, the melodramatic gesturing. Yet the poetic imagery works in another direction, not so much in its actual verbal suggestions as in its rising energy and human comprehensiveness. And at least Antony acts all his own parts. His chief reason for scorning Octavius Caesar is that he plays simply the role of cunning policy spinner and refuses to prove himself in any other capacity:

> his coin, ships, legions,
> May be a coward's, whose ministers would prevail
> Under the service of a child, as soon
> As i' the command of Caesar: I dare him therefore
> To lay his gay comparisons apart
> And answer me declin'd, sword against sword,
> Ourselves alone.

Of course, Caesar will not take so preposterous a risk—

> Caesar to Antony: let the old ruffian know,
> I have many other ways to die.

Antony has descended to "old ruffian" now: but it would never occur to Caesar that there is—perhaps must be—an element of the ruffian in every good soldier. He keeps his categories too separate for that kind of thought to be able to emerge. As for Caesar's "gay comparisons", it is only Antony's language that makes them so: the very notion is Antonine, not Caesarian.

The richness of Antony's humanity increases with the instability of his attitudes. His rage with the presumptuous Thidias, who dares to kiss Cleopatra's hand, is of course partly the result of Thidias' being Caesar's messenger and of Cleopatra's looking kindly on him—he himself shortly afterwards gives Cleopatra Scarus' hand to kiss. But more than that, it is a release of something humanly real within him, and his expression of it has a ring of appeal about it, appeal to our understanding of his emotional predicament, of the full human-ness of his situation:

> If that thy father live, let him repent
> Thou wast not made his daughter, and be thou sorry
> To follow Caesar in his triumph, since
> Thou hast been whipp'd for following him: henceforth
> The white hand of a lady fever thee,
> Shake thou to look on 't. Get thee back to Caesar,
> Tell him thy entertainment: look thou say
> He makes me angry with him. For he seems
> Proud and disdainful, harping on what I am
> Not what he knew I was. He makes me angry,
> And at this time most easy 'tis to do 't:
> When my good stars, that were my former guides,
> Have empty left their orbs, and shot their fires
> Into the abysm of hell.

It is interesting to compare this with the version in North's *Plutarch* from which Shakespeare took the incident. "He was longer in talke with her then any man else was, and the Queene her selfe also did him great honor: insomuch as he made Antonius gealous of him. Whereupon Antonius caused him to be taken and well favouredly whipped, and so sent him unto Caesar: and bad him tell him that he made him angrie with him, bicause he shewed him selfe prowde and disdainfull towards him, and now specially when he was easie to be angered, by reason of his present miserie."

The phrase "harping on what I am / Not what he knew I was" has no equivalent in Plutarch. Antony's consciousness of his different selves represents an important part of Shakespeare's intention. At the same time Antony's almost genial acknowledgement of his own weakness has not only an engaging confessional aspect but also draws on its rhythm and movement to achieve a suggestion of human fallibility which increases rather than diminishes Antony's quality as a man:

> He makes me angry,
> And at this time most easy 'tis to do 't: . . .

When Cleopatra approaches him, hoping that his angry mood has passed, he is still talking to himself:

> Alack, our terrene moon
> Is now eclips'd, and it portends alone
> The fall of Antony!

It is Cleopatra who is the moon—the changeable planet. (We recall Juliet's reproof to Romeo:

> O, swear not by the moon, th' inconstant moon,
> That monthly changes in her circled orb . . .)

But while he is lamenting Cleopatra's changeableness, she is awaiting the change in him that will bring him back to a full recognition of her love for him: "I must stay his time." He accuses her of flattering Caesar, and she replies simply: "Not know me yet?" To which in turn he replies with another simple question: "Cold-hearted toward me?" Her answer to this, beginning with the quietly moving "Ah, dear, if I be so, . . ." brings him round at once. "I am satisfied", is all he says to conclude the dispute, then proceeds at once to talk about his military plans. Having declared these, he suddenly realises just who Cleopatra is and where he stands in relation to her:

> Where hast thou been, my heart? Dost thou hear, lady?
> If from the field I shall return once more
> To kiss these lips, I will appear in blood,
> I, and my sword, will earn our chronicle:
> There's hope in 't yet.

He is both warrior and lover now, and well may Cleopatra exclaim "That's my brave lord!" This in turn encourages Antony to move to his third role, that of reveller:

> I will be treble-sinew'd, hearted, breath'd,
> And fight maliciously: for when mine hours
> Were nice and lucky, men did ransom lives
> Of me for jests: but now, I'll set my teeth,
> And send to darkness all that stop me. Come,
> Let's have one other gaudy night: call to me
> All my sad captains, fill our bowls once more;
> Let's mock the midnight bell.

More role-taking now takes place on a very simple and moving plane. Cleopatra adjusts herself to Antony's recovered confidence:

> It is my birth-day,
> I had thought t' have held it poor. But since my lord
> Is Antony again, I will be Cleopatra.

Cleopatra's reference to her birthday is almost pathos, but it rises at once to grandeur with "But since my lord / Is Antony again, I will be Cleopatra." The question posed by the play is, what do these two characters finally add up to? When Antony is Antony again and Cleopatra Cleopatra who *are* they? One cannot give any answer less than the total meaning of the play.

Enobarbus, the "realist", gives his comment on this dialogue. He knows his Antony; his shrewd and knowing mind give its ironic diagnosis:

> Now he'll outstare the lightning; to be furious
> Is to be frighted out of fear, and in that mood
> The dove will peck the estridge; and I see still,
> A diminution in our captain's brain
> Restores his heart; when valour preys on reason,
> It eats the sword it fights with: I will seek
> Some way to leave him.

But it is the realist who does not see the reality, and Enobarbus' death in an agony of remorse for having deserted Antony in the name of *Realpolitik* is Shakespeare's final comment on this interpretation.

The strangely haunting scene in which the soldiers hear the music which signifies the departure of "the god Hercules, whom Antony lov'd" projects the loss of faith in Antony's success even by those who love him: this is one soldier's view of their leader. Antony has already started to play an elegiac role before his men, and this is a consequence of it.

The death of Antony leaves a whole act for Cleopatra's duel with Caesar before she finally outwits him and dies in her own way and in her own time. It is an act in which she plays continuously shifting roles, and while these are obviously related to the exigencies of her conflict with Caesar and the fluctuations in her position, they also show her exhibiting varied facets of her character before deciding on the final pose she will adopt before the world and before history. She is not fooled by Caesar or by anybody, despite superficial evidence to the contrary. In the scene with Caesar and Seleucus where she is clearly playing a part designed to fool Caesar into thinking that she wants to live and make the best bargain possible for herself, she exclaims contemptuously to her ladies in waiting: "He words me, girls, he words me". Caesar is not an accomplished actor—he is not used to role-taking—and he gives himself away. "Feed and sleep", he tells Cleopatra, thinking that the exhortation will disarm and soothe her. But the words suggest the treatment one gives to a caged beast and give away, what Dolabella is easily charmed by Cleopatra into confirming, that Caesar intends to lead Cleopatra and her children as captives in his triumphal procession. This role, for all her infinite variety, is one Cleopatra will never play. If she does not arrange her last act properly, the Romans will put her in *their* play:

> Nay, 'tis most certain, Iras: saucy lictors
> Will catch at us like strumpets, and scald rhymers
> Ballad us out o' tune. The quick comedians
> Extemporally will stage us, and present
> Our Alexandrian revels: Antony
> Shall be brought drunken forth, and I shall see
> Some squeaking Cleopatra boy my greatness
> I' the posture of a whore.

The pageant of her death which she arranges is a sufficient anti-dote to this. Preceded as it is by the characteristically enlarging dialogue with the clown who brings the figs—enlarging, that is, the human impli-cations of the action—she goes through death to Antony whom at last she can call by the one name she was never able to call him in life—"Husband, I come". The splendour and dignity of the final ritual brings together in a great vindication the varied meanings of her histrionic career and temperament:

> Give me my robe, put on my crown, I have
> Immortal longings in me.

It is both a subsuming and a sublimating ritual. Love and loyalty and courage and queenliness are here together at last. And so is sexyness and sensuality, for this is a vindication through *wholeness*, not through a choice of the "proper" and the respectable elements only. Iras dies first and Cleopatra exclaims:

> This proves me base:
> If she first meet the curled Antony,
> He'll make demand of her, and spend that kiss
> Which is my heaven to have.

This almost flippant sensuality has its place in the summing up, which transcends morality. Charmian, who dies last, lingers to set her dead mistress's crown straight:

> Your crown's awry,
> I'll mend it, and then play.

"Play" means play her part in the supreme pageant of ceremonial death and at the same time refers back, with controlled pathos, to Cleopatra's earlier

> And when thou hast done this chare, I'll give thee leave
> To play till doomsday: . . .

When Caesar arrives, the striking and moving spectacle of the dead queen in all her regal splendour flanked by her two dead handmaidens forces even this cold schemer to see her in the great inclusive role she has arranged for herself. Love, which in the Roman view of the matter has hitherto been opposed to duty, the enemy of action and dignity and honour, is now at last, and by the very epitome of Roman authority and efficiency, pronounced to be part of history and of honour:

> Take up her bed,
> And bear her women from the monument;
> She shall be buried by her Antony.
> No grave upon the earth shall clip in it
> A pair so famous: high events as these
> Strike those that make them: and their story is
> No less in pity than his glory which
> Brought them to be lamented. Our army shall
> In solemn show attend this funeral,
> And then to Rome. Come, Dolabella, see
> High order, in this great solemnity.

"Famous", "high", "glory", "solemn", "order", "solemnity"—these are the terms which Caesar now applies to a love story which earlier he had dismissed as "lascivious wassails". Is the play about human frailty or human glory? We are left with the feeling that one depends on the other, an insight too subtly generous for any known morality.

HOWARD FELPERIN

A Painted Devil: "Macbeth"

'Tis the eye of childhood
That fears a painted devil.

—from *Macbeth*, II.ii.53–54

The last of Shakespeare's major trage-
dies to depend primarily on a native tradition of religious drama is also the
most widely and seriously misunderstood in its relation to it. Indeed,
Macbeth might well appear to be an exception to the principle of Shakespearean revision we have educed from the earlier tragedies. In those
plays, the effect of mimetic naturalization over and above the older
models contained within them had been achieved precisely by revealing
the moral oversimplification of those models, in sum, by problematizing
them. But *Macbeth* is unique among the major tragedies in having generated nothing like the central and recurrent problems that have shaped
interpretation of *Hamlet*, *Othello*, *King Lear*, and even *Antony and Cleopatra*.
Certain aspects of the play have of course received more than their share
of attention and are continuing matters of debate: the status of its witches
and of witchcraft; its topical relation to James I; the authorship of the
Hecate scenes, yet these are more pre-critical problems of background and
provenance than critical problems as such. For *Macbeth*, as Shakespeare's
one "tragedy of damnation," is so widely acknowledged to exist within a
relatively familiar dramatic tradition, that critical response to the play has
become almost a matter of reflex in assimilating the play to it. This would
seem to contradict the argument so far advanced that Shakespearean tragedy
is fundamentally and finally unassimilable to its models, and that this

From *Shakespearean Representation*. Copyright © 1977 by Princeton University Press.

unassimilability is what underlies and generates their problematic status and realistic effect in the first place. At the risk of bringing chaos into order by discovering problems where none have existed, I want now to re-examine the relation between *Macbeth* and its inscribed models. . . . It may turn out that those models are not quite the ones usually said to lie behind the play, and its relation to them not the clear and settled congruity that it is generally thought to be.

The tradition within which Macbeth is almost universally interpreted is that of orthodox Christian tragedy, the characteristic features of which are already well developed as early as Boccaccio and Lydgate and are familiar to all students of medieval and renaissance literature. It typically presents the fall of a man who may be basically or originally good but is always corruptible through the temptations of the world and his own pride or ambition. This action occurs against the structure of a fundamentally ordered and benevolent universe, which is finally self-restorative despite the evil and chaos temporarily unleashed within it, since crime will out and sin is always repaid. Of course the point in this essentially didactic genre is to illustrate the wages of human wrong-doing and the inexorability of divine purpose. That *Macbeth*, with its malign forces of temptation embodied in the witches, its vacillating but increasingly callous protagonist, and its restorative movement in the figures of Malcolm and Macduff, has affinities with this tradition is obvious and undeniable. The moral pattern of Shakespeare's play is not essentially different from that set forth in Boccaccio and Lydgate, and there is no lack of more immediate versions of it with which Shakespeare would have been well acquainted. He had drawn on *A Mirror for Magistrates* in previous histories and tragedies; several sixteenth-century moralities deal with the same theme; and the same pattern, though without political overtones, informs *Dr. Faustus*, a play with which *Macbeth* is often compared. Shakespeare's own early Marlovian monodrama, *Richard III*, falls squarely within this tradition of Christian tragedy, and its similarities with *Macbeth* were pointed out as far back as the eighteenth century.

Yet there is another dramatic tradition at work within *Macbeth* or, more accurately, a sub-genre of this same tradition, that is at once much older than these examples and more immediately and concretely present within the play. For here, as in *Hamlet*, Shakespeare allows the primary model for his own action to remain at least partly in view. We have seen how the cry of the elder Hamlet's ghost to "remember me" is more than a reminder to his son to avenge his death; it simultaneously conjures up the older mode of being and acting which would make revenge possible, which the action of *Hamlet* at once repeats and supersedes, and which points with all the intentionality and ambiguity of any sign toward the heart of the play's meaning. In *Macbeth*, too, the persistence of an older dramatic mode within the world of Shakespeare's play is no less explicitly recalled. Though there are many places in *Macbeth* that could serve as an entry into this older world, the two modern scholars who have consciously perceived its existence have both entered it through, so to speak, its front door, the "hell-gate" of Inverness with its attendant "devil-porter." For here too the purpose of the porter's request, "I pray you remember the porter" (II.iii.22), is more than to extract a tip from Macduff whom he has just admitted. The reference of his remark is ambiguous, as Glynne Wickham observes, "for it can be addressed by the actor both to Macduff and to the audience. As in the porter's dream, it is in two worlds at once; that of Macbeth's castle and that of another scene from another play which has just been recalled for the audience and which the author wants them to remember."

That other play, which Wickham advances as Shakespeare's "model for the particular form in which he chose to cast. Act II, scene iii, of *Macbeth*, and possibly for the play as a whole," is *The Harrowing of Hell* in the medieval English mystery cycles. Derived from the apocryphal *Gospel of Nicodemus* and adapted in two of the oldest rituals of the Roman Catholic liturgy, it is enacted in all of the extant cycles, though details of staging and dialogue differ from one to another. Between his crucifixion and resurrection, Christ comes to hell (represented as a castle on the medieval stage) and demands of Lucifer the release of the souls of the prophets and patriarchs. In all versions, the arrival of Christ is heralded by strange noises in the air and thunderous knocking at the castle gates. In the York and Towneley plays, the gate of hell has a porter appropriately named Rybald, a comic devil who breaks the news to Beelzebub of Christ's arrival and questions David and Christ himself as to his identity. Finally, Jesus breaks down the gate of hell, routs the resisting devils and, after a debate with Satan, who tries to deny the prophecies of his godhead, releases the prophets amid prayers and rejoicing. The Coventry version of the playlet, the one that Shakespeare is almost certain to have seen, is not extant, but there is no reason to think it was substantially different from the other versions. In fact, the Pardoner in John Heywood's *The Foure PP* (1529?), is described as having been on easy terms with "the devyll that kept the gate," since he had "oft in the play of Corpus Christi . . . played the devyll at Coventry," and is himself addressed as "Good mayster porter." With its castle setting, bumbling porter named Rybald, "*Clamor vel sonitus materialis magnus*" in the depth of night, and background of prophecy, the cyclic play of the Harrowing of Hell would have been easily evoked by the business of *Macbeth*, II,iii in the minds of many in Shake-speare's audience who still remembered the porter. Moreover, the memory of the old play would strongly foreshadow the outcome of *Macbeth* as well, since Christ's entry into and deliverance of the castle of hell also looks forward to Macduff's second entry into Macbeth's castle and triumph over the demonic Macbeth at the end of the play.

Though prefiguring the didactic superplot or counterplot of Macduff's liberation of Scotland and defeat of Macbeth, however, *The Harrowing of Hell* has little direct bearing on the main or central action of Macbeth's personal destiny within the play, aside from rather broadly associating him with Beelzebub or Satan. But there is another play, or rather pair of plays, in the mystery cycles that supply what *The Harrowing of Hell* leaves out in the action of *Macbeth*, namely *The Visit of the Magi* and *The Massacre of the Innocents*. The cycles are more varied in their dramatization of these episodes from St. Matthew than they are in the case of the deliverance from hell, particularly as to the outcome of the massacre, but all share certain elements that bear directly on Macbeth's career. In all of them, three wise men come to pay homage to a king born in Israel and descended from David, the prophecies of whose birth they rehearse to Herod. Outraged at these prophecies of a king not descended from him, which are confirmed by his own Biblical interpreters, Herod plans to murder the magi and all the children of Israel. The magi escape, warned by an angel, whereupon Herod sends his soldiers out to exterminate his rival, who also escapes into Egypt. The outcome of Herod's brutality—the murders are carried out on stage amid the pleas and lamentation of the mothers—though different in each version, is in all cases heavy with dramatic irony. The Towneley play, for example, concludes with a self-deluded Herod proclaiming that "Now in pease may I stand / I thank the Mahowne!" In the York and Coventry versions, the irony is more explicit, as the soldiers of the former admit under questioning that they are not sure whether Jesus was among the "brats" they have murdered, and in the latter a Messenger informs Herod that "All thy dedis ys cum to noght; / This chyld ys gone in-to Eygipte to dwell." In the Chester play, Herod's own son is murdered by his soldiers while in the care of one of the women. When told the news, Herod dies in a paroxysm of rage and is carried off to hell by devils. Even more pointed and ironic is the *Ludus Coventriae* version, in which Herod stages a feast to celebrate the success-ful execution of his plan to consolidate his reign and succession. Its mirth and minstrelsy are interrupted with the stage-direction, "*Hic dum* [the minstrels] *buccinant mors interficiat herodem et duos milites subito et diabolus recipiat eos.*" While the devil drags Herod away, the spectral figure of

Death, "nakyd and pore of array" closes the play with the inevitable
moral: "I come sodeynly with-in a stownde / me with-stande may no castle /
my jurnay wyl I spede."

The appearance of death at Herod's feast cannot help but recall
the appearance of Banquo's ghost at Macbeth's feast. For even though this
motif of death at the feast of life occurs only in this one version of the
Herod plays, it is a medieval topos which must have been available to
Shakespeare from other dramatic or pictorial sources, if not from this
particular play, since he had already employed it in Fortinbras' image at
the end of *Hamlet*:

> O proud Death,
> What feast is toward in thine eternal cell,
> That thou so many princes at a shot
> So bloodily hast struck?
>   (V.ii.353–356)

Indeed, the influence of the medieval cycles on *Macbeth* is not confined to
the pair of plays already discussed but can be traced to other plays within
the same cycles. Shakespeare's choric trio of witches, for example, are
anticipated not only by the three kings in *The Adoration of the Magi*, but
by the three shepherds and the three prophets in the play that precedes it
in the Coventry and other cycles, *The Adoration of the Shepherds*. There,
both the shepherds and the prophets are granted foreknowledge of Christ's
birth, both discuss his prophesied kingship, and in the Chester version,
both employ a form of paradoxical salutation similar to that of Shakespeare's witches:

> PRIMUS PASTOR: Haile, King of heaven so hy, born in a Cribbe . . . !
> SECUNDUS PASTOR: Haile the, Emperour of hell, and of heaven als . . . !
> TERTIUS PASTER: Haile, prynce withouthen peere, that mankind shall
>   releeve . . . !

Moreover, prophecies of the birth of a potentially subversive child trouble
not only Herod, but both Pharaoh and Caesar Augustus before him in the
Towneley cycle. Both follow the same, self-defeating course of attempting
to defy the prophecies through promiscuous slaughter. Certain details of
the Towneley play of Pharaoh may even find their way, from this or other
versions of the story, into some of Macbeth's most famous language and
imagery. His miraculous lines on how "this my hand / Will rather the
multitudinous seas incarnadine, / Making the green one red" (II.ii.60–62)
may well have their humble beginning in the reported outcome of Pharaoh's equivocations with Moses, the first of Egypt's plagues:

> Syr, the Waters that were ordand
> for men and bestis foyde,
> Thrugh outt all egypt land,
> ar turnyd into reede-bloyde.

Or Macbeth's anguished outcry, "O, full of scorpions is my mind, dear wife!" (III.i.36) may echo the same soldier's account of the third plague while internalizing it: "Greatte mystis [of gnats], sir, there is both morn and noyn, / byte us full bytterly." Even the plague of darkness may contain the hint for the dominant imagery of Shakespeare's play. It is not my intention to press these parallels as literal "sources," but it is important to recognize the close affinities of *Macbeth* with a series of Biblical tyrant plays, all repeating essentially the same story, each of whose protagonists—Satan, Pharaoh, Caesar, Herod—is a type of tyranny within a providential scheme of history. The apparently innocent request to "remember the porter" opens up an historical context for *Macbeth* that we have only begun to explore.

What, then, is the significance of these largely neglected models as they are deliberately recalled within Shakespeare's play? Glynne Wickham sums up their contribution to *Macbeth* as follows:

> The essentials that he drew from the play [of Herod] are the poisoning of a tyrant's peace of mind by the prophecy of a rival destined to eclipse him, the attempt to forestall that prophecy by the hiring of assassins to murder all potential rivals and the final overthrow and damnation of the tyrant. . . . Like Herod with the Magi, Macbeth adopts a twofold plan. He aims first at Banquo and Fleance; and, when this plan miscarries, he extends his net to cover all potential rivals and strikes down Lady Macduff and her children. The last twenty lines of this scene are imbued with the sharpest possible verbal, visual and emotional echoes of the horrific scene in Bethlehem. Young Seward's image of Macbeth as both tyrant and devil in Act V, scene vii, recalls the drunken devil-porter of Act II, scene iii, and thereby the two complementary images of the religious stage, Herod the tyrant and the Harrowing of Hell, are linked to one another in compressed form to provide the thematic sub-text of this Scottish tragedy. Pride and ambition breed tyranny: tyranny breeds violence, a child born of fear and power: but tyrants are by their very nature Lucifer's children and not God's, and as such they are damned. As Christ harrowed Hell and released Adam from Satan's dominion, so afflicted subjects of mortal tyranny will find a champion who will release them from fear and bondage. This Macduff does for Scotland.

The passage is worth quoting at such length because it so accurately reflects not only the indisputable elements Shakespeare takes over in

Macbeth from the medieval tyrant plays but the doctrinal message those plays were designed to illustrate and inculcate, a moral orientation that critics much less conscious of dramatic traditions and much more "modern" and secular in outlook than Wickham also find in *Macbeth*. But to assimilate the meaning of *Macbeth* to that of its medieval models, as Wickham and most other critics of the play more or less explicitly do, is not only to make Shakespeare's play less interesting than it is but to make it say something it does not say. Such an interpretive stance is based on a misunderstanding of the way any truly great writer uses his sources and models, as well as the way Shakespeare used his own in this play.

For the resemblances of plot structure, characterization, even language between *Macbeth* and the medieval cycle plays cannot simply be ascribed to a pious attitude and a parallel intent on Shakespeare's part in relation to his models. All these resemblances arise in the first place as a result of the efforts of characters within the work to turn the action in which they are involved toward or even into a certain kind of older action, to recreate their experience in the image of certain precedents for their own purposes, purposes which cannot be immediately identified with the author's and which the play as a whole may not ratify. We have seen this impulse at play within *Hamlet* and the previous tragedies, where Hamlet, Othello, and Lear all attempt and fail to turn the action into a version of the morality play, and it is no less present and pervasive in *Macbeth*, though here the particular medieval convention involved is a somewhat different one. For from the inception of the Scottish counterplot, Malcolm, Macduff, and the others are given to recreating present history in terms of medieval dramatic conventions. In Malcolm's depiction of him during the interlude at the English court, for example, Edward the Confessor is presented not as an historical monarch but as a type of royal saintliness, the dispenser of "The healing benediction" and possessor of "a heavenly gift of prophecy" (IV.iii.156–158). In contrast to the England blessed with such a king, Scotland has become, in Ross's account, a place "Where sighs and groans, and shrieks that rent the air, / Are made, not marked; where violent sorrow seems / A modern ecstasy" (IV.iii.168–170), that is, a hell on earth that cries out for the harrowing. Its ruler becomes, in Macduff's words, "Devilish Macbeth," "this fiend of Scotland" than whom "Not in the legions. Of horrid hell can come a devil more damned" (IV.iii.55–56). In the same highly stylized and archaic vein, Malcolm proceeds to characterize himself, first as a walking abstract and brief chronicle of vices exceeding even those of the collective portrait of Macbeth, and then as an equally abstract model of virtue allied to Edward the Confessor. To seek some naturalistic basis for his highly abstract "testing" of Macduff is futile, for like Hamlet's "portrait-test," its rhetorical and theatrical overdetermination will always be in excess of any personal motive that can be offered in so far as it is inspired by old plays rather than present feeling. Malcolm, like Hamlet, must go out of his way to abstract and depersonalize himself and his world as a necessary prelude to the scenario of redress being contemplated. He and his fellows must remake Scottish history into moral allegory, thereby legitimating themselves and their historical cause by assimilating them to an absolute and timeless struggle of good against evil. Malcolm and his party must, in sum, represent themselves and their world, in precisely the terms of the play's medieval models, that is, in the name of all that is holy.

This effort to abstract themselves to older and purer roles, however, is not the exclusive prerogative of the angelic party of Malcolm and his followers and not confined to the Scottish superplot. A complementary but antithetical project is already underway near the beginning of the play in Lady Macbeth's attempt to become one with a demonic role:

> Come, you spirits
> That tend on mortal thoughts, unsex me here,
> And fill me from the crown to the toe top-full
> Of direst cruelty. Make thick my blood;
> Stop up th' access and passage to remorse,
> That no compunctious visitings of nature
> Shake my fell purpose. . . .
>
> (I.v.38–44)

Her terrible soliloquy is appropriately cast in the language of the tiring room, as if its speaker were an actress beckoning attendants to costume her and make her up for the part she is about to perform, to "unsex" and depersonalize her into yet a fourth weird sister, even to dehumanize her into the "fiend-like" creature that Malcolm styles her at the end. All her efforts are bent toward making herself into a creature who trades lightly, even whimsically, in evil, and if her soliloquy echoes something of the incantatory tone of the witches' speeches, her utterances surrounding the murder reproduce something of their levity:

> Give me the daggers. The sleeping and the dead
> Are but as pictures. 'Tis the eye of childhood
> That fears a painted devil. If he do bleed,
> I'll gild the faces of the grooms withal,
> For it must seem their guilt.
>
> (II.ii.52–56)

Her entire effort of depersonalization lies compressed within the notorious pun: an inner condition of being ("guilt") is to be externalized into sheer theatrical appearance ("gilt"), not simply to transfer it onto others but to empty it of the substance of reality and make it (stage-)manageable. Her repeated assurance that "A little water clears us of this deed" (II.ii.66) would similarly transmute the red and real blood of Duncan not simply into gilt but into something as superficial and removable as the Elizabethan equivalent of ketchup or greasepaint: "How easy is it then!" There is bad faith here of course, in so far as her transformation never loses consciousness of its own theatricality and thus never becomes complete. She would qualify herself for murder by becoming a devil, but to her devils remain only "painted," thereby disqualifying herself for murder. Lady Macbeth's attempt to theatricalize herself into a callous instrument of darkness and thereby disburden herself of the horror of the time is doomed to break down, largely because it receives no external confirmation or reinforcement from her husband—since role-playing in drama as in culture does not go on in a vacuum—who is constitutionally unable to think of these deeds after these ways.

In contrast to her fragile and ambivalent commitment to a mode of imitation which is expedient, temporary, and only skin-deep, Macbeth's commitment is to a mode of vision in which sign and meaning coincide, role and self are indivisible, and an action is not imitated but accomplished, once and for all time. It is a way of thinking and seeing much closer to that of Macduff, who describes the scene of the murder as "the great doom's image" (II.iii.74), than to that of his wife:

> This Duncan
> Hath borne his faculties so meek, hath been
> So clear in his great office, that his virtues
> Will plead like angels, trumpet-tongued against
> The deep damnation of his taking-off;
> And pity, like a naked new-born babe
> Striding the blast, or heaven's cherubin horsed
> Upon the sightless couriers of the air,
> Shall blow the horrid deed in every eye
> That tears shall drown the wind.
> (I.vii.16–25)

In Macbeth's apocalyptic and allegorical projection of the deed and its consequences, Duncan becomes the Christ-like victim, and Macbeth the Judas-like traitor and Herod-like judge who will himself be judged. With its winds, weeping, pleading, and trumpet-tongued angels, the imagined scene conflates features of several typologically related cycle plays, notably those of the Crucifixion and Last Judgment. Within a mode of vision that blurs distinction between intent and action, subject and objects, illusion

and reality, even to contemplate such a deed is to shake and crack the
"single state of man" in which role and self were formerly united in the
figure of Duncan's trusted defender. "To know my deed," he tells his wife
after the murder, " 'twere best not know myself" (II.ii.72), and for Macbeth the rest of the play is dedicated to assimilating himself to the role he
has fully foreseen to replace his old one, to closing any gap that remains
between himself and it:

> From this moment
> The very firstlings of my heart shall be
> The firstlings of my hand. And even now,
> To crown my thoughts with acts, be it thought and done.
> The castle of Macduff I will surprise,
> Seize upon Fife, give to th' edge o' th' sword
> His wife, his babes. . . .
> No boasting like a fool;
> This deed I'll do before this purpose cool.
> (IV.i.146–154)

A new and antithetical unity of being is born. Macbeth expounds and
enacts a philosophy of language in relation to action that brings him into
line with every previous tyrant of the medieval and Tudor stage.
Tamburlaine's insistence on the instantaneous convertibility of his words
into deeds is notorious, but the same attitude underlies Cambyses' murderous demonstrations of his omnipotence, as well as the decrees of Pharaoh,
Herod, and Caesar that all the children shall be slain and all the world
taxed. In each case, the tyrant enacts a demonic parody of the divine
power he claims, namely the power to make the word flesh. By the end of
his play, Macbeth's assimilation of himself to the dictates of the tyrant's
role within the older drama being mounted by Malcolm and Macduff
would seem to be complete, their dramatic visions having joined into one.

Given that the Macbeths willingly take on and play out the roles
of "butcher" and "fiend-like queen" assigned to them in the apocalyptic
history of Scotland according to Malcolm and Macduff, how can we
contend that they are anything more than the walking moral emblems
that the latter say they are, or that their play is anything essentially
different from its medieval models? The answer is already implicit in the
nature of their role-playing. For the fact is that, despite the different
attitudes they bring to their role-playing and the different outcomes of it,
Macbeth and Lady Macbeth both have to strain very hard to play out
their respective roles, and neither is completely successful in doing so.
Lady Macbeth cannot fully become the fiend she tries to be, and Macbeth
cannot fully become the strutting and fretting Herod he thinks he is. In

the case of Lady Macbeth, her eventual madness is the index of the very humanity she would negate by turning herself into a pure and untrammeled role, the residue of an untransmuted humanity that had sought boldness in drink and was checked by remembered filial ties before performing the act that should have been second nature. Madness in Shakespeare's tragedies always attests to the incompleteness of an unreinforced role-playing, that technique by which the self in its naked frailty seeks refuge from the anxiety of such extreme and disruptive actions as revenge, regicide, or abdication through the adoption of an older and simpler mode of being. In this respect, the "antic disposition" of Hamlet, the madness of Lear on the heath, and now the quiet somnambulism of Lady Macbeth are very different from the behavior of Herod, who "ragis in the pagond and in the street also" when he fails to find confirmation of his absolute kingship in the prophecies, the wise men, and events themselves. For Herod does not and cannot *go* mad; he *is* mad. His "rage" is his role, and no matter how often he is traumatized, he will rebound with cartoon-like resiliency to his former outline, and rage again.

To define the truer madness that occurs in Shakespeare's tragedies, however: what is it but to be something other than role? Those who would follow Malcolm, Macduff, and the rest in equating Lady Macbeth with her fiend-like role and Macbeth with his role of butchering tyrant, and proceed to moralize or patronize them accordingly, are simply not listening:

> MACDUFF: Turn, hellhound, turn!
> MACBETH: Of all men else I have avoided thee,
>   But get thee back! My soul is too much charged
>   With blood of thine already.
>   (V.vii.3–6)

Macduff's challenge proceeds programmatically out of his own role of missionary, Christ-like avenger. Yet Macbeth's response proceeds not out of his assigned and chosen role of stage-tyrant, but out of an unsuspected reserve of sympathetic and spontaneous humanity that exists beneath it, a self still fragile and unhardened in evil even at this point, against his own and Macduff's protestations and accusations to the contrary. And Shakespeare's juxtaposition of the two reveals how inadequate and inappropriate are the moral terms deriving from the didactic drama of Satan, Pharaoh, Herod, Cambyses, even Richard III, to the drama of Macbeth.

Shakespeare makes it clear that Macbeth's play is in a fundamental sense *not* their play, despite the efforts of the characters within it, including Macbeth, to conform it to an orthodox tyrant play, and the many resemblances that result. Consider, for example, the nature of the prophecies and the manner in which they are accomplished. Just as Herod had questioned the Magi (and in one version his own interpreters), Macbeth questions the witches. He is shown in a highly archaic dumb-show an emblem of a "Child Crowned, with a tree in his hand" and another of a "Bloody Child," with accompanying glosses to the effect that "none of woman born / Shall harm Macbeth" and "Macbeth shall never vanquished be until / Great Birnam Wood to high Dunsinane Hill / Shall come against him" (IV.i.80–81, 92–94). Malcolm's camouflaging of his troops with the foliage of Birnam Wood identifies him with the crowned child bearing a branch, Macduff's Caesarean birth identifies him with the bloody child, and together they do indeed overcome Macbeth, with all the irony of a violated nature having her vengeance on the man who has violated her workings in himself. Yet even as these prophecies come true, they do so with an air of contrivance and artificiality quite alien to the inevitability of those of the cycle plays. On the religious stage the prophecies had had a literal transparency that those of *Macbeth* no longer possess. No interpretive effort is necessary to reconcile what was predicted (a king is to be born who will supplant Herod) and what occurred; or the literal meaning of the prophecy (Christ will supplant Herod) and its moral meaning (good will supplant evil); or the signs in which the prophecy is expressed (a star in the sky like a "sun"; a word in a sacred text) and their significance (the "son" of God, the "word made flesh").

In *Macbeth*, by contrast, a strenuous interpretive effort is necessary to reconcile the portentous emblems and pronouncements of the witches' dumb-show with their human and natural fulfillments, though we are largely unconscious of that effort when we make it. This is not simply a matter of the trickiness traditionally associated with prophecies of demonic origin. For not only are the prophecies of *Macbeth* not transparent and univocal as the prophecies of the Herod plays had been; strictly speaking, they do not even come true. It is not Birnam Wood but Malcolm's army bearing branches from Birnam Wood that comes against Macbeth at Dunsinane. Macduff may have been "Untimely ripped" from his mother's womb, making him something of a man apart, but that hardly qualifies him as one not "of woman born," the immaculate and other-worldly avenger of a fallen Scotland. It is only when we suppress their literal meaning (and our own literalism) and take the prophecies solely at a figurative level that they can be said to "come true" at all, let alone be made to illustrate the kind of moral logic we like to read out of them. In his handling of the prophecies so as to reveal their "double sense," their disjuncture of literal and figurative meanings, Shakespeare has introduced an element of parody, of fallen repetition, into his play in relation to its medieval models.

Yet this parodic discrepancy between Christian vision and Shake-spearean revision which runs through the play does not in the least prevent the Scottish resurgents from blithely conducting themselves and their counterplot as if no such gap existed and the two were one and the same, even though their own elected roles and exalted design are compro-mised by it. We might think, for example, that Macduff's unexplained abandonment of his own children and wife to Macbeth's tyranny, though ultimately providing him with the most natural of motives for revenge, could scarcely strengthen his claim to the exalted, impersonal role of Scotland's avenger prescribed by the play's Christian model. After all, even on the medieval stage it is the epic, superhuman Christ of the Apocalypse who harrows hell, and not the more human figure of the gospels. But for the Scottish resurgents, these deeds must not be thought of after these ways. It is precisely their capacity to sublimate their naked frailties into the service of a missionary role and a divine plan that constitutes their real strength and the prerequisite for their success. Macduff's personal guilt and grief are instantly transformed, at Malcolm's prompting, into the "whetstone" of his sword in the impending divine conflict, for which "the pow'rs above / Put on their instruments" (IV.iii.248–249). As such an "instrument" of righteousness, Macduff "wants the natural touch" (IV.ii.9) in more ways than his wife imagines. His unhesitating absorption into his role is never more astonishing than when he finally presents his own nativity legend, however literally lacking it may be, as the necessary credential for defeating Macbeth, however invincible in combat he once again appears. The same absence of self-doubt or self-consciousness in his new kingly role also characterizes Malcolm (whose single act prior to the mounting of the counterplot was also one of flight), particularly in his disposition of that "Which would be planted newly with the time" (V.viii.65) after the final victory. His announced intent of rewarding his followers with promotion to the rank of earl and of punishing his foes ("The cruel ministers / Of this dead butcher and his fiend-like queen" [V.viii.68–69]) sets the seal on the new historical order of his reign as a secular imitation of divine judgment. Yet the scene is also an eerie and unsettling repetition of an earlier scene in the play. For Malcolm's language and gestures cannot help but recall those of Duncan after the victory over Cawdor and Macdonwald, a new era of freedom and love that proved only too fragile and temporary, anything but an apocalyptic triumph of good over evil. The battle toward a civilized and humane order, like all the play's battles would seem only to have been lost and won after all. The arrival of

Malcolm and Macduff at Dunsinane is decidedly not the harrowing of hell or the coming of Christ, though its partisans behave as if it were.

Of course it is not really surprising that Macduff and Malcolm never come to perceive, much less feel, themselves to inhabit the gap between the heroic and archaic roles they adopt and the precarious selves that adopt them. For they are ultimately akin to such earlier Shakespearean tragic foils as Laertes and Edgar, un-self-conscious and un-self-questioning imitators of an inherited and wholly conventional way of acting, two-dimensional characters in a three-dimensional world. It makes no difference whether we say that such foils seem cardboard or cut-to-pattern because they are supporting actors or that they are doomed to be supporting actors because they are cardboard and cut-to-pattern. For it is precisely the conventionality of Laertes' rant and Edgar's mock-madness that throws into relief the dimensionality of Hamlet's and Lear's more demanding experience. We can accept in them an unreflectiveness, even an insensitivity that is harder to accept or understand in Shakespeare's protagonists themselves. We are not unsettled when Laertes acts like Laertes, rants for revenge and leaps into his sister's grave. The cat will mew, the dog will have his day. It is much more unsettling, however, when Hamlet acts like Laertes, betrays the very depth and sensitivity that distinguishes him from Laertes, and does the same. Similarly, no one is shocked when Macduff enters with "the tyrant's cursed head" atop a pike and apocalyptically proclaims that "The time is free" (V.viii.55), nor when Malcolm lends his blessing to the deed and the sentiment. For that judicial brutality and the ritual language that surrounds it proceed directly out of the ingenuous repetition of convention that we have come to expect from these characters and violate nothing that has been shown to exist in either of them. Macbeth's brutalities, by contrast, and the self-brutalization that makes them possible are profoundly disturbing to us, not simply because they remain so disturbing to him, and not simply because they represent, as one critic puts it, "murder by thesis"—for what else is Macduff's decapitation of Macbeth?—but because they betray precisely that fullness of humanity with which Shakespeare has endowed *him* in contrast to his foils. In his strenuous effort to become the complete tyrant, to achieve the demonic equivalent of his angelic foils' un-self-conscious conventionality, Macbeth must go out of his way to ignore the gap he senses between the pious and preordained view of things and the way things are, must do willfully what the others do quite naturally.

The question arises, then, why does Macbeth accept his destiny as a latter-day Herod, when he is not Herod? For no less remarkable than Macduff's unhesitating conviction that his birth carries the necessary credential for defeating him, is Macbeth's unresisting acceptance of it and the consequent slackening of his "better part of man." Why does Macbeth acquiesce to prophecies that require his cooperation to be fulfilled? The answer to these questions, I would suggest, lies in the mode of vision that we have already seen him bring to his experience before the murder of Duncan. He simply cannot do otherwise, not because his actions are compelled from without—the prophecies are not theologically binding like those of the cycle plays but psychologically self-fulfilling—but because he has long since internalized his society's way of seeing and thinking. Both before and after the murder, Macbeth's is a primitive and animistic world of portents and totems, of stones that "prate" of his whereabouts, of a bell that summons to heaven or hell, of knocking that might raise the dead, of the crow turned emblem of darkness, of night that is synonymous with evil, of accusing voices and menacing visions, a world become archaic melodrama burdened with significance. This "overperception," in which distinctions between subject and object, man and nature, illusion and reality, past and present—all the potential distinctions of our modern critical and historical consciousness—are lost, is characterized in its essence by Lady Macbeth, when she reminds her husband that " 'Tis the eye of childhood / That fears a painted devil," that "these flaws and starts . . . would well become / A woman's story at a winter's fire, / Authorized by her grandam" (III.iv.63–66). Yet it is just such a childlike and superstitious vision that finally binds everyone else in the play, including Macbeth, into a society as traditional and cohesive as a tribe or a clan. It is the vocation of the ruling and priestly class of such a society to paint, fear, and punish the devils who endanger that cohesiveness and their own power, and this is exactly what the Scottish thanes do, from the suppression of Macdonwald and Cawdor to the overthrow of Macbeth. The act of mounting atop a pole Macdonwald's and Macbeth's painted images, or better still their heads, is necessary as a totemic deterrent to tyranny, a public symbol of the inviolability of the social order and a glaring reminder of the inevitability of the moral law that sustains it: the wages of ambition is, and always must be, death. Macbeth had been an integral part of this social order, as Cawdor had been, so it is in no way surprising to see them both attempt to conform their careers to the sacred fictions they were born into and carry around within them, Cawdor by repenting like a morality protagonist and Macbeth by remaining the arch tyrant to the end. Macbeth and Macduff understand one another perfectly, across the moral gulf that separates them, for both speak the primitive language of the tribe.

This is not to suggest that Shakespeare is simply holding up to ridicule the sacred myths, symbols, and forms that so pervade *Macbeth*. It is Marlowe, not Shakespeare, who is given to expressing an adolescent contempt for religion as something invented to "keep men in awe." The play is much more than an easy demystification of the ritual forms that dominate the consciousness and condition the actions of virtually all its principals, for it shows those forms to be at once quite arbitrary and fictive in themselves but wholly necessary and "real" in the social function they serve. In this respect, the play presents a stylization not only of Shakespeare's own society, where these Christian, ritual forms still prevail, but of all societies. It would be the height of ethnocentric naivete to view the "ecstatic" or "nostalgic" community depicted in *Macbeth* as any more primitive in its constitution than later, more "enlightened" societies in which heads are no longer mounted on poles. The gibbet in the eighteenth century—some of whose Shakespearean criticism does indeed condescend to his Elizabethan "barbarism,"—or the electric chair in the twentieth are designed to serve the same necessary function of deterring deviance within the community and to preserve the same necessary fiction that crime must inevitably be followed, as the night the day, by punishment. Moreover, the play depicts the impulse constitutive of every society to make its particular social forms and institutions, which are always arbitrary in so far as they are man-made, seem as necessary as natural forms and processes themselves, indeed a logical extension of them:

> I have begun to plant thee and will labor
> To make thee full of growing.
> (I.iv.28–29)

> What's more to do,
> Which would be planted newly with the time—
> As calling home our exiled friends abroad. . . .
> (V.viii.64–66)

> My way of life
> Is fall'n into the sear, the yellow leaf. . . .
> (V.iii.22–26)

Within a world that sees itself through the ritual forms of the medieval drama, in which the book of human history and the book of nature are one volume of God's making, it is almost a reflex of all its members to describe the social and historical process of meting out rewards and punishments, for all its demonstrated fallibility, in an imagery of unfailing natural process. But to dismiss this impulse as a version of nostalgic fiction or pathetic fallacy is to misunderstand the play. For like Macbeth's, Duncan's, Lennox's, and the others' investment of the natural world with human attributes, these efforts to endow the human and historical world with a serene inevitability that properly belongs only to non-human nature is more than fiction and less than truth, another aspect of the persistent recreation of the sacred, the remystification of the merely secular, that defines the world of the play in its essential doubleness.

It is this radical equivocation of *Macbeth* in relation to its medieval models, the double sense in which it at once recreates those models through the communal effort of its characters and reveals them to be a means of social and institutional legitimation, that makes the play so susceptible to pious mystification or ironic demystification. Of these possibilities for misinterpretation, the pious reading has of course prevailed. The play is generally regarded as a humanization and vivification, through the flesh and blood of Shakespeare's mature language and dramaturgy, of the bare skeleton of its stagy and didactic antecedents. In this view, their homiletic intent though it may be softened is not fundamentally questioned or altered in the process of benign and respectful transformation. The "good" characters are granted just enough of a depth they do not possess, and the "evil" characters are denied just enough of the depth they do possess, to flatten the play into a consistent domestication of a wholly traditional moral design. But surely it must be otherwise, for in what does Shakespeare's humanization of his sources consist but the putting into question of their conventional roles and forms? To the extent that the figures who carry around with them that older moral design as a sacred and un-self-conscious trust are made to appear conventional, predictable, and bidimensional by contrast with the figures with whom they share the stage and who are restless in their roles, however strenuously they attempt to conform to them, that older moral design can no longer be authoritative. Critics have always been responsive to the interiority of Macbeth's struggle, but they have been reluctant to recognize that it is achieved precisely at the expense of his status as a moral emblem or example. Yet he becomes something much more interesting to us than any moral emblem in the process, and not because, as the critical commonplace would have it, evil is intrinsically more interesting than good. Macbeth is more interesting than his prototypes and foils, not because they are good and he becomes evil—for Herod is hardly "good"—nor even because they "are" and he "becomes"—for his change is in many ways regressive—but because he cannot take his nature for granted. He cannot quite rest content in an action in which his role and his nature are determined in advance, but must continuously re-invent himself in the process of acting them out.

It is in this that Macbeth's "modernity" consists and that his case bears directly on our own, at least to the extent that we are as fully human as he is. In this respect too, he becomes a very different kind of dramatic model, a type of modernity whose compelling interest for the playwrights who follow Shakespeare will cause him to be imitated again and again.

The simplifications that have become doctrine in the tradition of interpretation of *Macbeth* are the result not only of a failure to establish the play's relation to its models in its full ambivalence, but of a failure to identify the play's primary models in the first place. Just as *Hamlet* has less to do with Senecan revenge drama than with native morality tradition, so *Macbeth* has less to do with the morality play than with the tyrant plays of the Biblical cycles. Its nearest contemporary analogue is not Marlowe's *Faustus*, with which it is often compared as a parallel study in the psychology of damnation, but *Tamburlaine* or even *Edward II*, those early Elizabethan history plays which, like *Macbeth*, are modeled on the medieval tyrant plays that are the authentic prototypes of Elizabethan historical tragedy. The morality play is a misleading model in the interpretation of *Macbeth* in so far as it presents a world already more cerebral and voluntaristic than the cultic and animistic world of the cycles. It emphasizes, that is, freedom of moral choice within a mental setting, as opposed to the communal and typological destiny unfolded in the cycles. This misplaced emphasis on moral choice within *Macbeth*, where it receives little of the extended deliberation accorded to it in *Hamlet*, may well arise from the forced imposition of morality conventions upon the play and may well underlie all the misguided adulation of the bland and reticent Banquo and the equally misguided pity for Macbeth. For Macbeth's choices and actions, as I have tried to show, are not free in the way the morality protagonist's are, but are largely determined by his own and his society's expectations soon after the play begins. The universe of *Macbeth* is not ultimately and comically free, as it is even in those variations of the morality (like *Faustus*) where the protagonist persists in choosing wrongly and thus qualifies as an object of tragic pity, but is conditioned by forces largely outside his control. Of course those forces are no longer the benign and providential ones embodied in the figures of God and his angels who descend from above upon the human community below. Rather, they are disruptive forces that periodically and inexplicably bubble up, as it were, from within human nature and society, as the witches who incarnate and herald them, seem to do from within the earth itself. Unlike the morality protagonist, who is confronted at all points with a clear choice between moral meanings already established by generations of sophisticated theological apologetics, Macbeth, and the protagonist of Elizabethan historical tragedy generally, must struggle with meaning as it ambiguously unfolds in the world. It is only by confusing these two dramatic modes that such reassuring commonplaces as "the Elizabethan world picture" or "the great chain of being" could misleadingly have been applied as a norm in the interpretation of Shakespeare's histories and tragedies in the first place, as if the "natural condition" they present were order and the life of man could be analogized to the life of nonhuman nature. In our own struggle with the meaning of *Macbeth*, the proper identification of those models actually implicit within the play thus proves crucial and affirms once again the interdependence of literary history and interpretation.

A. D. NUTTALL

"Othello"

Shakespeare's play about Venice, *Othello*, has been the occasion of a classic dispute in Transparent criticism. There is disagreement about the hero: is he, in fact, heroic? Othello's speech at the end of the play causes most of the trouble:

> Soft you; a word or two before you go.
> I have done the state some service, and they know't—
> No more of that. I pray you, in your letters,
> When you shall these unlucky deeds relate,
> Speak of me as I am; nothing extenuate,
> Nor set down aught in malice. Then must you speak
> Of one that loved not wisely, but too well;
> Of one not easily jealous, but, being wrought,
> Perplexed in the extreme; of one whose hand,
> Like the base Indian, threw a pearl away
> Richer than all his tribe; of one whose subdu'd eyes,
> Albeit unused to the melting mood,
> Drops tears as fast as the Arabian trees
> Their med'cinable gum. Set you down this;
> And say besides that in Aleppo once,
> Where a malignant and a turban'd Turk
> Beat a Venetian and traduc'd the state,
> I took by th'throat the circumcised dog,
> And smote him—thus.
>   (He stabs himself)
>   (V. ii. 341–59)

T.S. Eliot in 'Shakespeare and the Stoicism of Seneca' observed that in this speech Othello seems to be 'cheering himself up': 'He is endeavouring

to escape reality, he has ceased to think about Desdemona, and is thinking about himself.' F.R. Leavis in his 'Diabolic intellect and the noble
hero' picked up a word applied by Eliot to the Stoic hero, 'self-dramatization',
and said that this speech by Othello, though it begins in quiet authority,
ends precisely in self-dramatization: no tragic hero this, but one who has
learned nothing from his misfortune and would rather rant than think. On
the other side stands Dame Helen Gardner. In her article, 'The noble
Moor', she reaffirmed the essential nobility of Othello, his generosity, the
greatness of his heart, his absoluteness and disinterestedness; and many
felt that the cynics had been silenced.

My general argument has been that Shakespeare's mimesis is unusually comprehensive. He moves forward on a total front. He imitates
individuals but he also imitates contexts. My response to this disagreement of Transparent critics is to stand further back for a while. There are
more things in this play than the figure of Othello, and it may be that in
understanding some of them we shall understand him. To begin with we
may be utterly formalist and ask what kind of play *Othello* is.

Shakespeare's plays have come down to us in the triple division
into comedies, histories and tragedies laid down by the editors of the First
Folio. There is in this division a large measure of editorial accident, for
the three categories are not co-ordinate. *Richard II* is, clearly, a history,
but, equally clearly, it is also a tragedy. Indeed it is formally a better
tragedy than *Othello* in that it deals with the fall of a prince. *Othello*, on
the other hand, is about an almost bourgeois Italian household, a misunderstanding and a murder at a level which involves no repercussions
among nations. Its social milieu is that normally inhabited by comedy.
This social difference is enough to stamp *Richard II* as central tragedy and
Othello as peripheral tragedy.

Othello, to be sure, is not the only Shakespearean tragedy to deal
with upper-middle-class goings-on. *Romeo and Juliet* refers to a similar
section of society, but then it has long been commonplace to observe that
Romeo and Juliet opens like a comedy. The long dynastic rivalry of
Montagues and Capulets brings us nearer to the proper political stature of
central tragedy than anything that can happen behind Othello's closed
front door.

But there is the phrase 'domestic tragedy'. Is this appropriate to
Othello? The phrase 'domestic tragedy' is commonly used to connote a
distinct genre: all those Elizabethan and Jacobean plays which dealt with
real-life murders and scandals, such as Jonson's and Dekker's *The Lamentable Tragedy of the Page of Plymouth*, Yarrington's *Two Lamentable Tragedies*,
A Yorkshire Tragedy (about a man who murdered his two children) and

Arden of Faversham (about the murder in 1551 of Thomas Arden by his wife), Wilkin's *The Miseries of Enforced Marriage*, Heywood's *A Woman Killed with Kindness*. It is fairly obvious that these plays catered for appetites which are served today by the more sensational Sunday newspapers. The title pages of these domestic tragedies repeatedly strike a note of prurient censoriousness which is immediately recognizable. *Othello* is not in any straightforward manner a member of this class, although we may note in passing that both *The Miseries of Enforced Marriage* and *A Woman Killed with Kindness* deal, like *Othello*, with the then uncommon theme of marriage. Moreover, Michel Grivelet has pointed to the popularity among writers of domestic tragedy of the *novellas* of Bandello, Boccaccio and Cinthio. The principal source of *Othello* is a novella by Cinthio. Again, the stories of domestic tragedies tend to crop up later in ballads. This is true of *Arden of Faversham* and it is also true, as it happens, of *Othello*.

The authors of these plays seem not to be have used the term 'domestic tragedy' themselves. The word 'domestic' was used of 'what goes on in a house' (in accordance with its etymological derivation from *domus*, 'house') and also of national as opposed to foreign affairs. Thomas Heywood does occasionally play on this ambiguity, but in the only place where he uses 'domestic' to designate genre ('domestic histories') he is referring to chronicles of England. The earliest example in the *Oxford English Dictionary* of *domestic* as opposed to *regal* (where the *Dictionary* offers the slightly misleading gloss 'devoted to home life') is from Davenant's *Playhouse to be Let:*

> Kings who move
> Within a lowly sphere of private love,
> Are too domestic for a throne.

Nevertheless, it is plain that the idea of a contrast between the tragedy of courts and the tragedy of private, household events was current in Shakespeare's time. The unknown author of *A Warning for Fair Women* (1599) refers to his play as 'a true and *home-born* tragedy'. Yves Bescou has remarked that in *A Woman Killed with Kindness* the house is itself a principal character. But in the common run of Elizabethan domestic tragedy there is admittedly little sense of tension between the idea of tragedy and the idea of domesticity.

Here Shakespeare is unlike the rest. For if we say that *Othello* is his domestic tragedy we must note that in this case the term connotes a paradox, domestic and yet a tragedy, tragic and yet domestic. If this is acknowledged the phrase has a certain utility as a description of the play. Thomas Rymer's celebrated attack on *Othello*, published in 1693, turns primarily on the fact that the play is bathetically domestic. Speaking of its moral, he says,

> First, This may be a caution to all Maidens of Quality how, without their Parents consent, they run away with Blackamoors. . . . Secondly, This may be a warning to all good Wives, that they look well to their Linnen.

Othello's tragedy indeed is strangely—and formally—introverted; it consists in the fact that he left the arena proper to tragedy, the battlefield, and entered a subtragic world for which he was not fitted. *Othello* is the story of a hero who went into a house.

Long ago A.C. Bradley observed that, if the heroes of *Hamlet* and *Othello* change places, each play ends very quickly. Hamlet would see through Iago in the first five minutes and be parodying him in the next. Othello, receiving clear instructions like 'Kill that usurper' from a ghost, would simply have gone to work. Thus, as the classic problem of *Hamlet* is the hero's delay, so the classic problem of *Othello* is the hero's gullibility. The stronger our sense of Othello's incongruity in the domestic world, the less puzzling this becomes. Certainly, *Othello* is about a man who, having come from a strange and remote place, found his feet in the world of Venetian professional soldiership—and then exchanged that spacious world for a little, dim world of unimaginable horror. 'War is no strife/To the dark house and the detested wife' comes not from Othello but from a comedy, but it will serve here. Its note of peculiarly masculine pain and hatred can still score the nerves. It is therefore not surprising that Shakespeare avails himself of the metaphor of the caged hawk. Desdemona says, 'I'll watch him tame', at III. iii. 23. The real process of taming a hawk by keeping it awake and so breaking its spirit is described at length in T.H. White's *The Goshawk* (1953). Othello turns the image round when he says of Desdemona,

> If I do prove her haggard,
> Though that her jesses were my dear heart-strings,
> I'd whistle her off and let her down the wind
> To prey at fortune.
>
> (III.iii.264–7)

He speaks formally of Desdemona, but it is hard not to feel that in the last words it is his own dream of liberty which speaks.

Othello is also about insiders and outsiders. The exotic Moor finds when he leaves the public, martial sphere that he is not accepted, is not understood and cannot understand. The Venetian colour bar is sexual, not professional. Iago plays on this with his 'old black ram . . . tupping your white ewe' (I. i. 89–90) and the same note is struck by Roderigo with his 'gross clasps of a lascivious Moor' (I. i. 127). Othello's gullibility is not really so very strange. Coal-black among the glittering Venetians, he is visibly the outsider, and in his bewilderment he naturally looks for the man who is visibly the insider, the man who knows the ropes, the sort of man who is always around in the bar, the 'good chap' or (as they said then) the 'honest' man. And he finds him.

There are two schools of thought on the sort of actor who should play Iago. School A chooses a dark, waspish fellow. School B chooses a bluff, straw-haired, pink-faced sort of man, solid-looking with no nonsense about him. In production School B triumphs, for the role, cast in this way, becomes both credible and terrifying. Although Iago is everywhere spoken of as a 'good chap', he has no friends, no loves, no positive desires. He, and not Othello, proves to be the true outsider of the play, for he is foreign to humanity itself. Othello comes from a remote clime, but Iago, in his simpler darkness, comes from the far side of chaos—hence the pathos of Shakespeare's best departure from his source. In Cinthio's *novella* the Ensign (that is, the Iago-figure) with a cunning affection of reluctance, suggests that Desdemona is false and then seeing his chance, adds, 'Your blackness already displeases her.' In Shakespeare's play we have instead a note of bar-room masculine intimacy, in assumed complicity of sentiment. Iago says, in effect 'Well, she went with black man, so what is one to think?' (III. iii. 232–7). Othello's need to be accepted and guided makes him an easy victim of this style. The hero is set for his sexual humiliation.

From the beginning of the play Othello is associated with outdoor weather, with openness: 'The Moor is of a free and open nature' (I. iii. 393); 'But that I loved the gentle Desdemona,/I would not my unhoused free condition/Put into circumscription and confine/For the sea's worth' (I. ii. 25–8). Note the important word 'unhoused' and the powerful emphasis on the last four monosyllables. In II. i, set on the quayside in Cyprus, the language bursts into profusion of images of wind and weather, before it brings Othello down from the high seas into the encircling arms of his wife. The effect is best represented by sporadic quotation: 'What from the cape can you discern at sea?/Nothing at all, it is a high-wrought flood./I cannot twixt the heaven and the main/Descry a sail./Methinks the wind hath spoke aloud at land;/A fuller blast ne'er shook our battlements./. . . The chidden billow seems to pelt the clouds;/The wind-shaked surge, with high and monstrous mane,/Seems to cast water on the burning Bear,/And quench the guards of th'ever fixed Pole. . . . The town is empty; on the brow o'th'sea/Stand ranks of people, and they cry "A sail!". . . . Great Jove Othello guard,/And swell his sail with thine own powerful breath,/That he may bless this bay with his tall ship,/Make love's quick pants in Desdemona's arms. . . . O my soul's joy!/If after

every tempest came such calms' (II. i. 1–6, 12–15, 53–4, 77–80, 182–3).
The diminuendo is marvellously managed: the bay becomes the arms of
Desdemona, the tall ship Othello himself. When, in III. iii, Othello
thinks his married happiness is irretrievably lost, he makes a formal speech
of valediction. This speech turns insensibly from a farewell to married
contentment into the real farewell, the real loss, which is the loss of
that military action and freedom in which alone Othello's true personality
could move:

> I had been happy if the general camp,
> Pioneers and all, had tasted her sweet body,
> So I had nothing known. O, now for ever
> Farewell the tranquil mind! farewell content!
> Farewell the plumed troops, and the big wars
> That makes ambition virtue! O, farewell!
> Farewell the neighing steed and the shrill trump,
> The spirit-stirring drum, th'ear-piercing fife,
> The royal banner, and all quality,
> Pride, pomp and circumstance, of glorious war!
> And O ye mortal engines whose rude throats
> Th'immortal Jove's dread clamours counterfeit,
> Farewell! Othello's occupation's gone.
> (III. iii. 349–61)

The word 'big' in line 353 is exactly right. He is surrounded by things
which are too small to fight with, things like handkerchiefs. When, later
in the same scene, he envisages a dark release from the dreadful circumscription of the house, once more a great flood surges in the language of
the play:

> Like to the Pontic sea,
> Whose icy current and compulsive force
> Ne'er feels retiring ebb, but keeps due on
> To the Propontic and the Hellespont;
> Even so my bloody thoughts, ...
> (III. iii. 457–61)

Othello's gradual disintegration is mirrored in his style of speech, at first
swiftly authoritative, then broken and at last full of a barbaric extremism.
The thing is done slowly through the play, but there are certain speeches
in which the entire triple development is gone through in little. When
near the beginning of the play the truculent gang comes crowding in with
weapons and torches, Othello easily controls them:

> Keep up your bright swords, for the dew will rust them.
> (I. ii. 59)

When he is brought before the Duke and the Senators in I. iii he is at first similar. Asked to account for his conduct he gives the reverend 'signiors' a very gentlemanly account (smooth, unflustered, almost majestic) of the way he won Brabantio's daughter (I. iii. 128–70). There is no sign of any break in this style until we reach line 260. Here Othello's language suddenly becomes problematic, so much so that most editors assume that the text is corrupt. The speech appears in Alexander's edition of the *Works* in the following form (Desdemona has just asked to be allowed to go with him to the wars):

> OTHELLO: Let her have your voice.
>   Vouch with me, heaven, I therefore beg it not
>   To please the palate of my appetite;
>   Nor to comply with heat—the young affects
>   In me defunct—and proper satisfaction;
>   But to be free and bounteous to her mind
>   And heaven defend your good souls that you think
>   I will your serious and great business scant
>   For she is with me.
>
>   (I. iii. 260–8)

The crux occurs in the baffling third and fourth lines, which remain puzzling even after they have been amended and repunctuated, as here, by a modern editor. In the case of this play, it is not easy to determine whether the first Quarto of 1622 or the Folio of 1623 has the higher authority. In the crux before us, however, this thorny problem fortunately does not arise, for the two are virtually identical. The first Quarto gives: 'Nor to comply with heat, the young affects in my defunct, and proper satisfaction'. The difficulties are evident. Is 'affects' a noun, in apposition to 'heat', or a verb (the relative pronoun 'which' having been elided) which would turn 'young' into a noun, the object of 'affects'? Should we change 'my' to 'me' (as Alexander did) so that we can read 'the young affects in me defunct' as an absolute construction, equivalent to 'the youthful passions being dead in me'? Does 'proper' mean 'legitimate' or 'my own'? Quite obviously, the sentence is a mess. But a Transparent reading may suggest that nevertheless we can accept it as it stands; that is, if we look *through* the fractured form to the possible person we may understand the forms as we never could if we looked at form alone.

A certain meaning comes through, and indeed it is strange. Othello seems to be saying, 'Do not think that I am asking for this out of lust, for I am past all that, rather I am interested in Desdemona's mind.' This does not have to be a full profession of impotence (though the powerful word *defunct* might be held to imply that), but only of diminished desires, but this in a newly married hero is sufficiently arresting. Attempts to make *defunct* bear some such meaning as 'discharged' or 'freed' by analogy with the Latin *defunctus periculis* ('freed from perils') will not do. This sense is not found elsewhere in English and, even in Latin, only emerges when there is an accompanying ablative (*periculis*). If Othello had said, 'defunct *from x*', this gloss might have been defensible, but he did not. No audience hearing these words would understand 'discharged'. Othello, beginning to explain that his request does not arise from lust, for the first time loses control of his sentence and so, we may infer, of his thoughts. Why?

Desdemona has just intervened in the men's world of senatorial debate with a sexual candour almost as startling as Othello's sexual retreat:

> My heart's subdu'd
> Even to the very quality of my lord:
> I saw Othello's visage in his mind;
> And to his honours and his valiant parts
> Did I my soul and fortunes consecrate.
> So that, dear lords, if I be left behind,
> A moth of peace, and he go to the war,
> The rites for why I love him are bereft me,
> And I a heavy interim shall support
> By his dear absence. Let me go with him.
>   (I. iii. 250–9)

There is no serious doubt that 'rites' in line 257 is a reference to the consummation of the marriage. This is what throws Othello off balance. She began by speaking of his mind—that part was excellent, carried no danger in terms of the stereotype of the lascivious Moor—but then she asked to be allowed to consummate the marriage. Othello's status in Venetian society is strong as long as it is kept separate from questions of sexuality. His speech is a stumbling, eager attempt to quash the implication of lasciviousness and to recover balance by catching at Desdemona's initial emphasis on mental affinity. The two speeches, Desdemona's and Othello's, are chiastically arranged: ABBA, mind, desire, desire, mind, but Othello's answering version is strangled and broken. To emend is to make it smooth. But the very roughness can be seen as correct, if one intuits a person in the part.

The editorial questions may still need answers (I think 'affects' is probably a noun and that 'proper' means here 'my own') but an actor can deliver the speech as given in the first Quarto, if he is allowed to stammer or hesitate. It remains true that the speech, thus unamended, would count as the most extreme piece of naturalistic confusion in the canon (though

Leontes' speech, 'Affection! thy intention stabs the centre' in *The Winter's Tale*, I. ii. 138–46, comes very close). The collapse of Othello's language is microcosmic of the collapse of his personality in the entire tragedy.

Othello was perplexed in the extreme before Iago went to work on him. Marriage itself disoriented him. Naturally, his valediction of marital happiness became a valediction of the military life. It was there that he last knew himself. We are now in a position to return to his final speech before he stabs himself (V. ii. 341–59). Othello quietly stops the captors who would lead him away; he speaks briefly of his service to the state and then asks that, when the story of his actions and his fate is told, it should be fairly told; if it is fair, it will tell not of a pathologically jealous man but rather of a confused man, one who threw away a treasure and weeps for it; moreover the story should also include the slaying of the Turk long ago in Aleppo. As he tells of the slaying of the Turk, he kills himself on the clinching word 'thus'.

In this speech the pathos of the outsider reaches a climax. It is true that Othello has not attained full understanding, but there is a kind of dignity, for that very reason, in 'perplexed in the extreme' (V. ii. 349). In the course of the speech his mind flinches away from the mangled, unintelligible scene around him, back to his heroic past, when he had an honoured part to play. It is no accident that Othello's memory, in its search for a feat proper to be remembered, should light on the slaying of the turbanned Turk. To assert his Venetian status to the full he needs as enemy a spectacularly foreign figure. Yet, as we watch him, we *see*, not a Venetian but—precisely—a spectacularly foreign figure. That this is art of the highest order rather than accident is brought home by the conclusion of the speech. For at the moment when Othello comes, in his remote narrative, to the slaying of the foreigner, before our eyes he stabs himself, in a horrific parallelism. It is as if as his last act of devoted service, his last propitiatory offering to the state, he kills the outsider, Othello.

Let us now turn to the questions we posed at the outset. Is the rhetoric of his speech self-dramatizing, histrionic, or is it noble? I answer, it is noble, but its nobility is tragically deracinated. I said before that Othello's tragedy lay in the fact that he left the arena proper to tragedy. The logical 'shimmer' of this suggestion affects our perceptions of his final speech. Nobility thus isolated and astray is infected with absurdity, but the very absurdity is tragic. Othello's rhetoric is the rhetoric of a shame-culture. . . . Othello's shame-culture is more primitive, more thoroughly pre-Stoic than Coriolanus's, and his difference from the society around him is also greater.

Othello is actually *simpler* than those around him. A shame-culture identifies glory and virtue. The manner in which this survived in Shakespeare's time (and, to some extent in ours) was in the notions of honour and reputation. Thus Cassio harps desperately on his 'reputation' as 'the immortal part' of himself (II. iii. 253–7). But it is in Othello that we find the notion of reputation, not as something extrinsic but as the centre of his moral identity, operating with enough force (as Iago knows) to kill him. At I. iii. 274 Othello says, in the first Quarto, 'Let . . . all indign and base adversities/Make head against my reputation.' There he is insisting still on a confidence which is seriously threatened. But then, in a marvellous scene, Iago gets to work within Othello's mind, thinking his thoughts aloud for him and he knows well on which nerve he should press:

> But he that filches from me my good name
> Robs me of that which not enriches him
> And makes me poor indeed.
>
> (III. iii. 163–5)

In the world of professional military action Othello was a human being. When he passed through the door of the house he became a kind of nothing. The word 'occupation' is in our day and was in Shakespeare's a relatively colourless word (it had a few extra meanings then, but that is by the way). Shakespeare is therefore doing something very deliberate when he places it at the climax of Othello's speech of valediction at III. iii. 349–61: 'Othello's occupation's gone.' He is making sure that we notice that the idea of profession or métier has an ethical status in Othello's mind which it does not naturally have in ours.

Venice in Othello is the same city we [see] in The Merchant of Venice. Othello is thus no feudal baron or chieftain, but a professional mercenary, paid by the state. Thus a certain continuity of economic reference links the two plays. But in Othello Shakespeare plays down the references to money. Instead he develops at greater length something which is also present in The Merchant of Venice. At III. iii. 31 Antonio said, 'the trade and profit of the city/Consisteth of all nations.' Venice is the landless city where different kinds and races meet in a strangely abstract effort of aggrandizement. The sea is the medium of their wars as money is the medium of their wealth. This, in The Merchant of Venice, yielded the endlessly fruitful contrast between a Jewish and a Christian consciousness. In Othello it permits the study of a primitive consciousness yoked to the service of a complex, civic society. Venice is for Shakespeare an anthropological laboratory. Itself nowhere, suspended between sea and sky, it receives and utilizes all kinds of people.

Othello in his last speech is reverting to the earlier phase. Utterly beaten by his domestic environment, he goes back into his heroic past and delivers his formal vaunt (characteristic of the shame-culture hero from the boasts of the Homeric warrior to the *beot-word* of the Anglo-Saxons, and thence to the 'I killed me a b'ar when I was three' of the American folk hero) though, at the beginning of his speech at least, Othello is restrained by his civilized environment. The speech, properly delivered, should not sound more and more shrilly histrionic as it goes on. On the contrary, it should gather strength and confidence. The actor must draw himself up to his full physical height. Of course there is immense pathos. For—though we dispute their judgement—we are now in a position to account for the reaction of Eliot and Leavis. Othello's behaviour, if judged by the *mores* of the city, *would* be merely theatrical. It may really have a therapeutic function, if not of 'cheering him up,' of galvanizing muscles trained to kill. But ultimately all talk of self-dramatization is a product of the discrepancy between Othello's own nature and the place in which he finds himself. Shame-culture is more concerned than later cultures with outward behaviour; indeed, it locates identity in outward features. Thus for a shame-culture what in us would be artificial posturing may be a means of recovering one's true self. For all the pathos of incomprehension Othello is at last more authentically himself than at any time since the beginning of the play. This recovery of self, however achieved, corresponds to the 'moment of insight' customary in tragedies and successfully prevents *Othello* from turning into a 'sick' paraphrase or serious parody of tragic form. The core of Othello's nobility is real. He has reached a clearing in the forest, a small but sufficient open space in the labyrinth. He has come to a place where, once more, he has a job to do—a job like the jobs he did before—and he knows how to do it well. It is to kill himself. His words recall his feats against the foreign dog and his conclusion is another feat, both like and horribly unlike those.

Thus *Othello* joins the basically economic insight into cultural variation which we find in *The Merchant of Venice* to the contrast of heroic and civic cultures which is so finely treated in the Roman plays. Although Othello postdates Coriolanus and is more primitive than he, there is nevertheless implicit in what I have been saying a shadowy version of the 'evolving human nature' we [see] in the Roman plays. The civic state naturally succeeds the heroic. Othello does not merely belong to another culture but to an earlier one. In the first of the three great dramatists of ancient Greece, Aeschylus, there is virtually no distinction between motive and public situation (this is a continuation of a shame-culture refusal to separate inner and outer). The dilemma of Orestes is essentially public: one god says 'Do this,' another god says, 'Do that.'

There is no question of attributing hesitation or procrastination to Orestes as a feature of his character (indeed, he can hardly be said to have character). This holds to some extent for Othello, or for Othello's conception of Othello. Remember here Bradley's remark, cited earlier, about Hamlet and Othello changing places. One thing Othello does not suffer from is hesitation or infirmity of purpose. Between the thing which is to be done and the doing of it no mental shadow falls.

At a later stage of cultural evolution people become aware that their actions are not only provoked by the outside world but are also inwardly motivated. The notion of self, as we saw, begins to contract. The shame-culture hero *is* his strength, his gleaming arms, even, at times, his cloud of assisting goddesses. Later we begin to assume that the self is separate from such external factors; we say 'Oh, yes, she did well in the four-hour examination, but that's just because she happens to have a strong constitution—it's not *merit*.' I suppose this is the present phase for most of us. Can one *imagine* a further phase? By continuing the trend, we would get an even more narrowly contracted ego, perhaps one which might even view its own motives as separate from itself. Certainly a person like that would seem civilized—rather horribly so—and would be a proper product of a world grown very old.

One cannot ascribe to *Othello* as developed a conspectus of evolving human nature as we find in *Julius Caesar* and *Coriolanus* but it may be, nevertheless, that in *Othello*, some four or five years later than *Julius Caesar*, Shakespeare began to push harder at the idea I have just let fall. If Othello is the underevolved man, who is overevolved? The answer is Iago. For if the workings of Othello's mind recall the oldest literature we have, Iago's evoke a literature as yet unwritten, the literature of existentialism, according to which any assumption of motive by the ego is an act of unconditional, artificial choice. Mark Antony is strange but Iago is far stranger. Mark Antony exploits the emotion he really feels; Iago chooses which emotions he will experience. He is not just motivated, like other people. Instead he *decides* to be motivated. He concedes that he has no idea whether Othello has had sexual relations with his wife. He simply opts, in a vacuum, for that as a possible motive.

I think I know how this astonishing idea occurred to Shakespeare. In the seventh story of the third decade of the *Hecatommithi* of Giraldi Cinthio, the following passage occurs (I quote from the careful translation by Raymond Shaw, given in an appendix to M. R. Ridley's New Arden edition of *Othello*):

> The wicked ensign, caring nothing for the loyalty due to his wife or the friendship, loyalty and duty he owed the Moor, fell passionately in love

with Disdemona and turned all his thoughts to seeing whether he might enjoy her. . . . Everything that the ensign did to kindle in her a love for him was useless. So he imagined that the reason was that Disdemona had become enamoured of the captain and so decided to put him out of the way. Furthermore he changed the love that he bore the lady into the bitterest hatred.

The important phrase is 'So he imagined' and the crucial word is 'so'. The Italian, which Shakespeare may have read, reproduces this feature. I assume that in fact it is merely verbal slackness on Cinthio's part. But, taken literally, it implies that the ensign *deliberately* imagined that something was the case, and this impression is reinforced by the active voice of 'changed' a few lines below where we might have expected 'his love changed'. Most readers would hardly notice these two tiny anomalies. But Shakespeare, I suspect, did notice them, and paused in his reading. For here is the germ of the existentialist Iago.

Chronology

1564	Birth of Shakespeare at Stratford-upon-Avon; christened April 26.
1582	Marries Anne Hathaway in late November.
1583	Birth of daughter Susanna.
1585	Birth of twin daughter and son, Judith and Hamnet.
1588–89	Shakespeare's first plays are performed in London.
1593–94	Publication of *Venus and Adonis* and *The Rape of Lucrece*, both dedicated to the Earl of Southampton.
1594	Helps to establish the Lord Chamberlain's company of actors.
1595	*Romeo and Juliet.*
1596	Death of his son, Hamnet.
1597	Purchases New Place in Stratford.
1599	*Julius Caesar*; construction of the Globe Playhouse.
1601	*Hamlet*; Shakespeare's own father dies.
1603	Death of Queen Elizabeth I; James VI of Scotland becomes James I of England; Shakespeare's company becomes the King's Men.
1604	*Othello.*
1605–06	*King Lear; Macbeth.*
1607	*Timon of Athens; Antony and Cleopatra.*
1608	*Coriolanus.*
1609	Shakespeare's company purchases Blackfriars Playhouse.
1611–12	*The Tempest*; Shakespeare retires to Stratford.
1616	Death of Shakespeare at Stratford, April 23.
1623	Publication of Folio edition of Shakespeare's plays.

Contributors

HAROLD BLOOM, Sterling Professor of the Humanities at Yale University, is the author of *The Anxiety of Influence, Poetry and Repression* and many other volumes of literary criticism. His forthcoming study, *Freud: Transference and Authority*, attempts a full-scale reading of all of Freud's major writings. He is the general editor of *The Chelsea House Library of Literary Criticism*.

G. WILSON KNIGHT is Emeritus Professor of English at Leeds University. His many influential books include *The Wheel of Fire, The Burning Oracle, The Mutual Flame, The Christian Renaissance* and *The Starlit Dome*.

HAROLD GODDARD was head of the English Department at Swarthmore College from 1909 to 1946. He is remembered not only for *The Meaning of Shakespeare*, but also for his writings upon American Transcendentalism.

HARRY LEVIN is Irving Babbitt Professor of Comparative Literature, Emeritus, at Harvard University. His books include *The Question of Hamlet, The Gates of Horn, The Overreacher: A Study of Christopher Marlowe* and *Shakespeare and the Revolution of the Times*.

The late A. P. ROSSITER was lecturer in English at Cambridge University and the author of *Angel With Horns*.

ALVIN B. KERNAN is Professor of English at Princeton University. His books include *The Cankered Muse* and *The Plot of Satire*.

KENNETH BURKE is the author of such crucial works of theoretical and practical criticism as *Permanence and Change, The Philosophy of Literary Form, A Grammar of Motives* and *The Rhetoric of Religion*.

NORTHROP FRYE is University Professor of English, Emeritus, at the University of Toronto. His epoch-making books remain *Fearful Symmetry: A Study of William Blake* and *Anatomy of Criticism*. Later studies include *The Secular Scripture* and *The Great Code: The Bible and Literature*.

DAVID DAICHES is Regius Professor of English, Emeritus, at the University of Edinburgh. His books include studies of Willa Cather and Robert Burns, and *The Novel in the Modern World*.

HOWARD FELPERIN is Robert Wallace Professor of Post-Medieval Literature at the University of Melbourne, Australia. He is the author of *Shakespearean Romance* and *Shakespearean Representation*.

A. D. NUTTALL is Professor of English at the University of Sussex. His books include *A Common Sky* and *A New Mimesis*.

Bibliography

Bamber, Linda. *Comic Women, Tragic Men*. Stanford, Calif.: Stanford University Press, 1982.

Baroll, J. Leeds. *Artificial Persons*. Columbia, S.C.: University of South Carolina Press, 1974.

Bayley, John. *Shakespeare and Tragedy*. London: Routledge & Kegan Paul, 1981.

Bethell, S.L. *Shakespeare and the Popular Dramatic Tradition*. Durham, N.C.: Duke University Press, 1944.

Bevington, David, ed. *Twentieth Century Interpretations of Hamlet*. Englewood Cliffs, N.J.: Prentice-Hall, 1968.

Bowers, Fredson. *Elizabethan Revenge Tragedy*. Princeton, N.J.: Princeton University, 1940.

Bradbrook, Muriel C. *Themes and Contentions of Elizabethan Tragedy*. Cambridge: Cambridge University Press, 1979.

Bradley, Andrew C. *Shakespearean Tragedy*. London: Macmillan, 1915.

Brooke, Nicholas. *Shakespeare's Early Tragedies*. London: Methuen & Co., 1968.

Bullough, Geoffrey. *Narrative and Dramatic Sources of Shakespeare*. London: Routledge & Kegan Paul, 1973.

Bush, Douglas. *English Literature in the Earlier 17th Century*. Oxford: Clarendon Press, 1945.

Campbell, Lily. *Shakespeare's Tragic Heroes*. New York: Barnes & Noble, 1952.

Cavell, Stanley. "Epistemology & Tragedy: A Reading of *Othello*." *Daedulus* (Summer 1979).

Champion, Larry. *Shakespeare's Tragic Perspective*. Athens, Ga.: University of Georgia Press, 1976.

Charlton, Henry B. *Shakespearean Tragedy*. Cambridge: Cambridge University Press, 1948.

Clemen, W.H. *The English Tragedy Before Shakespeare*. London: Methuen & Co., 1961.

Cole, Douglas, ed. *Twentieth Century Interpretations of Romeo and Juliet*. Englewood Cliffs, N.J.: Prentice-Hall, 1970.

Colie, Rosalie. *Shakespeare's Living Art*. Princeton, N.J.: Princeton University Press, 1974.

Croce, Bendetto. *Ariosto, Shakespeare and Corneille*. New York: H. Holt & Co., 1920.

Danson, Lawrence, ed. *On King Lear*. Princeton, N.J.: Princeton University Press, 1974.

———. *Tragic Alphabet*. New Haven: Yale University Press, 1974.

Dean, Leonard, ed. *Twentieth Century Interpretations of Julius Caesar.* Englewood Cliffs, N.J.: Prentice-Hall, 1968.

Eliot, T.S. *Elizabethan Essays.* London: Faber & Faber, 1953.

Ellis-Fermor, Una. *The Frontiers of Drama.* London: Methuen & Co., 1948.

Evans, Bertrand. *Shakespeare's Tragic Practice.* Oxford: Clarendon Press, 1979.

Evans, Gareth L., *The Upstart Cow.* London: J. M. Dent & Sons, 1982.

Fiedler, Leslie A. *The Stranger in Shakespeare.* London: Croom Helm, 1972.

Foakes, Reginald. *"Macbeth," Stratford Papers on Shakespeare.* Toronto: W.J. Gage, 1963.

―――. "An Approach to Julius Caesar." *Shakespeare Quarterly* 5 (1954).

Gardner, Helen. *The Business of Criticism.* Oxford: Clarendon Press, 1959.

―――. "The Noble Moor." *British Academy (Proceedings),* vol. 41 (1956).

Greenblatt, Stephen. *Renaissance Self-Fashioning.* Chicago: The University of Chicago Press, 1980.

Goddard, Harold C. *The Meaning of Shakespeare.* Chicago: The University of Chicago Press, 1951.

Harbage, Alfred, ed. *Shakespeare: The Tragedies.* Englewood Cliffs, N.J.: Prentice-Hall, 1964.

Harrison, George Bagshawe. *Shakespeare's Tragedies.* London: Routledge & Kegan Paul, 1951.

Holloway, John. *The Story of the Night.* London: Routledge & Kegan Paul, 1961.

Kermode, Frank, ed. *King Lear: A Casebook.* New York: Macmillan, 1969.

―――. *Shakespeare, Spenser, Donne.* London: Routledge & Kegan Paul, 1971.

Kernan, Alvin B., ed. *Modern Shakespearean Criticism.* New York: Harcourt, Brace & World, 1970.

Knight, George Wilson. *The Imperial Theme.* London: Methuen & Co., 1951.

―――. *The Wheel of Fire.* London: Methuen & Co., 1949.

Knights, Lionel C. *Further Explorations.* London: Chatto & Windus, 1965.

Kott, Jan. *Shakespeare Our Contemporary.* London: Methuen & Co., 1965.

Lawlor, John. *The Tragic Sense of Shakespeare.* New York: Harcourt Brace, 1960.

Leavis, F.R. "Antony and Cleopatra and All for Love." *Scrutiny* 5 (1936).

Mason, Harold A. *Shakespeare's Tragedies of Love.* London: Chatto & Windus, 1970.

MacCallum, M.W. *Shakespeare's Roman Plays and Their Background.* New York: Russell & Russell, 1967.

McElroy, Bernard. *Shakespeare's Mature Tragedies.* Princeton, N.J.: Princeton University Press, 1973.

Muir, Kenneth. *Shakespeare the Professional and Related Studies.* Totowa, N.J.: Rowman & Littlefield, 1973.

Murry, John Middleton. *Shakespeare.* London: J. Cape, 1936.

Nevo, Ruth. *Tragic Form in Shakespeare.* Princeton, N.J.: Princeton University Press, 1972.

Ornstein, Robert. *The Moral Vision of Jacobean Tragedy.* Madison, Wisc.: University of Wisconsin Press, 1960.

Ridler, Anne, ed. *Shakespeare Criticism, 1935–1960.* Oxford: Oxford University Press, 1963.

Righter, Anne. *Shakespeare and the Idea of the Play.* London: Chatto & Windus, 1961.

Rosen, William. *Shakespeare and the Craft of Tragedy.* Cambridge, Mass.: Harvard University Press, 1960.

Schwartz, Murray M. and Kahn, Coppelia, eds. *Representing Shakespeare.* Baltimore & London: John Hopkins University Press, 1980.

Sisson, Charles J. "The Mythical Sorrows of Shakespeare." British Academy Lecture. London: 1932.

Snyder, Susan. *The Comic Matrix of Shakespeare's Tragedies.* Princeton, N.J.: Princeton University Press, 1979.

Spivack, Bernard. *Shakespeare and the Allegory of Evil.* New York: Columbia University Press, 1958.

Spurgeon, Caroline. *Shakespeare's Imagery.* Cambridge: Cambridge University Press, 1935.

Steiner, George. *The Death of Tragedy.* New York: A. Knopf, 1961.

Stoll, Elmer Edgar. *Art and Artifice in Shakespeare.* Cambridge: Cambridge University Press, 1933.

Stroup, T.B. "Cordelia and the Fool." *Shakespeare Quarterly* 12 (1961).

Ure, Peter. *Shakespeare: Julius Caesar, A Casebook.* New York: Macmillan, 1969.

Van Doren, Mark. *Shakespeare.* New York: Holt, Rinehart, Winston, Inc., 1939.

Welsford, Enid. *The Fool.* Gloucester, Mass.: Peter Smith, 1966. (1st pub. 1935).

Whitaker, Virgil. *The Mirror Up to Nature.* San Marino, Calif.: Huntington Library Publication, 1965.

Wilson, Harold S. *On the Design of Shakespearian Tragedy.* Toronto: University of Toronto Press, 1957.

Acknowledgments

"*King Lear* and the Comedy of the Grotesque" by G. Wilson Knight from *The Wheel of Fire* by G. Wilson Knight, copyright © 1930 by Oxford University Press. Reprinted by permission.

"*Romeo and Juliet*" by Harold Goddard from *The Meaning of Shakespeare* by Harold Goddard, copyright © 1951 by The University of Chicago Press. Reprinted by permission.

"Interrogation, Doubt, Irony: Thesis, Antithesis, Synthesis" by Harry Levin from *The Question of Hamlet* by Harry Levin, copyright © 1959 by Oxford University Press. Reprinted by permission.

"*Troilus and Cressida*" by A. P. Rossiter from *Angel With Horns*, edited by Graham Storey, copyright © 1961 by Longman Group Ltd. Reprinted by permission.

"*Othello*: An Introduction" by Alvin B. Kernan from *The Tragedy of Othello*, edited by Alvin B. Kernan, copyright © 1963 by Alvin Kernan. Copyright © by Sylvan Barnet. Reprinted by arrangement with New American Library, New York, New York.

"*Coriolanus* and the Delights of Faction" by Kenneth Burke from *Hudson Review* 2, vol. 19 (Summer 1966), copyright © 1966 by University of California Press. Reprinted by permission.

"My Father As He Slept: The Tragedy of Order" by Northrop Frye from *Fools of Time—Studies in Shakespearean Tragedy* by Northrop Frye, copyright © 1967 by University of Toronto Press. Reprinted by permission.

"Imagery and Meaning in *Antony and Cleopatra*" by David Daiches from *More Literary Essays* by David Daiches, copyright © 1968 by David Daiches. Reprinted by permission of David Daiches.

"A Painted Devil: *Macbeth*" by Howard Felperin from *Shakespearean Representation* by Howard Felperin, copyright © 1977 by Princeton University Press. Reprinted by permission.

"*Othello*" by A. D. Nuttall from *A New Mimesis* by A. D. Nuttall, copyright © 1983 by A. D. Nuttall. Reprinted by permission of Methuen & Co., Ltd.

Index